THE CONSTANT
OUTSIDER

THE CONSTANT OUTSIDER

Memoirs of a South Boston Mechanic

THOMAS M. CIRIGNANO

To order additional copies of this book, contact:
Xlibris Corporation
1-888-795-4274
www.Xlibris.com
Orders@Xlibris.com
46186

Contents

Dedication

To my wife Diane and my son Ken

*I am grateful that I survived all the events in my life
to be able to spend these years with both of them.*

Foreword

By Izzy Kalman:
Nationally Certified School Psychologist

It is an honor for me to be writing this opening to Tom Cirignano's wonderful book, *The Constant Outsider*. He asked me to read his manuscript because years ago he used the information on my website, www.Bullies2Buddies.com, to teach a young friend how to stop being bullied. With society's current zero-tolerance-for-violence policies, Tom knew he couldn't just tell this kid to do what worked for him—beat the crap out of the bully—without getting in trouble, so he found my less violent approach on the Internet. Respecting my opinion, he asked me to review his book, a labor of three years of love.

Frankly, when I saw the title, *The Constant Outsider*, I was worried. I thought to myself, "Oh, no. Another whiny book telling of the horrors of bullying and how it scars a person for life. How am I going to tell Tom that I don't think the world needs another book like this?" Fortunately, I quickly found I had nothing to worry about. There is not a whiny note in the book. How wonderful the world would be if everyone faced life with Tom's attitude.

To my even greater surprise, it turned out to be a book I couldn't put down. I spent every spare moment reading it till I was done. There isn't a boring paragraph.

While Tom insists on calling this autobiographical work *The Constant Outsider*, you will find that he does an amazing job of becoming an *insider*. Without ever going to therapy or counseling, he developed the character traits that made people like him, respect him, and even risk their lives for him. The story about his first job as a young teen at the local drugstore, going after a group of thugs who robbed the store is both amazing and hilarious. Reading the book made me fall in love with Tom, and I immediately decided I must make this man my friend. And I'm sure you will fall in love with him too. God must also love Tom, or Tom wouldn't have survived all his close brushes with death. He/She must enjoy watching Tom's adventures and doesn't want the series cancelled.

Tom's book is full of important messages about life, though he is not preachy and rarely gives outright advice. He does strongly recommend that we go through the same process he did, of just sitting down, recalling our personal life stories, and writing them down for posterity. I know this is a wonderful idea, though I have never done so and hope that I will before I become too senile.

While he has always been remarkably courageous, Tom has not always had the wisdom to match. He wants young people to learn from his foolish mistakes, most importantly: *don't drink and drive!* Tom was very lucky, but we can't all be. Also important: don't risk your life for nonsense. Again, Tom has been lucky, but his ruined back is a reminder of the foolishness of doing things just to impress others.

And if you feel tremendous pain, don't be a hero. Swallow your pride and get yourself to the emergency room. One of Tom's final messages in the book: If you eat a gallon of fruit salad, stay close to a toilet!

And I personally could have used the advice his dad gave him, "Don't ever get involved in owning a bar!" I made this mistake between the years 1981-83, and I'm fortunate I survived intact.

There is much to learn from Tom's life that is less obvious. A major topic in mental health in recent years is *resilience*. In fact, the theme of the upcoming (2008) annual convention of my primary professional association, the National Association of School Psychologists, is resilience. For the past several years, we have been witnessing horrible actions committed by young people who obviously lack resilience. They are treated badly by people and, not being able to handle the accumulating pain, they crack and go on killing sprees. Hoping to prevent such horrific acts of violence, mental health scientists are trying to figure out how to promote resilience in our children so they will be able to bounce back from the inevitable hardships of life.

Unfortunately, resilience is not something easily taught. To develop the capacity to bounce back from pain, you have to *experience* pain. Yet the same organizations trying to figure out how to promote resilience are simultaneously trying to create an environment that is completely safe. They believe that children should be spared not only from physical pain, but emotional discomfort as well. Schools are outlawing not only dodge ball; their anti-bullying laws make it a crime for anyone to say or do anything that might upset anyone.

Instead of promoting resilience, these efforts are creating a generation of emotional marshmallows—a generation of children growing up believing they are entitled to a life without any abusive experiences. How is this generation going to manage when they grow up, get married and have children, and discover what abuse is really like!

Tom wasn't spoiled by emotional overprotection. Growing up in a violent environment, he knew the government could not always be counted on to protect people from each other. His early experience witnessing a senseless death dispelled any illusion he may have had that life is supposed to be fair. Painful as it is, this understanding is liberating, for the belief that life is supposed to be fair is the anathema of resilience. Life is inherently *un*fair. But if you believe it is supposed to be fair, you will become upset whenever you experience inequity—and it will happen all of the time. When you realize that life is not fair, you are no longer upset by the fact that life didn't deal you the best hand.

Another trait necessary for resilience is a sense of humor—specifically, being able to laugh about yourself. There are two sides to humor. One is laughing at other people when they look stupid, clumsy, or miserable. That is easy to do. Whenever we laugh at jokes, political satire, comedy, or *America's Funniest Home Videos*, we are laughing at other people when *they* look bad.

The other side of humor is being able to laugh at ourselves when *we* look bad or tolerating others laughing at us. That is the hard side of humor. But that is the side of humor that is necessary for resilience—we have to be able to laugh at ourselves. No one is perfect.

We all look like fools sometimes. But when we take ourselves too seriously—when we demand that people treat us like we are perfect—all people need to do is make fun of our imperfections and we go bonkers. Unfortunately, today's anti-bullying policies are encouraging us to take ourselves so seriously that we shouldn't tolerate anyone making fun of us. Fortunately for us—and especially for Tom—he never takes himself too seriously. He is able to relate his most humiliating experiences and take pleasure in letting us laugh at him.

Perhaps the most important—and difficult—lesson we can learn from Tom is to be forgiving and accepting of people even when they are mean to us. It's no big deal to be tolerant of people when they are nice to us. That's easy; it comes naturally to us. The challenge—and the key to harmony—is to be tolerant of people even when they are mean to us. And until we die and go to heaven, we are going to encounter people being mean to us.

Mental health organizations are declaring that no one has a right to abuse, harass, or bully us in any way. Unwittingly, they are weakening us. By promoting the irrational belief that we are entitled to a life in which everyone is always nice to us, we become furious whenever someone is mean to us. "How dare you treat me that way!" Our ensuing anger promotes continued hostility. Instead, learn from Tom's example. When he first entered high school, two students subjected Tom to a terrifying rite of passage that today would have gotten those kids expelled from school, or worse. But Tom took it in good humor, and instead of getting angry—which would have turned these kids into Tom's bullies—they became his buddies. Regardless of the situation, Tom accepted people for the way they were, with all their human imperfections, and as a result, they were always happy to be his friends.

This is not to say that Tom was a wimp. On the contrary, he is remarkably tough and brave. When people went too far with him, he mustered the courage to fight and let them know he is not someone to be messed with. But his tolerant attitude meant he did not have to do this often. I must admit though, it would have helped had someone taught him in his childhood that he didn't have to get upset by verbal insults. It would have spared him some unnecessary fights. Despite what we are being taught today, you don't *have* to get angry when people insult your ethnic group.

The last of Tom's traits I would like to mention is his humility. When you read this book, you will be impressed by his courage, tolerance for pain, resourcefulness, and growing wisdom. But there is no self-aggrandizement. You get the feeling that Tom doesn't realize what a rare and remarkable person he really is. Tom is truly your ordinary everyday saint and hero.

The Constant Outsider is useful not only as a study of individual character. It is also an anthropological study of life in the inner city. People who grew up in South Boston will especially enjoy the book, but it should resonate with anyone who has grown up in any inner city. You get to see that even in neighborhoods ruled by thugs, there are sets of ethics that develop naturally without government imposition. People are much more interdependent, and have more intensive relationships, than in our sanitized suburbs. In fact, you realize that dangerous as it is, life in the inner city can be more "real" than life in the suburbs. Safety is not exciting, and a government protecting us from each other and taking care of us does not create a strong sense of community. Tom, after moving to the relative safety of the suburbs, actually moved back to South Boston, and the book makes it easy to understand why he would do such a crazy thing. And it wasn't, as Tom portrayed it, just to save some time commuting to and from work. Life in the inner city really *was* more meaningful.

The single most important insight I gained from *The Constant Outsider* is why young people would want to join gangs. Gangs are dangerous. They have enemy gangs and live in a constant state of warfare. Belonging to a gang, you could be injured, jailed, and even killed. Why would anyone in their right mind want to join one? What is their appeal?

It's this. Think of your friends. How many of them would risk their lives to help you? You probably don't really know. In fact, you may have found that often when you ask friends for help, they find ways to weasel their way out. We refer them to government agencies for help rather than sharing our resources with them. But when you are part of a gang, you know that your gang brothers will stand up for you in the most primal way. What a feeling of security, belonging, and pride you must get when your mates display their readiness to risk their lives for you when you are threatened by an enemy! This happens to be the same glue that is known to hold squads of soldiers together. With their very existence depending upon each other, they form bonds of an intensity rarely experienced in civilian life. The danger of the gang membership makes this feeling of intense solidarity available in nonmilitary life as well.

Tom Cirignano is a man for all of us, and *The Constant Outsider* is a book we can all relate to. I hope that you will enjoy it as much as I did.

December 5, 2007

Author's Note

I decided to title this book *The Constant Outsider* because as a very young boy, I came to an upsetting conclusion. For reasons unknown to me at the time, nobody was going to make it easy for me to be accepted by my peers. I would need to work extra hard in order to fit in. I'm sure that many readers will find that they too have experienced a similar situation, some possibly from the opposite side of the fence. Years would pass before I would come to understand that there were many reasons for my ostracism, several of which were beyond my control. While searching for ways to be accepted, I sometimes made reckless choices as you will read. One of the most important questions we must all answer for ourselves in life is the following. To what extremes will we go in order to just fit in? The answer to that question leads us to serious choices that every person, not just inner city kids, have to deal with over and over again.

For a very long time I believed my life's experiences were, more than likely, typical and ordinary. As I grew older and learned how other people's lives had evolved, I realized that my life has been anything but ordinary or typical. Numerous people and events had a major impact on forming the person I was to become. They would form the way I would perceive myself, the world, and life itself.

When you are a child and have witnessed someone lying on a neighborhood sidewalk near death at the hands of another human being, that vision stays with you forever.

When you have had contact with admitted killers, people who even bragged about the fact, those memories have a lasting impact as well.

I have met many people who have never had a gun pointed at them. Because that was a far too regular occurrence with me, I realized that my life has been rather unique. Even more astounding to me is the fact that many people that I know have never even been in a fistfight. Their reality and perception of what constitutes a typical and ordinary life was very different from my own. Fights were commonplace both where I grew up and where I worked for most of my life. Murder was not a rare occurrence.

The majority of my youth and working years were spent in South Boston, Massachusetts. It was a section of the city that always seemed to operate under its own set of rules. For almost twenty years, I ran an automotive repair business on East Third Street. The very nature of my business made it almost a certainty that I would eventually come in contact with just about everyone in town. Some very interesting and violent people enjoyed hanging out at my shop. Through those acquaintances, I was given several opportunities through which I could easily have become immersed in underworld activities. There were occasions when I could have become involved without even realizing it. The more direct offers of easy money, excitement, and prestige were very tempting to a person such as me, who longed to fit in. It was sometimes very hard and also dangerous saying no to certain people. I instinctively knew that once I cooperated and did this one "thing," saying no would not be an option from that day forward. Sometimes, I had to walk a fine line in order to coexist with those who thrived in the lawless environment which surrounded me.

I have had more than my fair share of close calls that could easily have proven fatal. The list is awfully long for just one person to have experienced. Those incidents have often left me wondering if there was a special reason that I was allowed to survive.

As I look back, it's apparent to me that much of what happens to a person in life does depend on the environment to which he or she is subjected. But even more important are the choices that person makes within their allotted environment. I know my life would have been totally different had I played into some of the unique opportunities that my environment offered. Choosing to grasp all of those opportunities would have been the easy way. In life, it seems that it is always easier to say the word "yes" to people, and never easy to say the word "no." The hard part of saying the word "yes" sometimes comes later.

Although I'm not a famous or infamous guy writing the story of his life, I believe that some real value can be found in the pages of this book. My experiences show that choices come with consequences. Thankfully, the book also illustrates that even if you make some really bad choices you may still be okay as long as somebody "up there" likes you.

*Please Note: In many instances throughout the book, I have altered the names of the people mentioned. (Those altered names first appear in quotation marks.) I did this because often those individuals were the only bad apple from an otherwise respectable, loving, and hardworking family. Possibly, some of the people that I talk about have turned their lives around, and therefore it is not my intention to embarrass anyone or their families. I suppose you could say that the names have been changed to protect the innocent and the guilty. Regardless of the fact that names were changed, the accounts are true. There are events in this book that I have never shared with anyone before.

I kept many of these things to myself for decades because I found them far too difficult or disturbing to talk about. As hard as it was to write some of those experiences down, I felt that these events could not be omitted if I were to write an honest work. My friends and family will be hearing about many aspects of my past for the very first time as they read this book. I'm sure there will be several surprises in store for them. I hope they can accept that I was much younger when many of the events in this book took place and just be thankful that I am much wiser now.

To me as the author, the following feature is possibly the most significant aspect of this book. **At intervals as you read, you will find several pages designated for "Reader's Notes." It is my sincere hope that you will use these pages as an opportunity to record the most memorable events of *your* life**. Write about the significant people and life altering events that you have never recorded or maybe felt unable to share with your loved ones. As I did so, I found that recalling such things and documenting them was an extraordinary experience.

Have you ever felt like "the constant outsider" during your lifetime? If so, explore the choices you felt compelled to make in order to fit in with those around you. Share your regrets as well as your triumphs of will. As you lay in bed, something important will come to mind that should be included in your notes. Don't wait until morning to write those things down. Trust me. The thought will be *gone* when you awaken. Keep a notepad and pen on your nightstand. If you remember it, it is important. You will gain a deeper understanding of yourself if you invest the time to do this. You may want to just write short notes in the book as a reminder of things to write about later. Then go into the details of those events in a separate notebook. Who you are today was significantly shaped by the situations, people, and choices of your past. Whether or not you share the results of your writings with family or friends is entirely up to you, but one thing is for sure; you may find out that your life has been anything *but* typical and ordinary.

Acknowledgements

My sincere gratitude goes out to all of the friends and family members who have encouraged me to put these experiences into book form.

The notes I had saved throughout the years were laborious to organize and put into words. I must thank my son Ken and my wife Diane for their work in helping with that task and for Diane's editorial expertise.

Thanks also to my sister Fran for being the first person to read the very rough draft and for her enthusiastic encouragement to continue. I thank my brother John and my son Ken for bringing these old and badly faded photos back to life via their computer skills.

Sincere thanks to my good friend Donna Cipullo-McHugh for her advice and encouragement.

A big thank you goes out to Donna Theisen and Dary Matera, coauthors of *Childlight* and *Angels of Emergency*. I appreciated your opinions and advice. Donna showed me that if you believe in your work and don't give up, good things will happen.

Thank you, Alberta Sequeira, author of *A Healing Heart*, for holding a seminar to help new and aspiring authors. Your straightforward information, expertise, and the unselfish giving of your time and were all greatly appreciated.

Thank you, Izzy Kalman, Nationally Certified School Psychologist and author of *Bullies to Buddies: How to Turn Your Enemies into Friends*. Even though we had never actually met, you agreed to make an exception to your rule and read my book after viewing a summary. It meant so much to me that after reading the book, you believed in it, and me, enough to volunteer to write the foreword. Thanks!

Suggested/Related Reading

I would like to recommend the following reading, as the subject matter strongly relates to, or sheds light on aspects of *The Constant Outsider*. I truly found each of these books fascinating.

All Souls: *A Family Story From Southie*
By Michael Patrick MacDonald

Black Mass: *The Irish Mob, The FBI and A Devil's Deal*
By Dick Lehr and Gerard O'Neill

Brutal: *The Untold Story of My Life Inside Whitey Bulger's Irish Mob.* By Kevin Weeks and Phyllis Karas

A Criminal and an Irishman: *The Inside Story of the Boston Mob-IRA Connection*
By Patrick Nee, Richard Farrell, and Michael Blythe

The Brothers Bulger: *How They Terrorized and Corrupted Boston for a Quarter Century.* By Howie Carr

For anyone (young or old) dealing with a bullying situation, I highly recommend the following book. It can change your life.

Bullies to Buddies: *How to Turn Your Enemies Into Friends*
By Izzy Kalman: Nationally Certified School Psychologist
On the web: *www.Bullies2Buddies.Com*

Chapter I

Learning To Stand Up For Myself

At the time I was born, my family owned a well-kept two family home located at 60 Stanton St. Dorchester, Massachusetts. There were churches on both ends of our street with a third church, St. Matthew's, along with its Catholic grammar school located in the middle of the block. Our family had moved there from South Boston, where my sister Eleanor (Dolly), my brother John, and the closest sibling in age to me, my sister Frances, were born. John was out of the house and in college when I was very young, and Dolly, being thirteen years older than I, was usually out of the house working. There were eight years separating me and Fran, so I was more like an only child. In fact, Fran got married and moved out at the ripe old age of eighteen. I was just ten when she left.

Dorchester was a predominantly Irish section of Boston at the time. My family and I are 100 percent Italian. My dad, Vito, was born near Naples, Italy, in Avelino. He arrived in the United States at age six. The Fiumedoros, my mom Eleanor's side of the family, emigrated from that same part of Italy shortly before she was born.

I remember first feeling like an outsider when I was very young. I never felt like I really fit in with the neighborhood kids. They would stick to their small groups whose members had names like Foley, Kelly, McDonald, and the like. There were some rare occasions that I got to play ball in the street, I guess because they needed an extra guy to even out the teams. I was left wondering many, many days as to why I was not liked or made to feel like one of the gang. I wasn't the tough outgoing type like most of the kids on my street seemed to be. Looking back, it's possible there was a little envy as a reason that certain kids didn't warm up to me. My father owned an auto repair business in South Boston, and when things were slow at the shop, he would ask his mechanics to build me something. At the time, my father's brother, Tony, and long time employee Ken Saunders were the mechanics at the shop. Uncle Tony was one of my favorite people, and he and Ken were very ingenious with the crude materials they had to work with at the shop. When I was fairly young, they built me a wooden pedal car with a fancy paint job that could fit three kids. When I was ten or twelve, he had them build me a real go-cart with a five horsepower engine. I would noisily cruise along the neighborhood sidewalks on it until the cops chased me home. I can't remember any of the other kids in the neighborhood having elaborate toys like these.

It would have been very difficult for my family to be liked in the neighborhood because my father was continuously engaged in confrontations with neighbors over their parking in front of our house or blocking our driveway. Parking was at a premium in the city. The streets were lined with two and three-decker homes, some of which had driveways and garages. I don't remember any other families arguing in the street over people blocking their driveways. It's possible they did single us out for trouble because we were Italian.

My dad guarded what he considered his territory like a pit bull. I can't count the number of horrible arguments he got into and how close they always came to a physical fight. Even though he was only five feet nine inches tall, he never backed away from a confrontation. In fact it seemed to me that he sought out conflict. One guy who lived right next door was over six feet tall. That neighbor was hotheaded just like my father and seemed to go out of his way to park in front of our house or block our driveway. Dad would tell me, "Go next door, and tell that guy to move his car." I remember really hating it when he would send me next door to be the bad guy. When the neighbor wouldn't come out to move his car as fast as Dad thought he should, there would be a big scene. Their voices could be heard from a block away, and my stomach would be tied in knots. The neighbors, including their kids, must have resented me as well because of these ongoing feuds. I can just imagine what might have been said about us as they sat around their dinner tables.

On many a late afternoon, I would be looking out of the front window to watch for my dad to arrive home from work. I wanted to see if he was going to be in a good mood or a horrible mood when he arrived. On a good day, he would smile and greet me with a loud "Tommio!" He might even hand me a silver dollar with which a customer had paid him that day. On a bad day, you could immediately recognize it by the scowl on his face. He would start yelling at anyone he encountered. On far more days than normal, it was the latter situation. I now believe that it was his uncontrolled medical problems that caused his unpredictable mood swings. They were beyond his control. He was a diabetic who totally ignored his doctor's instructions, eating anything and everything he wanted. He *raised hell* if Mom tried to feed him healthily by trimming the fat off his steak.

"That's the best part!" he would yell. One day, Vito came home from work to find a neighbor's car once again parked in front of our house. Dad backed in, purposely smashing the grill of the car with the trailer hitch that was mounted on the back of his Jeep. A while later, the neighbor sent one of his kids over to tell my dad that they saw him hit his car and demanded a copy of my father's license and insurance information. My dad, in turn, sent me over to retrieve the other guy's license and insurance information. I brought the papers to Vito as he sat in his big recliner, smoking a cigar. He glanced at the papers and stated, "This guy's car is registered in Plymouth! It's not even registered here in Dorchester where he lives!" Back then, people would register their cars using the address of a relative who lived somewhere out in the country. They did this in order to illegally trim hundreds of dollars from the city auto insurance rates that they normally would have to pay. Vito sent me back over to the neighbor's house with instructions to tell him, "Go ahead and file a claim if you want, but my dad said he would report to the insurance company that you live in the city, not the country." No claim was ever filed against my father's insurance.

A few months later, during a snowstorm, my father was parked in the garage behind our house. It was barely light out, and it was time for him to leave for work. I was shocked to see that a neighbor had his car parked on the street, blocking our driveway! My dad had previously had run-ins with this neighbor as well. I guess he was sick and tired of sending me over to tell neighbors to move their cars because there was no request of me to do so this time. We had about six inches of snow on the ground, and my dad had a plow mounted on his Jeep. As I stood in our living room, looking out the window, I wondered what would happen next. I heard the Jeep roaring down the driveway with the snowplow down, scraping the pavement.

I remember saying to myself, "Where does Dad think he's going? The driveway's blocked!" Vito kept his foot on the gas. He plowed the snow along with the guy's car all the way across the street, into a big snow bank against a tree! Then he just backed up and drove off to work. Once again, my gut was tied in knots. I went to school that day really scared that another huge argument or a physical fight was going to result later that day. Surprisingly, I don't remember any follow-up confrontation or anything being said about what happened. Also, I don't remember anyone blocking our driveway ever again.

Looking back, I'm sure incidents like plowing a neighbor's car out of the way most likely fueled resentment of our family. The kids on our street often made me feel unwelcome. One of them would take the lead, and the others would follow suit. I would sometimes get punched for no reason, pushed, or called names. I was young at the time, and I would go home very upset. My mom was the great protector. She would ask me what was wrong, and I would tell her, "So and so hit me." She would grab me by the arm and take me directly to the house of the boy who had punched me. She would knock at their door and be very upset with the mother or father of the boy, telling them in a loud voice, "Leave my son alone!" Not a word of this would ever reach my dad. I'm sure he would have told me to punch the kid back as hard as I could. Mom really thought she was doing the right thing, and I loved her for fighting for me. As you can guess, Mom's visits to my tormentor's households only fostered further resentment. It didn't stop the taunting and hitting.

Finally, one day, I had had enough. This one neighborhood boy, who went by the name of "Kelly," was constantly taunting me with ethnic insults, and then he would run away if I chased him.

I was not a fast runner. These incidents had gone on for so long that I finally decided that if he said anything bad to me the next time I saw him, I was going to chase him down if it killed me. Even though he was faster than I was, I figured if I just kept running after him, he would sooner or later run out of breath. I was not going to stop till I caught him, no matter how much I hurt. Sure enough, he said something derogatory about me being of Italian decent, like "hey wop," and my blood boiled. I chased him for the longest time as he ran ahead of me laughing. It felt like my chest was going to explode, but I kept running. This was my day to take a stand.

I couldn't believe it when Kelly started looking back at me and slowing down as he ran. He was running out of steam! We were almost at the end of our street, and I was going to catch him! When I got my hands on him it was the best feeling in the world. I slammed him to the ground and jumped on top of him, holding one side of his face to the pavement. I was mad as hell, yelling inches from his ear, "If you EVER call me a name again, I will punch your face in!" I could see the shock and fear in him, and it felt good. It also felt good knowing that some of the other kids from the neighborhood had observed this new me, and they would now think twice about antagonizing me. Instead of being the victim, I was in control for the very first time in my life. It was a much-better feeling than running home with my tail between my legs. But this did not come easy to me because I was not naturally aggressive or violent. I realized that these were skills I had to learn in order to survive. That boy called "Kelly" was the very first person that I had ever fought back against. I think it's quite a coincidence that to date, the very last person I have gotten into a physical confrontation with was also of the same name. That fight would happen in South Boston, almost twenty years later. The second "Kelly" didn't get off nearly as easily, and that felt *really* good.

Unfortunately, while still quite young, I observed a horrifying incident that will always be etched into my memory as if it happened yesterday. When I was ten or eleven years old, I was walking along Norfork Street heading toward Codman Square. I noticed some people gathering on the opposite side of the street, so I crossed over to see what was going on. There, lying on her back on the sidewalk was this truly beautiful teenage girl with long black hair. She was lying there motionless, looking half-alive, half-dead with blood flowing freely from several knife wounds in her chest. She had probably been just walking home from Dorchester High School, but now she was lying in a pool of her own blood. She seemed totally oblivious to the several people that had gathered around her. They stood there in silence, doing nothing. She was looking directly into my eyes, and I could see the life slowly draining out of her stare. Upon seeing this, I can't explain how I felt. Nobody was making any attempt to help her, and at my age, I had no idea what to do. I get a sick feeling in my stomach even today as I write this. As I stood there, an ambulance finally pulled up. The paramedics wasted no time loading her onto a stretcher. She didn't acknowledge the ambulance personnel at all. Her eyes were still wide open and fixed *upon me.* Her head was lying limply to its side. It was as if her eyes were saying to me, "Why did this happen to me?" That bewildered stare followed me as they slid her into the back of the ambulance with a loud thud that made me quiver. Her stare stayed with me through numerous sleepless nights. I still think of her occasionally to this day. I never even mentioned this incident to my parents. In fact, I have never told anyone about what I saw that awful day, until writing it here. It was so devastating to realize that one human being could be capable of doing this to another. What had this beautiful young girl done to deserve to die like this?

What kind of person could plunge the blade of a knife into the body of another? Those questions lingered. This was something a young child should never have to see.

If you dared to venture out of your immediate neighborhood in Dorchester, you risked running into trouble with kids from surrounding areas. I had started going to a boys club to use their swimming pool. It was located several blocks away from my home, so I would ride my bike to the club, by myself. As I was riding along one day, a gang of boys blocked my path in the street. Two of them grabbed onto me, and others were holding the handlebars of my bike. I was defenseless and unable to escape. They threatened me, telling me never to come down their street again because the next time they saw me, they would beat me up "real bad" and take my bike. I was around eleven or twelve years old, and they were fourteen or fifteen. They would not let me pass, and I had to turn around and find another route to the club. I had no doubt that they meant what they said. Another route that I attempted had a vicious dog that would chase my bike and attack me as I tried to pass by. Eventually, after running into similar situations on other streets, there was no way to get where I wanted to go. That was the end of the boys club.

As is true almost everywhere, there were some really nice families in our neighborhood. One family even sent over a fresh loaf of Irish bread one day, right out of the oven. I remember being very surprised that someone had done something nice like that. It was a totally foreign experience. I was especially surprised because a week or so earlier, my mom had made one of her visits to their front door, with me in tow, because their son had punched me in the face for absolutely no reason as we stood in the street waiting to order from the ice cream truck.

I attended St. Matthew's Catholic School, right there on Stanton Street. We all wore uniforms, and I could walk home for lunch, which was nice. At the entrance to the school, there was a fence made out of narrow diameter pipe. The top rail of the fence was about two and a half to three feet off the ground. One day after school, I was walking the top of the pipe fence as if it was a tightrope. I had seen a couple of the "cool" guys do it, so of course I wanted to show that I was "cool" too. There were several boys and girls watching me as I tried to make my way down the entire length of the fence. The pipe must have been damp because without warning, my foot slipped off the top edge of the fence. I came down hard, directly onto the pipe, with my body perfectly parallel to the ground. The pipe had caught me right in the middle of my spine. I fell to the ground in excruciating pain, unable to breathe, make a sound, or move for what seemed like forever. The kids who were watching me stood around laughing while I lay there in agony. Nobody came over to offer help or to show concern. After several minutes, I was finally able to get to my feet. The pain in my back was intense, but I was able to stand. As usual, whenever I hurt myself, I was too embarrassed to tell my parents what I had done, so I lived with the constant pain, never mentioning anything about my accident. As the weeks passed, the pain finally subsided. I fell from that fence when I was in the fourth or fifth grade. Years later, when I was a senior in high school, I was diagnosed with scoliosis. While looking at my x-rays the doctor asked, "When did you break your back?" I found out then that I had actually fractured a vertebra during that fall at St. Matthew's. The fracture had healed, but scoliosis caused my back to grow crooked. Back problems would haunt me for the rest of my life.

At St. Matthew's School, there were kids from all over the Boston area and from some of the more well-to-do suburbs as well. One good friend that I made was named Michael Kearney. He was from Randolph, a rather rural suburb at that time. I loved visiting Mike's house in Randolph. The suburbs seemed like a different and kinder world. The first and only time I ever played spin-the-bottle was at Mike's house with the girls from his neighborhood. We were in either the sixth or seventh grade. That's a fun fact to remember because later in life, Mike became a Catholic priest and eventually was monsignor of his own parish.

There were plenty of other nice kids at St. Matthew's beside my friend Mike, but there were also a few that were very aggressive. "Paul" and "Robert" were pains in the neck, literally. Somehow, many of the other kids managed to fly under their radar and not be bothered, but I had no such luck. It was as if I had a big target on my back that said, "Please mess with me." They were probably good kids now that I think back, but they would continually punch all the boys really hard in the arms and shoulders. They would also *leap* onto your back, choking you from behind when you didn't expect it. These were two of the biggest boys in the school, and it was really hurting my back having them jump on it. I told them to stop day in and day out, but they just laughed and kept it up. I suppose I was giving them the response and reaction that they craved. Nobody ever stood up to them or fought back against the abuse they constantly dished out. Finally, one day I decided that I'd had enough of this. When Paul jumped on my back from behind, I mustered up all my strength, reached back and grabbed him, and flipped him over my shoulder. I slammed him onto the blacktop of the schoolyard. I knew I had hurt him pretty badly because he stayed there on the ground for quite a while, rolling around with the wind knocked out of him.

Then his sidekick, Robert, having seen what I had just done to his buddy, did the exact same thing that Paul had done. He leapt on my back from behind! I immediately did exactly the same thing to him, flipping him onto the pavement really hard, directly next to Paul. I remember actually feeling bad about doing this as they both lay there. The bell rang, and I went right into the school, leaving them to get up on their own. Nobody ever said anything to me about that incident that I can remember, but they never messed with me again. The three of us actually got along very well from that point on. Now that I was accepted by them, and perceived as one of the tough guys at school, this opened up a whole new set of problems for me. Guys would send a friend of theirs over to me and say, "So and so doesn't think you're so tough, and he wants to offer you out," meaning they wanted to meet me after school and fight. You had to say okay or be called chicken. The first time that happened to me was with a boy I had never had any words with. He just wanted to fight me for some unknown reason. The combatants would always meet at the corner of Norfolk and Stanton streets, in front of "the black people's church," as we called it. We would never fight near our own church for fear of getting in trouble.

This was my first time in a scheduled fistfight. I thought that somebody should probably state the rules of the fight like they do on television. I started with "no kicking in the balls" and "no pushing in the bushes," but before I could finish what I was saying, I saw this fist *winding up,* as if in slow motion. Then, with a loud *"smack",* my opponent had hit me square in the face with all his might. Because I lacked any actual fight experience, I had made no attempt to duck and took the full force of the punch. I didn't go down, but there was definitely a loud buzzing noise in my head.

I was stunned at what had happened. Instinctively, I lunged at my opponent, tying him up and prevented him from throwing any more punches. I found that I was stronger than he was, and I threw him to the ground and straddled him, holding his arms pinned to the ground. He couldn't move or throw any more punches. I just held him in that position underneath me while making sure that every drop of blood that came from my nose and my mouth dripped directly onto his face and white shirt. I had him down, and he was helpless. I could have pummeled him from my position, but I chose to just let him wear lots of my blood. To enjoy hurting someone who was now helpless and no longer a threat was just not in my make up. After he was covered with blood, enough so that it was even grossing *me* out, I said to him "Want to quit?" and he nodded yes. I let him up and that was that. My "second," who I think was my friend Mark, offered me his fancy white linen handkerchief to clean my face. Remarkably, I was free of any signs of blood on my clothes. My opponent, who had not been hit by one actual punch, was a bloody mess. I was so terrified that my dad would notice my fat lip when he got home from work that I avoided facing him as much as possible that entire day and night. He never noticed. A great lesson was learned that day in the fight—watch out and be prepared for the "sucker punch!" Learning how to duck wouldn't be a bad idea either.

There was no shortage of Italian bashers at St. Matthew's School. One Irish kid who was pretty tall and fat used to greet me every morning by calling out loudly as I approached "Hi, Guinea! Hi, Guinea!" I never responded to him, but I would be boiling mad inside. I'm sure he could tell from the look on my face every morning that it bothered me tremendously. All I could think about on countless nights as I tried to get to sleep was someday hitting this jerk as hard as I could.

It was the only thing I could think of that might stop him. I planned time and time again to carry out his punishment, but for the longest time, I just couldn't bring myself to do it. Then one morning, as I approached the school entrance, I heard his nasty ethnic taunts, and my blood *boiled* once again. The time was right. With nobody else around, I walked right up to him, looked up at his fat, grinning, freckled Irish face, and without saying a word, punched him as hard as I could right in the gut. A punch in the face would have left evidence that could get me in trouble with the nuns. Like a tree that had been struck by lightning, he fell slowly backward over the pipe fence and onto his back. This was the same fence where he and his friends had stood laughing at me the day I broke my back. *He* was now the one on the ground who couldn't breathe, and he wasn't laughing now. Once again, the taunting ended.

There were other incidents at school that I won't be able to forget. While chasing another habitual tormentor, I was running full speed along the back alleyway of the school when the fleeing boy tipped a barrel over, right into my path as he ran past it. I ran directly into the sharp top edge of the barrel, at a full gallop, and it caught me directly where a guy hates to be hit. I will remember the intense pain of that morning for the rest of my life.

The Sisters of St. Joseph were very strict, and in those days, they were free to dish out plenty of corporal punishment. I was the recipient of more than my fair share of it. In trying to make up for feeling unpopular in the neighborhood, and for other reasons, I would joke a lot in class and try to make people laugh. I was the class clown. The tactic worked great with the kids, but I was always in trouble with the nuns. Out of frustration with my behavior, my first-grade nun actually picked me up by the head.

With my feet dangling in the air, she banged my head against the blackboard two or three times before putting me back down. If a nun did that to me as a student today, she would be arrested, and the school would be renamed St. Thomas's after I won it in a lawsuit.

All through grammar school, I would be the one getting the ruler smacked on my hands, staying after school, or having to write one hundred times on the blackboard some foolish sentence that they thought would instantly cure my behavior. My mom was regularly called to the school for conferences regarding my behavior. My older sister Dolly was even stopped on the sidewalk one day as she walked past the school on her way home from work. A nun informed her that my teachers had serious concerns over my behavior. I realize now that one of the reasons I resorted to constant misbehavior in class was to compensate for and draw attention away from my struggle with undiagnosed dyslexia. When asked to read aloud, I had to exert a great effort to concentrate on each letter individually. This prevented me from reading as quickly and clearly as the other students in my class. I literally prayed that I would not be called upon to stand up and read, and I would cringe when my name was called. I stumbled over words and got extremely nervous and embarrassed. I could never understand how the other kids were able to read so effortlessly. I was especially in awe of the girls in my class. They could read in such a flowing and relaxed manner and sound as if they were having a regular conversation. That was just amazing to me. I thought I must be stupid, so I made up for it by clowning around even more. Numbers were, and still are, a struggle for me. If I don't concentrate on each number one at a time when copying a phone number, I will mix up the numbers. Dyslexia really slowed me down.

Another setback at school was when the nuns noticed that I was naturally left-handed. I could write beautifully using that hand. After being sternly informed that "The devil writes with his left hand," I was forced to learn to write with my right.

I recently finished reading a book about "Sammy the Bull" Gravano. He was John Gotti's right-hand man. He was a mob enforcer turned informant. Sammy was personally involved in numerous murders. His testimony put John Gotti in prison while earning his own eventual freedom. I was stunned as I read his story and saw the *numerous* similarities in our childhoods. Both of us grew up in tough inner city neighborhoods where Italian kids had to stand up for themselves and fight to be accepted. We were both undiagnosed dyslexics who became class clowns in order to help cope. We both had the same trouble reading and working with numbers. Both of us were presumed to be slow learners because of our unheard-of learning disability. He was kept back in the fourth grade, and I was kept back in the third. We were both ridiculed by other kids because of being kept back. Both of us had fathers who ran small businesses. Both of our fathers were on good terms with the local "wise guys," but both fathers chose to keep a safe distance from the serious illegal activities of those groups. The vast differences in the way our two lives evolved were the direct result of the choices we each made along the way. One wrong choice and everything can change.

Outside of school, there were times when I would hang out with the kids on my street, depending on how hostilities were running among the adults. One day, I went next door looking for a boy I had met who was there visiting relatives. His grandparents had a very old barn in their yard. As I entered the doorway to the barn, it was very dark inside. My eyes had not had time to adjust to the darkness from the bright sunlight outside, so I was unable to see at all.

Out of nowhere, I felt a hard and painful bang to my forehead that knocked me backward. I exited the barn into the daylight to find that I could barely see through the stream of blood that was running over my eyes. I had never experienced any sensation like this before, and it was very scary. As I was trying to make my way home, I got to the end of the neighbor's driveway at the street. My sister Fran, who was sitting on a porch across the street, spotted me with the blood streaming down over my face. I heard her scream "TOMMY! TOMMY!" She ran over and helped escort me home. From the amount of blood, and my resulting appearance, you would think I had been mortally wounded. As it turned out, the boy in the barn had thrown a brick at me as I entered through the doorway into the darkness. The pointy corner of the brick hit me just right in order to make a puncture wound to my head. It was a surprisingly small, but deep wound that bled like hell. I can't recall ever getting a good explanation as to why this boy threw the brick at me, other than his claim that I had frightened him when I entered the barn.

My older siblings and I, enjoying a day at Boston Common in 1953.
Eleanor (Dolly) on left, John and Frances.

One of the cars built for me at the shop when things were slow.

Mom and Dad at Walden Pond near Concord Mass., taken one month before they were married in 1938. They made a handsome couple. This pond was the subject of Henry David Thoreau's prose.

Chapter II

First Close Call and Other Assorted Mischief

Growing up in Dorchester was different back in the 1950s and 60s than it is today. All the neighborhood kids played games in the street. We all rode bikes with no helmets. Lots of times, we rode two kids on a bike. We sometimes got hurt, but nobody ever got sued.

My first brush with death came when I was riding double on the crossbar of my friend's bike. We were on one of the steepest hills in Dorchester, coming down Milton Avenue where it meets Gallivan Boulevard. As we were heading down the hill, both his front and rear brake cables gave out. We were terrified as we picked up speed, going faster and faster. Both of us were squeezing the brake handles as hard as we could, but they did nothing to slow us down. I remember staring to our left at the granite stone wall that lined that side of the street as we flew by it. We had to quickly decide if it would be better to intentionally crash into that stone wall or take our chances trying to make it across one of the busiest boulevards in the city while dodging the traffic. The stone wall didn't look too appealing as it was zooming by, and the bottom of the hill was approaching really fast. We had a huge decision to make as we watched the cars and trucks speeding through the intersection below us.

At around forty miles per hour, should we attempt the almost impossible hard right turn, and try to mesh in with the flow of traffic, or turn left, which was a far less drastic angle to turn, and hope there would be no traffic in our path? I screamed, "GO LEFT!"

In an instant, we had veered, at a high rate of speed, directly into the oncoming traffic of the boulevard! It must have been a worst nightmare for those drivers as we suddenly appeared out of nowhere, coming right at them. Several cars swerved frantically to avoid hitting us. I can still remember the frightening sound of all the screeching tires. We found ourselves in a head-on-collision course with a large white plumbing repair truck that was approaching us at around fifty miles per hour! Add our speed of around forty to his speed, and we would have hit with the force of a ninety-mile-per-hour impact. Thank God, the driver slammed on his brakes and swerved hard to his left just prior to hitting us. It would surely have been a fatal collision for me and my friend if that truck driver hadn't reacted so quickly. Instead of hitting the truck head-on, we hit the side of the truck with a tremendously hard glancing blow. The bad part was that my right leg caught one of the heavy L-shaped metal brackets that were mounted on the side of the truck. The brackets were loaded with long lengths of pipe. My buddy and I went flying through the air and tumbling down the roadway. We came to rest at the side of the road next to each other. Miraculously, my friend was not really hurt. I had taken the brunt of the collision with my leg, and I was now rolling around on the ground in *excruciating* pain. It was the most intense pain I had ever experienced in my life, bar none. One driver who had stopped on the side of the road after seeing the accident was standing there *yelling* at us, saying "You stupid kids! What's the matter with you, trying to cross a busy highway like that?" I was obviously experiencing intense pain, but instead of trying to help, this guy was *yelling* at me!

I picked up the largest rock I could reach in the gutter next to me, and threw it at him as hard as I could. I continued to roll around on the pavement in pain as I screamed at the man, "I am hurt bad, and you're *yelling* at me? You asshole! Do you think we did this on purpose?" The man whose truck we had run into was doing his best to comfort me. After a few minutes, the pain started to subside. I couldn't walk, but I kept insisting that I didn't want an ambulance. The truck driver helped me to his truck and loaded me into the passenger seat. He then drove me directly to my house. With my arm over his shoulders, he helped me hop to the front door of my house. He explained to my mother how the accident had happened and told her, "Your son is really lucky to be alive. He missed the front of my truck by six inches!" He was a really nice guy, and I was sorry I had put him in the position of hitting a kid on a bike. I admitted to my mom that the accident was entirely our fault because of the bad brakes on my friend's bike. The driver told us he was very sorry it happened, and off he went. How differently things would have been handled if that accident had happened today. That driver never would have dared put his hands on a kid he had just hit with his truck. There would have been an ambulance, police, and lawyers coming out of the woodwork. Things were simpler and more honest back then.

After an hour or so at home, things were getting much worse. My leg had swollen to twice its normal size, and it was pitch black from my ankle to my waist. The pain had become unbearable again. I never would have believed that human flesh could turn completely black. My dad was called home from work, and I was taken to the Carney Hospital. The x-rays showed a hairline fracture of the femur, just above my knee. Because the bone hadn't broken completely in two, my leg was Ace bandaged instead of having a cast put on it.

I was given pain medication and crutches along with instructions to use ice packs and keep weight off my leg for a few weeks. I never dared to ride double down a steep hill again.

Living in the city, and not having many friends to hang out with, I had to come up with fun ways to occupy myself. I guess the lesson here is that parents should pay attention to what they leave within reach of their children. My dad was an avid hunter and kept several guns in the house. He had a really pretty pearl-handled 9mm Colt automatic that he carried when hunting. He used this gun to finish off any game that the original rifle shot hadn't killed. Somehow I found out where he kept this loaded handgun. It was hidden behind one of the drawers in his bureau with a big wad of household money sitting right next to it. When nobody was home, I would take out the gun and remove the clip. Then I would eject the bullet he kept ready in the chamber so I could play with the empty gun. I was around eleven or twelve at the time. When I would hear somebody coming home, I would rush to reinstall the clip and load a bullet back in the chamber so it would be exactly as he had left it. Another *fun* thing that I can't believe I never got caught doing was even more dangerous. I would take my father's Springfield .22 caliber long rifle from his closet and retrieve some bullets as well. I would use my teeth to remove the projectile from the shell. Then I would get a candle and press wax into the opening of the shell where the lead shot had been. Of course, I left all the gunpowder in the shell. I would then take the gun and the modified ammunition out on the back porch of our house and load the rifle with my homemade blanks. From our back steps I would aim the rifle up into the sky and fire off a few rounds and then quickly go back into the house. I can't believe that in the middle of the city, with tenants living right upstairs and with hostile neighbors all around, I didn't get into major trouble doing this.

The shots were certainly loud enough, and the neighbors must have heard them. While making those blanks, if one of those bullets had experienced just a small spark as I removed the projectile from the shell using my teeth, it would have been the end of me for sure. Thinking about the dangerous things that I used to do should be incentive enough for gun owners to lock up your weapons, for your kid's sakes. Kids are naturally curious and you never know what goes on when they're home alone.

Another pastime, one I wish I never adopted, was smoking. All the men around me smoked. It seemed like a natural next step to growing up. I noticed that all of the tough and "cool" kids in the neighborhood smoked. My smoking started out rather innocently, but it gradually evolved into a lifelong habit. There were always several packs of unfiltered cigarettes around our house. I would just check the pockets of my dad's jackets or the glove compartment of his car. If that failed, there were always the cartons in his trunk that I could tap. I would steal one or two of his Luckies or Pall-Malls and hide behind our garage either alone or with one of my friends to smoke. Sometimes I would make a small campfire around which we would sit and puff away. When we were done smoking around the fire, we would get rid of the evidence by throwing all the burnt embers over the fence into the neighbor's yard. Of course, we would first put out the fire with whatever *liquid* was readily available.

Well, one day, we apparently had not done such a great job making sure the fire was really out before tossing the remnants over the chain link fence. About an hour or so after our little smoking party, I heard loud voices resonating from out behind our house. When I checked out the commotion, I saw several people, including my mom, running to the back corner of the neighbor's property.

From all adjoining yards, people were dumping buckets of water over their fences trying to put out a good-sized blaze that had engulfed the neighbor's yard. Thank God, his garage was made of concrete block! Somehow, my mom instinctively knew that I was the one responsible for the fire because she chased me all around the house with her big rolling pin in hand. She finally cornered me in the bathroom. The rest I'll leave to your imagination. I was only nine or ten years old when this happened. I can still remember the corny cowboy outfit I was wearing that day.

I kept our parish priests pretty busy with my confessions. The ritual would go something like this. "Bless me Father, for I have sinned. It has been one week since my last confession. I swore seven times, I lied twice, I stole six cigarettes from my father, and I set my neighbor's yard on fire." I had to say a lot of Hail Marys and Our Fathers as my penance. When my nicotine addiction reached the point that I had to steal entire packs of cigarettes from Dad to satisfy my cravings, the resulting guilt was too much to handle. Plus the priests were piling up the penance on me. I started to save up my candy money and, at age twelve, began buying my own packs of Pall-Malls.

Dorchester's Junior Firemen

Sporting their own fire truck, and firemen's hats, these youngsters have adopted a worthwhile project in the vicinity of Stanton st. They labor to keep yards and sidewalks free of leaves, rubbish and other debris that could catch fire. This group includes Jil Buonopane, 8; Tom Cirignano, 1(Kenny Coppenrath, 11, ar brother, Paul, 7. (Globe Photo l Joseph Dennehy)

Ah, the good old days.

This newspaper clipping fails to mention that I was given this cleanup duty after sneaking cigarettes behind the garage and accidentally setting the neighbor's yard on fire.

Chapter III

My Introduction to Southie

I was very young when I started spending quite a bit of time in South Boston. My dad's gas station/repair shop, named Emerson Auto, was located at the corner of East Third and Emerson Streets. He had purchased the business in 1947 when it consisted of just the tiny front office and two gasoline pumps. Eventually, he went on to buy three adjacent triple-decker houses, one at a time. He would knock down each newly acquired house in order to add one more bay to the shop. He did this three times over the years. Because of the street configuration, the building was V shaped. The front part of the building was very narrow, but the structure got wider and larger as you made your way back into the shop areas. There was a pit in the second bay with a vehicle inspection station and a lift in the third section. In the rear bay, which was the largest, we stored the very first tow truck that my dad had purchased. It was a 1942 Ford, two-ton bomb carrier from World War II. Dad said it had been imported from England. It had six-wheel drive and a huge snowplow I imagine was used to plow runways during the war. The rear boom had been modified from its former use as a bomb carrier into a tow-truck configuration. That old vehicle always generated lots of interest whenever we took it out for a spin, which was only once or twice per year. It was used for the bigger jobs when a regular tow truck couldn't handle the load. My dad told me that years ago, a tugboat had sunk directly under the Summer Street Bridge. A pair of regular tow trucks working from the bridge above was unable to raise the boat. Vito told me he brought our old Ford down there and secured it to several of the iron bridge supports, using heavy chains so the truck couldn't move. He used the front winch of the truck, with its ultra-low gear ratio and thick steel cable, to slowly raise the tugboat up to water level. Once at the surface, the tugboat was slowly drained. The leaks were plugged, and finally the boat was able to be moved.

Emerson Auto was also proud of its other resident antique, a beautiful large roll-top desk that was in the front office when Dad originally bought the business. Customers would continually comment on the desk, saying it didn't belong in a gas station. I still cherish that old turn-of-the-century desk. It now resides in my home as a wonderful reminder of my years at the garage. I traced its origin to a Chicago company where it was built around the year 1900. The desk is shown in the author photo on the back cover.

My father was a very enterprising man. For a while, he had owned and operated a bar on the west side of Southie, called the Strand Café, but that was before my time. One piece of advice he passed along to me as a result of that experience was, "Don't ever get involved in owning a bar."

Starting when I was around eight years old, Dad would insist that I go into the shop with him. I would protest, but I was forced to accompany him to work on most Saturdays and on many days during the school's summer vacations. I remember one morning when Dad and I were driving into work, we stopped, as was usual, to get coffee at a small variety store in Southie. He sent me in to get coffee to go.

In the store talking to the owner was a large guy, maybe in his twenties, with a very bad complexion. His nose was totally black and had a row of surgical stitches completely encircling it. It had obviously been reattached to his face. He was telling the owner of the store how his nose had been bitten off in a fight the day before. It was as if he was describing a baseball game rather than a horrible experience. The doctors had sewn his nose back on, but from what I could see, it didn't look like it was going to take. That day, I couldn't stop wondering how somebody could be that vicious to go as far as to bite someone's nose off in a fight. I immediately began to hate being in South Boston. I knew that the kids in Dorchester were tough, but I would soon find out that these Southie guys made Dorchester kids look like Girl Scouts! In Dorchester, you might get pushed and punched, but in Southie, if you were to get into a scrape, these kids wanted to do permanent damage to you. As I began to see fights on the streets around the gas station, I soon realized that if one combatant went down, he could count on getting booted full force in the face by his opponent. I didn't want to mess with any of these guys.

Even dogs were different here in the city. Many people allowed their dogs to roam free in the streets. One large and ruggedly built dog that lived close by was named "Rex." He looked like a shepherd mix, and he proudly displayed the scars of several gruesome fights. Although he was very friendly to me and other humans that he knew, he would turn into a bloodthirsty aggressor at the first sight of a strange dog. Any dog unlucky enough to be walking through the neighborhood was in for the fight of its life. It didn't matter if the dog was bigger than Rex or if it was a little poodle being led on a leash by its owner. It was in for a grizzly lesson. If I noticed a strange dog approaching from way down the street, I could do nothing but sit back, knowing what was about to happen, and helplessly wait for the attack to commence. Rex would go into attack mode, and the hair would stand straight up on his back as he honed in on his prey. Rex would go right for the neck. If the dog was light enough, it would be in Rex's jaws, being whipped back and forth like a bloody rag. His victims would end up shrieking and crying loudly, totally helpless. Somehow they would be let go when they were sufficiently injured or on the brink of death, never to venture into the neighborhood again. My dad really surprised me one day when he unexpectedly sprang into action and showed great compassion. Rex had spotted a beautiful full-sized collie that had unwittingly ventured into Rex's personal "no fly zone." With hair raised, Rex charged to the attack. Because these were both very large dogs, it was a ferocious and noisy fight. As usual, within a minute or so Rex was getting the better of the collie. He was doing an awful job on this beautiful dog when my dad suddenly grabbed the large broom that we kept in the office, and without a word, he swung the door open and darted across the street. With a cigar in his teeth, he went off, yelling and swinging the broom wildly in the air as he ran. He was trying to scare the dogs into quitting the fight, but his ominous display went completely ignored. As he reached the scene of the fight, he was in full forward motion when he tripped over the curbing of the sidewalk. I couldn't believe my eyes! He flew head first, right *onto* the two fighting dogs with broom still in hand. If those dogs had turned on him, he would have been easy prey. I think both dogs were shocked when Dad landed right on top of them with all his weight, yelling like he was. Within a split second, they shot off in separate directions, leaving Dad on his hands and knees on the sidewalk. Vito got up off the pavement and brushed himself off.

As he walked slowly back toward the office with the broom under his arm, he paused in the middle of the street and re-lit the stogie that was miraculously still in the corner of his mouth. To him it was just another day at the office. To me it was something I would remember for the rest of my life. Although that incident was very scary to observe at the time, looking back and knowing that he wasn't hurt, the vision of this memory still makes me laugh.

With regard to the kids my age that lived around the gas station, I was once again cursed by my father's actions. It was just as it was at home. Kids were not allowed to play ball near the gas station. If they did, Vito would yell at them in a very mean way with a scowl on his face. Halfball was a popular game in the streets of Southie. The kids would cut a pimple-ball in half and use a broken-off broomstick as a bat. I could see that there was a real knack to pitching that halfball. It was a side-arm pitch, and some of the boys were very good at it. Although I was never invited to play, or even spoken to by those kids, I enjoyed watching them play the game. I would gaze at them through the rock-and-bullet damaged wire mesh windows of the shop, often wishing I was one of them. It was similar to the feeling I had experienced many times when seeing the little leaguers in their wonderful uniforms, playing on the baseball fields near Dorchester High. All the parents would be watching their sons play ball and cheering them on as I walked by. I would wonder why those boys were so special that they got to play baseball. It was never even suggested to me that I could do that if I wanted to. Somehow, for me it was not an option.

When it would snow, my dad would plow all the snow away from the gas pumps and the four bays of the garage. With two and three family dwellings lining the streets, no matter where you pushed the huge piles of snow you were encroaching on somebody else's territory.

People would place a chair in the parking spot they had shoveled out and they defended that spot to the death. We not only had our personal cars to park in the street but also all the customers' cars that were left with us for the day. The continuous arguments and confrontations with the neighbors around the shop were very tense situations for a young kid to observe. I would stand there watching the arguments, frozen and silent, wearing the oversized and grungy, hand-me-down coveralls of some long-departed employee. I must have really stood out to the neighborhood kids as clearly being different. I remember one pair of coveralls I had to wear had the name "Shorty" embroidered on it, which was appropriate. It was the story of me being *the constant outsider* all over again. I was the son of the mean Italian guy from out of town who made his living in this neighborhood and made life miserable for the surrounding residents and their kids.

Even the air hose that we kept out front by the gas pumps was cause for conflict. Many folks would pull up to fill a low tire, and Vito would rush out to tell the person, "You're blocking my pumps! Go get your air where you buy your gas!" He would go as far as to disconnect the air hose while in mid-use, if the person made any remark in response that he didn't like. It was always a loud yell of "HEY!" or "WHOA! WHOA! You can't park there!" Some of those people that were being yelled at were not the type of people you wanted to be pissing off.

In later years, as the running of the business was transitioning to me, I would strive to find a way to be accepted by the people in Southie and reduce the amount of conflict and stress. It was important to me.

Please, don't get me wrong. I loved my father dearly. My father had many good traits. It's just that people skills were not his strong suit.

On the good side of the scale, he would never pass a Catholic church without tipping his hat, and you had better do the same or you'd get a reminder smack. He never drank or swore when around his wife and kids. On Sundays, we were always out somewhere as a family, either visiting relatives (who had no idea we were coming), ice skating, tobogganing in the Blue Hills, or going to the beach. I think a lot of his temper problems stemmed from being diabetic. He never took care of himself, and I think fluctuations in his blood sugar level may have been the cause of his angry disposition. That condition ended his life at the age of sixty-nine. He always did what he thought was right and I never once saw him take advantage of any customer. He was brutally honest in his opinions, and people either hated him or really loved him. There were plenty of both.

On any given day, there were always guys who would spend quite a bit of time hanging around the shop. They would tell stories about the old days in Southie, sometimes reminiscing about Vito's prize-fighting days. When he was a teenager, he fought in boxing matches that were held adjacent to the South Boston courthouse. After winning several of those fights he would sell the gold watches he had won, in order to help support his parents' large family. He was one of ten children. Dad had to lie about his age and use the borrowed name of *Joe Monaco* in order to enter those boxing matches. He hadn't yet attained the minimum required age of sixteen when he began fighting. He once confessed to one of my sisters that he would steal fish off the wagons of street merchants in Southie when he was a young boy, in order to help his family. I would also hear stories about the many street-fights that he had been in when he first started out in business for himself. He began with a horse and wagon selling ice and coal. The Irish vendors didn't take kindly to my dad taking business away from them, and it resulted in some pretty serious confrontations.

I found out the extent of some of his legal problems a few years later when I applied for a license to carry a concealed handgun. I needed to get a copy of any criminal records that may have existed on me, so I went to the South Boston courthouse to ask for a copy of my record. I knew I didn't have a record except for numerous speeding tickets, so I was shocked when they handed me a very long sheet of paper, listing numerous offences! There were several assault and battery charges and even assault and battery on a police officer. Then I noticed the name on the report was not mine. It was Vito's. I had heard the stories about fights with other icemen in the streets and even a fight during which ice tongs were used as weapons, but here was the proof of his stories in front of my eyes. Instead of keeping that report and really being able to read the entire thing, I regret that I handed the report back to the clerk, saying they had made a mistake, and that it was not my record.

Dad always gambled for as long as I can remember. Playing cards for money and betting the thoroughbreds were things he truly enjoyed. In the 1960s, he became a racehorse owner, and as such, many conversations at the shop would revolve around the horses. At times he owned as many as five horses that were running at various tracks simultaneously, but mostly at Suffolk Downs. I believe *Solicitation* was the most victorious horse he ever owned. After "claiming" this horse, she went on to win several races in a row. That horse and my father were the subjects of some great articles in the sports sections of the Boston newspapers. I wish somebody in the family had saved those clippings. We would thumb-tack the articles on the parts cabinet in the gas station office, where they would eventually get old and disappear.

I remember a few times during those years when the phone at the shop would ring, and Dad would listen very intently to the caller.

After a few seconds, he would hang up without saying a word, turn to me, and say that the guy on the phone had tipped him off by telling him, "Vito, don't bet your horse today." The mysterious caller would then just hang up. All the other owners and trainers at the track knew that my dad would routinely bet around a thousand dollars to win on his own horse when his entry had a good chance of winning. After one of those phone calls had ended, Dad told me that somebody, out of courtesy, had saved him from making a bad bet. With a frown of disappointment on his face he once said, "Somebody must have gotten to my jockey and paid him to hold my horse back." There was quite a bit of shady goings-on within the horseracing industry back then, and it was beyond his control. One trainer that I got to know well during my visits to the track with Dad was later relieved of his trainer's license, after being caught drugging horses. That gentleman had absolutely none of the outward characteristics you would attribute to a criminal.

My older brother John, who also worked at the gas station when he was young, told me that he vividly remembers times when a stranger would come into the shop and whisper something in Dad's ear and then leave. John said there would then be a flurry of phone calls to the local bookies from the guys who happened to be hanging out at the garage.

Recently, John told me that contrary to what I believed, he didn't mind working at the shop or working with my dad. He said he loved driving the tow truck and working in the shop. But, a career at the garage, or becoming a Doctor, as my father insisted upon if he was going to pay for John's college, was not in the cards. John had his own plans in mind for the future, which was to become a physicist. That decision caused friction between the two of them, to say the least. To his credit, John went on to earn several degrees in physics and business management, all of which he paid for on his own.

The silver lining to that storm-cloud is the fact that he never would have met his soul-mate, his wonderful wife Florence Nicosia, had he not been working as a driving instructor in order to pay for college. Everything seems to happen for a reason. Anyway, John eventually ended up working with NASA on the Apollo lunar landing, and later, on the development of the Patriot Missile System. Meanwhile, I was fixing old broken-down Novas at the shop. A plaque ordered by President Nixon, thanking my brother for his work on the Apollo project, sits in John's office today.

The choices we each made led two brothers on totally different paths. One summer, I experienced what it was like to travel with thoroughbred racehorses from track to track. I would ride in the back of the large multi-horse trailers along with several horses and one of the grooms. My assignments at the tracks were mostly limited to walking and feeding. For me, as a young boy, those were sometimes quite scary tasks when dealing with those very high strung animals. More than once I came close to getting hurt while walking a horse that was worth a small fortune and belonged to somebody else. They would get spooked and rear up on their hind legs while towering above me, trying to break away. I knew I had better not let that happen, at any cost to myself. I ate at cafeterias that were full of jockeys in full garb. They were a very close-knit and tough-looking group that kept pretty much to themselves.

For as long as I can remember, there was a bookie joint located directly on the other side of the back wall of our shop. "Wally the Bookie" was situated on the first floor of the three-decker house that was attached to our building. If we had punched a hole in that rear concrete block wall, we would have had a private window through which to place bets. As a young boy, my dad would send me next door to place wagers for him. I have to admit, I felt very special being able to do this.

I don't think many kids were allowed through that door. There was a special knock, and then someone would check me out through the peephole and let me in. Wally took all kinds of bets such as horses, dogs, and the street number etc. The street number was actually called (pardon the expression) *"the nigger pool."* Somehow, you could decipher that street number by looking in Boston's *Record American* each morning. It was similar to the state's daily numbers game, except you got all the winnings in your hand, in cash, tax-free. You could also get a loan from Wally, if you were willing to pay interest of ten percent *per week*, I was told. It always amazed me as the years went by that Wally's operation was so wide open and well known. He was just one of many bookies working throughout Southie. Just about every bar in town had its own resident bookmaker, and everybody knew who it was. I could see Wally's doorway from where I pumped gas. At times I would see the steady stream of customers, which, to my surprise, included many respected community members such as fireman, etc. The only thing Wally's place was missing was a sign over his door saying "Place your bets here. We specialize in short-term loans."

SOLICITATION

Owner		6. Furlongs.
V.P.Cirignano	2nd. Broward	J.Kurtz up
Trainer	3rd. Bethpage	Time-1.13
J.A.Ruberto		Sept.18,1965

Dad (in the plaid shirt) standing with friends,
holding his pride and joy after a win.
Solicitation was one of the many racehorses he owned over the years.
Sometimes he would get an anonymous phone call at the shop. The
tipster would say, **"Vito, don't bet your horse today."**

Longtime customer and friend Nick Tammaro and his son posed with me when gas was just 27¢ per gallon. I'm the one in the middle, wearing hand-me-down coveralls.

Nick and I stood in the same spot again, years later.
Gas went up a little.

Chapter IV

First Jobs and First Contact With Killers

I do feel very fortunate that my dad taught me to work hard from a very early age. That lesson served me very well through the years. While other kids were out playing ball, he kept me busy cleaning his car, washing windows (no streaks allowed or do over), working in the yard, and even burying his pet fig trees well under the frost line before winter set in. On Saturdays, as usual, he would have me in Southie with him, working at Emerson Auto. But after school, while he was working, I was free to explore the possibilities in our Dorchester neighborhood.

Around the corner from our home, there were numerous mom-and-pop shops along the busy sidewalks of Norfolk Street. One was a Rexall Drug Store and directly next door to that was an upholstery shop. The drugstore had a soda fountain and ice cream counter where my family would always trek and pick up a hot fudge sundae for any family member who happened to be sick. Ice cream always seemed to make us feel better. Anticipating and receiving that special treat became a tradition in our family. I should have guessed that that drugstore would end up being a special place for me when the following happened one day.

I went in to buy a bag of chips, and reached into my pocket for my nickel (yes, a nickel). It fell from my fingers and hit the floor. After bouncing a foot or so into the air, it came back down and landed squarely on its edge! There was nothing sticky on the linoleum. It was as if some strange force had grabbed that nickel and abruptly stood it there at attention! I remember thinking to myself, "Wow! I could never do that again in a million years!" I wished I could just leave it standing there to show everyone what had happened, but I wanted those chips badly.

A very nice gentleman named Bernie Cohen owned the drugstore. He had known me from the time I was in a baby carriage. I was very excited one afternoon when Bernie unexpectedly offered me a job working the ice cream counter when I was only in the eighth or ninth grade. It was really fun making all those treats and soda drinks. I would work there from 6:00 to 9:00 PM. While manning the counter at the drugstore, I got to know the owner of the upholstery shop right next door. The owner of Granite Upholstery was named Harold Irving. He asked me if I could work for him a couple of hours each afternoon. I accepted that job offer as well, helping Harold in the shop and delivering furniture with him in his van. Those store owners were two of the nicest men I had ever met. They accepted me, treated me with respect, and showed confidence in me. They each gave a tremendous boost to my self-esteem.

The drugstore had just one other employee. Sheldon, the pharmacist, always kept to himself, working in the back room while I took care of customers at the counter out front. I guess, at the very minimum, I would have to describe my coworker as very eccentric. Although he was not a large man, he was a very scary-looking person, especially to someone my age. He said as little as possible and had a permanent scowl on his face. When he would look at somebody, his head was always tipped forward and to one side.

One eyebrow was always raised way up. If I greeted him when I arrived at work there would be no response, just that weird raised-eyebrow glance as he passed by. He walked around looking as if he were all tightened up, contorted, and leaning to one side. I had as little contact with him as possible. Now that I am an adult, I realize that he was probably harmless and suffered from some sort of malady.

Some very scary things took place at my very first job away from the family business. One evening, I was working the counter, but there were no customers in the store. As usual, Sheldon was in the back room out of sight. An older woman came into the store and she didn't look quite right to me. She had a glazed look in her eyes as she shuffled up to the counter. Suddenly, she dropped to the floor and began flailing crazily! Her arms and legs were all jerking wildly in every different direction, yet she appeared to be unconscious. I was scared to death! I had never seen anything like this in my life. Display racks were being kicked over, and things were falling all around her. I ran around from behind the counter and quickly moved everything out of her way, trying to prevent her from being hurt by falling items. At the same time, I was yelling for Sheldon to come out front! He walked out from the back and calmly surveyed the woman with his usual demeanor. He announced to me that she was having an epileptic fit. He said, "Just leave her alone till she comes out of it." Sure enough, after three or four minutes she stopped flailing and became coherent again. I helped her to her feet and Sheldon issued an order for me to escort her home. I had never been so nervous in my life. The woman lived several blocks away, and with every step we took along Norfolk Street, I was fearful of a repeat performance of what had taken place in the store. Thankfully, I got her into her house without any further problems.

To my surprise there was no *goodbye,* or *thank you* from the woman. She just entered her house and closed her door in my face, which I thought was strange. I had quite a story to tell Bernie when he came back to close up shop.

On another evening while I was working, a far worse incident occurred. It was dark outside and nearly closing time. The owner had not yet arrived, and I was alone in the front room of the store once again. Suddenly, four or five older boys came bursting through the doorway from the street. They didn't look like they wanted ice cream. I recognized one of them as "Larry." He was an Irish kid that I knew because his yard connected to mine at the back corner. Larry had a bad reputation and hung around with a very tough group of guys. A couple of years prior to this night, I had witnessed his cruelty firsthand. I had gone behind the garage in my yard to sneak a cigarette. On the opposite side of the chain link fence, in his yard, I saw that he had a cat with a rope tied around its neck, hanging from a tree limb. He was beating the frantically struggling cat with a big stick. I yelled at him saying, "What are you doing? Cut that cat down!" (Many of the kids in the neighborhood, including myself, carried some sort of folding knife). Larry seemed really embarrassed that somebody had caught him committing this horrendous act. He pulled out his switchblade and cut the rope with it. The badly hurt cat was somehow able to run away with bloodied fur and the rope still around its neck. Larry said to me that he had found the cat hanging there like that. I knew he was lying, so I saw no sense in asking him why he was hitting it.

Now, two or three years after that incident, Larry was in the drugstore store with his gang, and they were grabbing everything that wasn't tied down. The store was being robbed! They took the display racks off the counter and off the floor, which mostly held just snack foods and potato chips. They were stuffing their pockets with whatever they could grab.

One of the teenagers that I didn't know came around the end of the counter where I stood guarding the cash register. He grabbed a handful of condoms off the shelf behind the counter and stuffed them into his pocket. Then he turned toward me and the cash register. I yelled out to Larry by name, ordering him to stop and get out of the store. He knew then that I recognized him, and I knew where he lived. Thankfully, they stopped short of going for the cash in the register after I called Larry by name. I don't know how far I would have gone to protect that cash, but it most likely would have ended badly for me. They left abruptly, just the way they had come in, still laughing as they carried away all the things they had grabbed.

Surprised that Sheldon had not heard the commotion and come out front, I yelled back to him, shouting that we had just gotten robbed by a bunch of neighborhood kids. Sheldon slithered his way out of the back room, wiping his hands on a towel, and asked me if I knew any of them. I told him I did know one of them, but we were not friends. Sheldon told me that I better go after those kids and get all that stuff back. He warned me that I would most likely lose my job when Bernie came back.

I was scared that Sheldon was telling the truth about me losing the job, so I reluctantly went after the gang. He hadn't even called the police. I knew that those guys hung out under the footbridge that went over the railroad tracks on the opposite side of Norfork Street. That was the direction they headed in when they left the store with their arms full of stolen goods. Their hangout was a wooden platform constructed way up high in the iron girder framing of the footbridge. It was an invisible hiding place where you could watch the freight and passenger trains zooming past below you.

Rumor had it that the gang would drink and smoke up there at night. I also heard that on Sunday mornings they would peep through holes in the wooden decking above them, looking up the skirts of girls as they headed from the other side of the tracks to the various churches of my neighborhood. After word of this private spot circulated through the neighborhood, I had infiltrated the hideout a few times out of curiosity and to sneak a smoke. I never dared to go there at night when the gang was likely to be there. To get to their hangout, you had to walk across to the far end of the footbridge where the stairs started to descend. Then, in order to access the plywood platform on the underside of the walkway you had to climb over the railing and maneuver your way under the edge of the bridge. This required a very strong grip as you defied gravity. One slip of the hand and you would plummet to the tracks some twenty feet below. There would be no second chances if you experienced a mishap. For somebody with my fear of heights, it was one of the most frightening things I have ever done in my life. From a distance, I had observed how the gang accessed the platform. Of course, during my visits, nobody was around, and I would be alone. I truly had to force myself to make the dangerous maneuvers required in order to get to that spot. I *needed to* prove to myself that I could actually do it. In my head, I would repeat to myself, "I am just as good as those kids. If they made it under here, I can do it too." Getting back out was even more terrifying, but every time I successfully made it without falling, there was a huge surge of adrenaline and a sense of personal accomplishment.

As I crossed the footbridge the night of the robbery, I could hear the laughter and loud conversation of the teenagers below. They were not up in the platform this night because it could only accommodate two or three kids comfortably at one time. They were gathered down along the railroad tracks directly under the bridge.

I walked down the stairs and around and under the far end of the footbridge. I approached them in the dark, not knowing what their reaction would be. They were sitting around, drinking beer and crunching away on all the food they had stolen from the drugstore. I called out, "Larry," and they all stopped talking and looked at me. I'm sure they were quite surprised to see me standing there. I explained to them that the man in the back room at the drugstore knew who robbed the store because I yelled out Larry's name, and he sent me to retrieve all the things they took. Then I told them, "The guy at the store said if I don't bring the stuff back, I would be fired from my job, and they were going to call the cops to come right down to their hangout at the tracks." I assured them that nothing would happen to them, and the cops would not be called if they just gave me the stuff back and stayed away from the store. I couldn't believe it when they agreed to let me take as much stuff as I could carry back with me. I had several racks of snack food and as many items as I could possible manage to carry as I made my way back over the bridge. They had already consumed quite a bit.

Bernie was just arriving at the store to start closing up as I got back. I explained what had happened and he was very upset and concerned. He was glad that I made it back to the store safely, but he wished I hadn't gone after those guys. He said, "That was way too dangerous!" He made me promise not to ever put myself in danger again. Now, when I look back at the situation, I know I made a bad decision that night going after those kids. Bernie Cohan was a great guy, and I'm thankful to him for having faith in me and for giving me my first real job.

Just months after that robbery at the drugstore, a dead body was found under the footbridge on the tracks, right where I had confronted those guys. Somebody had been stabbed to death, and then their body was laid across the train tracks to make it look like an accident.

The train had done a good job dismembering and mutilating the victim, but the police were still able to determine that the person had actually been stabbed to death before being placed on the tracks. Larry and his friends were arrested on suspicion of murder. Maybe the evidence against them was not rock solid because I was told they were offered a deal allowing them to join the U.S. Army and fight in Vietnam in lieu of prosecution and probable hard time in prison. They took the deal. After hearing about that murder, I realized just how fortunate I had been to survive my confrontation with those guys down by those same tracks.

My job next door at Granite Upholstery was not nearly as exciting, although the owner was equally as nice as my boss at the drugstore. Harold Irving and I would load his handiwork into his van, and the two of us would deliver sofas and chairs all over the Boston area. On one unforgettable trip, we had to deliver a huge sofa to an apartment building. It had to go to an apartment on the fifth floor, but it just refused to fit into the elevator no matter how we tried. That was funny because we had somehow gotten it down in that same elevator a few weeks prior. I guess Harold had added too much padding when he reupholstered it. It was a heavy monster of a sleep sofa, but we carried it up the five flights of stairs. When we finished our climb, I was totally exhausted. Both Harold and I were panting and dripping with sweat from the struggle. At the opened door to the apartment, we found that the rather slender and attractive woman who owned the sofa was drunk as a skunk. She was standing there wearing only a short flimsy nightgown, swaying from side to side, unable to stay balanced. Apparently, she had been entertaining her equally drunk boyfriend by sharing a half gallon of whiskey while sitting on blankets on the living room floor. The apartment reeked of alcohol. Both of them were barely able to stand.

As we backed the newly covered sofa through the doorway and into the room, I heard a loud thump on the floor right next to me. The woman had fallen over backward at my feet. One of her legs was extended directly under the heavy sofa that we were carrying, so we couldn't put it down. Her nightgown had gone all the way up around her waist, exposing her most private parts for all to see. I was frozen where I stood, and I couldn't help but stare. The woman was so intoxicated that she didn't even try to cover herself as she made pathetic attempts to sit up. Harold and I had no choice but to stand there, holding the monstrous sofa as we watched this spectacle in disbelief. This wasn't exactly the way that I anticipated my first view of a woman's anatomy would come about. After what seemed like forever, her boyfriend *finally* assisted her in covering up and got her leg out from under the sofa. Harold, being the perfect gentleman, did not remark at all about what had taken place. He just politely asked the customer if she was all right. Luckily, Harold's check was already made out, and it was sitting on the kitchen table. She directed him to his payment and mumbled a barely audible thank you. I was happy to leave the stale alcohol stench of that apartment.

As Harold and I descended in the elevator, we were in total silence. I couldn't think of a word to say about what we had just seen. Then, as we were leaving the building, Harold turned to me and said, "I'm really glad you saw that. It's good for you to see how some people live." I didn't have any idea what the heck he meant by what he said, but I was kind of glad I saw it too.

Chapter V

Time To Leave Dorchester

During the mid 1960s, Dorchester was transitioning from being a mostly white area into being a predominantly black part of the city. This struck fear into most of the first- or second-generation immigrant families who had lived there for years. They feared the anticipated fall of property values and an increase in crime that had developed in other sections of Boston. Those feelings fueled a rapid exodus of white families who fled to the suburbs. Unfortunately, the ignorance of the times was evidenced by the way black people were portrayed by many white parents to their young children. They were portrayed as something to be feared and avoided. I'm pretty confident that the tendency of black families to distrust and misunderstand white people was just as common.

The incident that clinched my family's decision to move to the suburbs directly involved me. My sister Fran had sparked my interest in playing the guitar. She played and sang all the time when she was home, and she showed me a few chords that I could strum. Playing by ear came pretty easily to me. I could learn a song by listening to the record over and over again while playing along.

Soon after that, I became friends with another boy at St. Matthew's School who played guitar very well. His name was Billy Lydon. We learned to play all the popular tunes of the time such as "Walk Don't Run," "Wipe Out," and "As Tears Go By," etc. We sounded good enough that we ended up playing a few songs at our eight-grade graduation. After a while, I decided it was time I learned how to read music, so I began taking guitar lessons from a music teacher at Codman Square. I would take the city bus to my lessons from in front of the church where we used to hold our after-school fights. One afternoon, as I stood holding my guitar case waiting for the bus, I saw a fairly large group of black teenagers fooling around and loudly conversing as they approached me. They must have been walking home from Dorchester High School. There were four or five hefty-sized girls leading the pack, followed by four or five boys trailing a few steps behind. Without warning, as they reached where I was standing, the girls started swinging their purses around their heads through the air, hitting me with them over and over again. It felt as if there were rocks in their purses. I dropped my guitar case and did my best to block the blows. My suspicions were confirmed when I blocked one shot with my arm and saw some rocks fly out of the girl's purse. They apparently had planned ahead of time that they were going to attack somebody along their stroll home. I ended up down on the ground, pretty banged up, and bleeding around my forehead. The girls just continued on their way with the boys walking right behind them. The whole group thought this was great fun. One of the boys stopped beside where I sat on the sidewalk and said with a big grin on his face, "Hey, whitey, why didn't you fight back?" He said this as he picked up my guitar case and flung it about twenty feet up onto the cement stairs of the church.

I replied to him, "If I hit those girls, you guys would have killed me." He just laughed, and they all walked away. When I retrieved my guitar, I was glad to see that it was still in one piece with only the case showing damage. During this ordeal, there was the usual steady flow of traffic along Norfolk Street, but not one person dared to stop their car to intervene. I skipped my appointment and went directly home, telling my mom that I would not be going to any more guitar lessons. When she heard the reason why and saw that I was hurt, she said, "That's it! We're moving!"

Dad had brought up the subject of moving many times before this happened, but Mom was not eager to comply until this incident. She had fought the idea of moving to the suburbs because it meant there would be no more walking with her shopping carriage to Codman Square for groceries. To survive in the suburbs, she would have to get her driver's license at the age of fifty-two. She truly feared that scenario, but Dad made that a prerequisite to moving. As usual, he prevailed. The house was put up for sale, and we started looking for a home in the towns south of Boston.

While still living in Dorchester and awaiting the sale of our house, I applied to attend Boston Technical High School and was accepted. As a fitting initiation for me, "the constant outsider," some seniors forced me into a loose locker during my first day at the school. They locked me inside and slid the locker out a second- or third-floor window, balancing it on the windowsill. Through the vents in the door of the tediously placed locker, I could see the pavement far below me. They were tipping the locker up and down as if to slide it right out of the window. It was terrifying! I was gripping the clothing hooks within the locker as tightly as I could, praying that they wouldn't let me slide out that window to my death. It was a horrible thing to do to someone, especially with my fear of heights. After sufficiently scaring me, they dragged the locker back into the building and released me as they had a great laugh at my expense. The next morning, I spotted my opportunity for revenge. With no teachers in sight, I grabbed the water hose, which was mounted on the wall outside their classroom and turned it on. I stood in their doorway and thoroughly soaked the guilty parties. After my initiation and their soggy payback were history, I actually ended up being friends with a couple of those guys, even though they were older.

Remarkably, it didn't take me too long to feel comfortable at Boston Tech. During that first year of high school I somehow decided I would try to make some spending money by selling fireworks at the school. I would carry a small paper bag with me from class to class during the day, selling my goodies, and then return the bag to my locker and refill it for the next day. One morning, I left the bag under my desk when I went to the men's room. Upon returning, the bag was gone. Somebody had stolen it. I scanned the class carefully, but there were no obvious signs of who had taken the bag. A classmate that I considered to be a friend offered to help me find the thief. During that entire day we searched the book-bags of numerous kids that were in that class to no avail. Finally, as my friend and I sat next to each other on the gymnasium floor waiting for the final bell to ring, I had a thought. I turned to my *friend* and said, "You know? We've checked just about everyone's bag except yours." He immediately looked astonished, and said, "What are you talking about? I was the one helping you search people's bags all day!"

I grabbed his bag and opened it without asking. I was both shocked and disappointed to see that my bag of fireworks was in there! The dismissal bell rang at that very moment, so I removed my belongings from his bag as the students quickly emptied out of the gym to board their buses. He and I were not assigned to the same bus, so we went our separate ways. I arrived at home and stewed all night as to how I should handle this scum bag thief the next day.

We shared homeroom, so the next morning I arrived purposely early before the teacher had entered the classroom. My *ex-friend* came shuffling into class as if nothing had happened. As he was about to strut past my desk he smiled down at me and arrogantly said, "How's the firecracker business?" Upon hearing those words, and without a thought, I leapt to my feet, grabbed him firmly by his jacket and threw him over two rows of desks. He crashed to the floor and against the wall. He got up with a bright red face and went to his seat. No words were ever spoken between us again. I believe a lesson in crime solving was learned by me during that situation. Sometimes, the person who seems overly anxious to help solve a crime should be looked at as a prime suspect.

A week or so after that incident, my locker was well stocked with firecrackers, rockets, cherry bombs, and block-busters. I had continuously left those items there overnight, but this day I had a premonition. Something told me to take all the fireworks home. The very next morning, some friends met up with me outside the school with some disturbing news. They said, "Did you have anything in your locker that shouldn't be there?" I said, "No. Why?" They replied, "Right after you left school yesterday the principle and some other guys used a master key. They took everything out of your locker and searched it." *Somebody* had obviously dropped a dime on me and informed the principle of my little business. My gut feeling and premonition had served me well the previous afternoon. That was the end of my enterprise at school.

I needed to take a bus in order to get to Boston Technical High. That commute brought me through some of the most run-down and neglected sections of the city. I had never personally seen these areas except on television. Every morning and afternoon, the school bus would drive by abandoned commercial buildings and vacant three-deckers with graffiti-covered facades.

Some had no remaining windows or doors. These were parts of town that resembled a bombed-out war zone to me. I remember being so glad that my neighborhood didn't look like that. The fear that our neighborhood would eventually look like this was what fueled the "white flight" to the suburbs. It was scary just driving through those neighborhoods. As I finished my first year of high school, I was thrilled when the Dorchester house finally sold and it was *off to the country*!

Chapter VI

Welcome to the Suburbs

My dad's brother, Paul, had recently moved from the city and had a new home built in the suburban town of Braintree. That town is located about sixteen miles south of Boston. We had also been looking at homes in Braintree, and we ended up purchasing a lot on the same street as my uncle and his family. I had never even heard of Braintree before, but I anticipated that it would be an exciting change for us all.

During the construction of our new home, we would drive out to Braintree every Saturday afternoon or on Sunday after church, anxious to see the progress that had been made that week. Within months, our beautiful brand-new, split-entry ranch had been built. The builder's name was Mario Pettiti, and he was a very amiable person. Once we moved in, Mario offered me a job working on the remaining new homes that he was building on our cul-de-sac street. One of my assignments was to use a razor blade to scrape the excess paint from all the window glass after the painters had finished their work. Keeping an eye out for, and chasing away vandals that liked to do damage to the vacant homes was another duty. I would also have the task of snapping off and removing all the leftover metal wires that protruded from the concrete foundations after the forms were removed. I was paid very little, I'm sure, but I always enjoyed working, especially for somebody who actually paid and appreciated me. Maybe I also liked it because when I was working, I didn't have to deal with any other kids and worry about being accepted. My bosses accepted me with praise for a job well done. There were eight to ten new homes being built on our little street, so my new job kept me busy for quite a while.

It was June of 1968 when we moved into our new home. I had just turned sixteen years old. My family had never even seen a dishwasher before, but right there in our very own new kitchen, there it was. After a lot of coaxing, I talked Mom into trying out this modern marvel. All we had on hand was our regular dishwashing detergent, and we figured it would suffice. After loading up the dishwasher, we gave everything a good spraying of Palmolive Liquid, closed the door, and let it rip. **wow!** Within thirty seconds, we had suds pumping profusely from every edge of the dishwasher door! In a panic, Mom and I were frantically scooping suds into the sink using pots and pans as fast as we could. When everything we had access to was full, we started dumping buckets of suds out the back door. It was impossible to keep up. No matter what we tried, the machine just didn't want to shut off. Soon the entire kitchen was six inches deep in suds! Finally, we opened the door and the darn thing stopped. Over and over again we cleaned up all the suds and restarted the machine, thinking that most of the soap *must* be gone. We were so wrong. The suds came cascading out of the door again and again, overtaking all efforts to contain them. Mom and I were laughing so hard that we could hardly breathe. I jokingly said to her as we laughed, "I guess you need special *non-sudsing* soap for dishwashers!" It was fortunate for us that Dad wasn't home.

He would not have laughed at all. For years after this incident, Mom never tried the dishwasher again. It served as an extra kitchen cabinet from that day forward.

Our street was named Delta Road, maybe because of a stream, named Farm River, which bordered the rear of our property. Dad loved it when the builder informed us that "they can *never* build on the land behind your new home because it's all protected wetlands." In hearing those words, we thought we were assured of having a quiet and private sanctuary behind the house forever. With that in mind, my dad and I created a nice path through the woods, and a sitting area under the trees along the edge of the stream. I built a large stone fireplace for cooking out and for watching a relaxing fire with the babbling brook in the background. It was our own little piece of paradise. Unfortunately, after several attempts, the owner of the land on the other side of the stream managed to get the "wetlands" designation removed and twenty or so condos exist behind that house today. I guess what I learned from this is, you should *never say never*, or believe it when you hear it.

It felt wonderful to be living in the country. I was hoping that the kids in the suburbs would be different than the city kids I had known thus far in my life. I prayed they would be easier to get to know and get along with. It was time to try making friends.

Located directly across from the entrance to our little dead-end road was the Colbert School. Besides being an elementary school, it served a second distinctive purpose. It was the most popular hangout in town for a gang of kids with ages ranging from fifteen to twenty-six. Every evening around dusk, muscle cars would start pulling into the schoolyard and gather. From my corner bedroom of our new home, I could see and hear all the action clearly every night. It was only a few hundred feet away. The headlights would at times shine right at my window. On weekends, both day and night, it was an even wilder place.

There would be plenty of loud laughter, music playing, and engines revving. Guys burned rubber coming and going. Cops were pulling in and out quite often, and occasionally they would clear the place out only to have the cars start returning a half-hour later. Sometimes it appeared as if the cops hung out up there with the gang!

It seemed like such a cool place to hang out. I *had to* figure out a way to get to know these people! My first few attempts at making contact were, as you might expect, very disappointing. I would go for a walk up to the school after a few of the guys in the gang had already gathered. They would be hanging out on the steps of the school or talking from car to car. As I approached and walked by, I would glance over at them and give a small wave. All I got in return were cold stares and dead silence. I had been an outsider all of my life, but this was a new town and new people. This time, I was determined that I would not give up. I was going to do whatever I had to do in order to fit in. What would it take to be *liked* by these kids?

The one thing that I noticed during my first few walks to the Colbert was that just about everyone had a beer in their hand. It seemed that this was the common thread among the group. It wasn't going to be easy figuring out how I could break into this tightly knit family of friends. They most likely had been born and brought up in this town and probably had known each other their entire lives. I was at a huge disadvantage, but I couldn't allow myself to *not* be part of this gang that was so close to my house. Suddenly, an idea came to me. I would need to make a bold move.

At the age of sixteen, I was not a drinker, and nobody in my household drank either. To be accepted by this group I would have to change that fact. My dad had a few ancient and dusty cans of Miller High Life in the downstairs fridge. They were there just in case we ever had company that might want a beer.

That never really happened in my house, so that beer was several years old. I decided I would grab a few of those beers and bring them to the Colbert School. My master plan was to plant myself, along with my beers, on the front stairs of the school where the group usually gathered. I would go up there *before* any of them were likely to show up. This way, they would have no choice but to either join me there on the steps or stay away. I was so happy having come up with what I thought was a brilliant plan!

It was time to put my plan into action. I went up to the Colbert School late on a Friday afternoon, and sure enough, I was the first one to arrive. I claimed a spot on the stairs of the building and sat there sipping my awful tasting five-year-old beer. It wasn't long before the first car showed up. It was showdown time. That driver just looked at me and stayed put in his car. Soon another car, and then a third, showed up. They were parked closely together with their windows down. Sometimes glancing in my direction, they looked irritated as they conversed with each other. I was trying not to pay much attention to them, acting as if I couldn't care less if anybody was there while I sat drinking my beer. Finally, the three drivers got out of their cars all at once and approached me. I continued to sit there silently, minding my own business. They stood in front of me looking rather confused. One of them was a short but largely built guy with a mustache, a year or so older than I was. From his build and dark tan, I could tell that he worked in construction or some other physically demanding profession that required him to be out in the sun all the time. He said to me in a stern voice, "What are you doing here?" I replied in a non-confrontational way, "I live right down there, and I came up to have a couple of beers." He said to me, "Well this is our spot, and you have to leave." My heart was beating so hard that I thought it was going to jump right out of my chest, but I had made up my mind that I was not going anywhere. This was my one and only shot at getting in with this gang and I was not backing down, no matter what happened. I said to him "I have every right to be here! I'm not bothering you. I'm not going anywhere!" He repeated, "Get out of here! I mean it!" I said just as loudly, "Forget it! I'm staying!" I played tough, but I remember having to force myself to breathe. I had made a commitment to myself. I would not allow myself to be the constant outsider *here*, even if it killed me.

I was expecting to be in a fight, but instead, the guy surprised the hell out of me when he said, "Well, if you won't leave, I will!" I paused, initially not knowing how to respond to what I had just heard until finally I said, "Go ahead and leave, because I'm staying!" Unbelievably, he did leave! I think he expected his friends to follow suit and leave as well, but they hesitated. He just got in his car and drove away. To my surprise, the remaining two guys sat down and started laughing at their friend's reaction. They thought the situation was extremely funny! I offered them a couple of my beers. It felt so good when they accepted my offer, but after taking a swig, they spit it out and dumped the rest out on the ground, saying how horrible the beer tasted. I confessed that the beers were pretty old. One of the guys went to his trunk, which contained a cooler, and brought over three ice-cold, 16-oz. cans of Schlitz. Those beers tasted so much better than the crap I had brought up to the school. A few large gulps relaxed me almost instantly. I couldn't complain. The beer I had brought with me had served its purpose exactly as planned. I was on top of the world as I sat there getting to know those guys as we talked, laughed, and drank. Their buddy, who had driven away in a rage, came back an hour or two later, and they ribbed him about how he had acted. They vouched for me, saying I was "okay."

He had no choice but to join us. I felt great. As it turned out, I was correct about that guy having an outside and physically demanding job. His name was Fubsy, and his family owned an asphalt-paving business. Decades later, we are still good friends. My relationship with the gang at the Colbert School lasted for years. Many of the people I met up there ended up being the greatest friends I could imagine. In all, there were probably thirty guys and girls that regularly hung out "up the school."

Occasionally, a couple of the guys could get nasty with one another when they got drunk. They would try really hard to pick a fight or would become unmanageable. As time passed, it was those couple of troublemakers who ended up with real drinking problems that affected their lives very negatively. After not seeing one of those troublemakers for several years, I was sitting in the lounge at the Nii Hau Chinese Restaurant when he happened to come in. This was the lounge that had been a regular hangout for the Colbert Gang for many years. My old acquaintance's first request of me was to buy him a drink. His second request, which came after a few more drinks, was to drive him to the halfway house in South Boston where he was scheduled to check himself in that day. I accommodated both of his requests.

At the Colbert, our gang partied every Friday and Saturday night. On Sundays, the guys would be "up the school," waxing their cars and drinking beer as their girlfriends stood around chatting and looking great. You would hear and smell the burning rubber from the spinning tires as we came and went. I would usually walk up to the school because during my first three years hanging out with the group, I had no car of my own. Dad had forbidden me from buying one. But occasionally, I would be allowed to drive his Oldsmobile, and that car could burn rubber with the best of them.

When leaving the school, most of our trips were just short hops up to Rosie's Sub Shop, Sammy's Pizza Villa, or Granite Liquors.

If nobody of legal drinking age was available to buy beer for us, we would drive all the way into South Boston. My new friends knew of a liquor store that would send a man out to your car as you were parked on the side street around the corner from the entrance. That man would take your order and your money. Within a minute he would return to the car with your booze! There were no questions asked and no ID required. This all took place in broad daylight. The funny thing was, even though I worked in Southie, I didn't know anything about this west side liquor store or its special curbside service. My suburban friends had to introduce me to it.

Often, while parked up at the Colbert, there would be music blasting from a new 8-track tape player that somebody had just installed in their new car. Most of the gang members were from well-off families. Many had parents that owned businesses, such as construction companies, body shops, window companies, etc. These kids had lots of money to spend on toys. We literally didn't have a care in the world back then. We worried about nothing! Where did those days go?

The dirt road that led through the woods behind the Colbert School served as a great parking spot when guys from the gang would have a date. We would back our cars off of that road, far into the woods where the cops couldn't see us. Once hidden from view you could relax, have a beer, and of course, steam-up the windows.

At the end of that dirt road, you could walk through the woods to a reservoir. We would sometimes sneak over there and fish or swim until we were chased away by the water department guys.

On one sad day, the brother of one of our group went under and drowned while trying to swim across the pond. Several of us stood on shore and watched in horror as the police finally dredged his body out of the deep water using a grappling hook. It was a surreal sight as they struggled to load him into the boat and brought his body to shore. I don't think we ever swam there again. Thankfully though, it was rare that tragedy struck the Colbert Gang.

During those youthful years hanging out "up the school", the ultimate goal was to get plastered on Friday and Saturday nights. Usually we stayed around the Colbert, roamed the neighborhood on foot, of took short rides around town. It is truly a miracle that none of the gang who did drive after drinking ever killed themselves or anybody else. One guy did have a horrible motorcycle accident one night that resulted in him almost losing his life. His left leg and his masculinity were nearly severed. He had lost control of his bike and hit a guardrail, which sliced into him very badly. The only thing that saved his life and limbs was the fact that a medical professional happened to be driving past the scene of the accident as it happened, and stopped to help. That heroic doctor worked to control the profuse bleeding from his arteries until the ambulance arrived.

Sadly, like many high school seniors experience, two good friends from my senior class were killed in a car accident shortly before graduation. The accident happened solely because of speeding and not because of alcohol, from what I was told. They were not members of the Colbert Gang, but I knew them very well. Richard and Dominic were two good-looking Italian guys that were *the* most popular in Braintree High. They sat one on either side of me in accounting, and we had such a good time in that class. I was popular with them because I happened to be knowledgeable about accounting basics due to my time working at the family business.

In class, they would constantly look to me for help. On one of the rare occasions that Dad let me take his car out for the night, I happened to be not far down the street from where their accident occurred. After a long evening of partying with my friends, we were enjoying a late-night breakfast at Fasano's Diner. Somebody ran into the restaurant and announced that Dominic and Richard had just crashed into a stone wall down the street. One of them had died at the scene and the other was in very bad shape. An ambulance was en route to Quincy Hospital with the survivor.

From Fasano's Diner, I left my friends, jumped in my dad's car and drove to the scene of the accident. I couldn't believe my eyes when I spotted the engine of the car lying all by itself in the middle of the road. It was hundreds of feet away from the crash site. That was not a good sign. Then I spotted the unrecognizable car. It had gone completely over a tall stone wall and it was standing almost perpendicular to the ground, up against a huge tree. The entire car was bent into an inverted U shape. I became extremely distraught upon seeing this nightmarish sight. Without a second thought, I found myself recklessly speeding down the road, trying to get to Quincy Hospital. I needed to see if at least one friend had survived. I was only halfway to Quincy Hospital when I heard a siren and saw blue lights flashing right behind me. The Quincy Police pulled me over. I was obviously upset and remember tears running down my face. I was sobbing as I told the officer where I was going. He had apparently heard about the accident over the police radio and knew I was telling the truth. He also sensed that I was not just upset but also under the influence of the drinks I had consumed. That kind officer explained to me very sympathetically that he could not allow me to continue driving in the emotional and impaired state that I was in. Rather than arrest me, he gave me another option to consider.

He offered to take my keys away from me! He would allow me to sleep right there in my car for a couple of hours, along the side of the road. He wanted me to sober up and calm down. He explained that I would not be helping my friend by getting into an accident myself. "I will return your keys to you in two or three hours," he said. I agreed to comply and I thanked him.

As I lay down on the front seat of the car, the hours passed, but I didn't sleep. There was no way to stop pondering the awful event of that night. As promised, the Quincy Police officer returned my keys a few hours later. He sadly informed me that he had checked with the hospital and found out that the second person in the accident had also died. That officer was very compassionate. He told me there was absolutely nothing I could do for my friends that night, and he made me promise to go straight home. Once again, I complied. My high school graduation ceremony was a solemn event for me due to my two missing friends. I'm sure that if they had the chance, Dominic and Richard would change the choices they made that last night of their lives. They shared the same philosophy that I did at the time. We just wanted to graduate and get the heck out of high school, to start really living our lives. I got to do it. They didn't.

With regard to the Colbert Gang, somebody up there must have liked us, a lot. We were nuts behind the wheel. There were several total wrecks among the gang over the years, but these kids, including myself, always managed to walk away in one piece and then replace the wrecked cars with newer and ever faster ones.

Outside of school and work, the Colbert Gang filled the major part of my social life. Within a week or so of my acceptance into the group, I was officially initiated when I was escorted home by Bubba Belcher of the Braintree Police. As the cruiser pulled up to us at the school, my pal John hid his beer behind *my* back without me knowing it.

Bubba, not knowing me because I was new to the gang, called me over to the cruiser, and, of course, he saw the beer as soon as I stood up. I wasn't even drinking that day, but he tagged me as the owner of that beer. He gave me a choice to either get arrested, or be taken home to my parents. When we got to my house, he delivered me to my mother at the front door, explaining that I had been caught drinking. After Bubba left, I explained to my mom what had happened and she agreed, as usual, to not tell Vito when he got home from work. I could do no wrong in my mother's eyes. She was always there for me, without exception.

While still in the process of getting to know more new friends at the Colbert, I decided to give them a real treat. I had never given it much thought, but one day it dawned on me that 90 percent of the guys at the Colbert were Italian. Just about every single one of their last names ended in an *a*, an *i*, or an *o*. They would really appreciate what I had in mind for a surprise. Some thirty years earlier, my long-departed Italian grandparents had made two barrels of homemade wine. That wine was eventually put into gallon glass jugs. We had kept about twenty gallons of the red and white wine stored in our cellar in Dorchester since way before I was born. Now, those bottles had been moved to a dark chamber under the stairs of our new home in Braintree. To me, it seemed a shame to have all that wine go unused year after year. My parents certainly wouldn't notice if one gallon went missing. I had already been snatching pints of Seagram's 7 every so often from the cases my dad had stashed in the cubby hole right next to the wine. Customers and business owners would give my father booze every Christmas, and sometimes, a deal he couldn't refuse on a case of whiskey would present itself in Southie. All these goodies were there for the taking, and I, "the little rat," as my mom would affectionately call me, would help myself.

One Friday afternoon, I grabbed a gallon of grandma's white wine and brought it up to the schoolyard. I still remember how I carried it up to the school in a big brown paper bag, hoping I wouldn't drop it or shake up too much of the gross sediment that clung to the glass. As the guys started to show up, I made them wait to see what surprise I had for them in the bag until several of the crew had gathered. When they finally saw it, they were excited to be able to sample some real homemade thirty-year-old "Guinea White." The sun started to go down, and so did the wine. We passed that jug around over and over again. It was anything but pleasant to drink because it was as strong as any whiskey I had ever tasted. My head started spinning after just a few swigs. By the time the jug was almost empty, the front lawn of the school resembled the aftermath of a civil war battle with passed-out bodies strewn everywhere. All I could manage to do was lift my head off the grass enough to observe the carnage. That wine created quite a memory that we all talked about for a long time to come.

I adopted my new friends' partying habits pretty quickly. I was now one of them. For the first time in my life I was accepted into a real group of my peers. The Colbert Gang had quite the reputation around town as a wild group, yet we were basically left alone by the authorities to enjoy our hangout freely and with impunity. It helped that we had two nephews of the most powerful and influential man in the region hanging out at the school with us. Most of the regulars knew all the cops in town by their first names. One former Colbert regular was now a Braintree cop himself. The police would cut us lots of slack, but they had to chase us away from our hangout every so often to keep things from getting too far out of hand. I'm sure that the reason the surrounding neighbors weren't on the phone to the police very often was because most of those families had a son, daughter, or nephew that frequented the gatherings at the schoolyard, so we were tolerated.

One night, an irate neighbor who lived near the school came marching up the driveway with a very determined gait. I guess we were exceptionally noisy that evening. We could sense he was furious because he was clutching a baseball bat, and it was way too dark outside to play baseball. He walked right up to us, face-to-face, and declared that he had three young daughters at home, and his wife was trying to get them to sleep. He convincingly went on to say that if we didn't "knock off the noise" he was going to "bash our heads in." I remember admiring his courage, coming up there all alone and confronting six or eight young guys in the dark. I guess he came to us himself because he knew that calling the cops would be ineffective. We were polite to him (and his bat) and we promised to keep the noise down. Ironically, several years later, one of his young daughters, that couldn't get to sleep that night, ended up marrying a member of our gang who was several years older than herself.

I soon found out that living in Braintree didn't isolate my family from things you might expect to only happen in the city. Shortly after getting my driver's license, I was sitting in my mother's new station wagon up at the Colbert. I was the only person up there at the time, and I had parked alongside the brick building. I started to hear what I thought were firecrackers off in the distance. I paid no attention until I realized that something was hitting the building next to where I was parked. After the second or third *ping* against the wall, I knew that the noise was not firecrackers. Somebody was shooting at me! The shots were coming from quite far away.

I crouched down low behind the steering wheel, started the engine as quickly as I could, and drove away. I knew the direction from which the shots were originating, so I drove down the next roadway closest to the school to search for the shooter. There was a man outside working in his yard. I stopped and told him what had happened and asked if he heard where the shots came from. He pointed in the direction and volunteered to come with me. As the two of us headed that way we heard another shot within seconds, which sounded pretty close. We ducked down and made our way through some bushes to the edge of a large field and saw a young man wearing a red football jersey who was holding a rifle. He was apparently target shooting in the field, but also firing off shots at anything he felt like shooting at. Both of us started yelling to the teenager, saying something to the effect, "Hey! What are you doing? Those shots are carrying over here!" Once he heard us, he immediately took off running. We watched as he ran to a distant house and quickly entered the back door. After thanking the man for his help, I decided to go and confront the guy who was doing the shooting, so I drove to that house. I never even thought of calling the police. It turned out that I knew the teenager. He sometimes would hang out at the school. Claiming that he wasn't trying to hit me with those shots, he admitted that he was firing in that direction. He stated, "I didn't think the bullets would carry that far." Although he apologized rather convincingly, I always questioned in my mind whether he was being truthful. I was never quite sure that the incident was just an innocent error of judgment.

A few years after that happened, my mother was standing in our front yard on Delta Road when she heard what she insisted was a bullet whizzing by her head. She said she actually felt the breeze of the bullet as it passed her ear. It was that close.

I suggested that it was probably just a bee flying by her, but she was insistent that it was a bullet. Her suspicion was later confirmed. A neighbor, who lived a few houses away on the cul-de-sac, arrived home from work to discover a bullet hole in the front window of his house. The bullet had lodged in the television set in his living room. The trajectory of that bullet would indicate that the shot came from near the entrance of our street, maybe from a passing car. It could also have come from somewhere in the heavy brush adjacent to the Colbert School. It had not originated from anywhere near the field I had been fired upon from previously. The shooting that almost killed my mom still remains a mystery.

Another family who lived within view of the Colbert School was the target of a shocking crime. They seemed to be an ordinary family. The son occasionally would come up to the school and was liked by everyone up there, including me. When that boy was much younger, he was one of the youngsters I would have to chase away from the new houses being built on our street because he liked to throw rocks and break windows. Now he was an adolescent, and a good kid. We were stunned at the news that his father, who had been missing for a couple of days, was found in the trunk of his Cadillac, shot to death.

A few doors away from that house lived an older woman whom I got to know over time. I would stop and talk to her while walking the neighborhood. She confided in me one day that she was taking bets on the daily street number, and she invited me to solicit bets from people I knew. I could work with her if I wanted to make some extra money. Because of my history knowing bookies in Southie, I wasn't shocked by her offer, but I said, "No, thanks." The suburbs were not as laid-back and innocent as I had imagined they would be.

About two years after moving to Braintree, my back pain started progressively getting worse. It eventually got to the point it was painful just taking a deep breath, and I had developed a pronounced hump on the left side of my rib cage. I was diagnosed with scoliosis, and there was a chance that if I wore a Milwaukee brace for a year, it might stop the curvature from progressing. The hope was that the brace would save me from eventually requiring major surgery. I was sent to Massachusetts Hospital School in Canton to be fitted with the brace. I could continue my high school classes while I was in that hospital. It was a wonderful facility in a beautiful setting. Some patients actually had televisions in their rooms and could interact with their classrooms and teachers directly from their beds. That was quite amazing technology for 1970. There were students from all around the state. Many were severely disabled, and this is where they attended school. My first day at that hospital was quite shocking to me. During dinner, which was my first meal at the facility, I sat at a long table that was full of kids with various serious maladies. Right next to me sat a boy that had no arms at all. He was sitting there eating, using a knife and fork with his feet. He could use his feet just as proficiently as I could use my hands. It was amazing to watch him cut up the food on his plate, albeit quite unsettling as well, until I got used to seeing it. He was a very nice guy, and he started a conversation with me at the table. After dinner, he offered to show me around.

We went into the billiards room, and I began to shoot pool by myself. That's one thing my new friend could not do. Shortly after I began to play, a heavyset guy rolled into the room in a wheel chair. He was paralyzed from the waist down. His arms were twice the normal size due to the constant workout they got, wheeling his massive self around. I had seen him earlier that day when I happened to walk past his room at the hospital. The doorway to his room was decorated with three or four blown-up prophylactics. They were now huge balloons that had the *F* word, along with many other assorted profanities, written all over them in magic marker. When I first spotted them, I wondered why the hospital staff would allow such a thing to exist. It became immediately obvious that this paraplegic had an attitude. He was still rolling into the recreation room when he announced that he wanted to use the pool table. I said, "Fine, let's have a game." He said no. He wanted to use it alone, and he made it clear that I was not to ever play on that table without asking his permission. When he saw my hesitation to comply with his wishes, he wanted to fight me! He was insistent that we go outside, where he was going to kick my ass! I think he had lived there at the hospital school for a long time, and this was his territory. I couldn't picture myself out in the courtyard, fighting with a guy in a wheel chair, so I backed off and let him have his way. This maniac became furious when I refused to fight him. He said to me, "I'm going to sneak into your room while you're sleeping and slash your throat!" Needless to say, I didn't sleep very well during my first few nights at the hospital. It also became obvious to me why the nurses allowed this guy to put up whatever obscenities he wanted to at the doorway to his room. He was an angry and disturbed human being, someone to be avoided if possible.

Within a few weeks, and after being fitted and briefed on my new hardware, I was back home wearing a huge and cumbersome back brace. It went from under my chin and around my neck to all the way down over my hips. It was very uncomfortable, constructed of steel rods in the back and front with pads and straps to pull my spine in the corrective directions. I was in that contraption for an entire year, only taking it off to shower.

The brace didn't stop me from partying with my friends at the Colbert. Fubsy, being the fun guy that he was, renamed me "Nick the Neck" after seeing me in the back brace. That nickname stuck, but when the brace came off a year later, my friends shortened it to just plain "Nick."

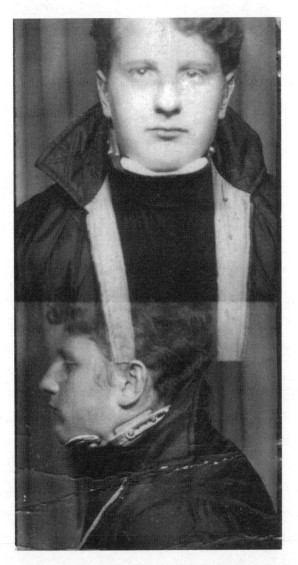

I wore this Milwaukee Brace for one year in a failed attempt to prevent my scoliosis from progressing. It extended from under my chin, to over my hips.

Freedom from the brace meant it was back to the usual antics, which included some wild driving. There was a quarter-mile drag strip in Braintree that was located near the Blue Hills Cemetery. A few years prior, a major highway had been constructed, and some roads had been redirected. That roadwork resulted in a perfectly straight, paved section of roadway being abandoned. This newly dissected road-to-nowhere measured just over a quarter mile, and it dead-ended with a mound of soil that was eight to ten feet high. A few hundred feet beyond that barrier was the new interstate. The highway department had inadvertently created the perfect drag strip! There was enough room off to the sides to allow spectators, and after the finish line, there was *usually* ample distance in which to stop safely. The "quarter mile" became a regular gathering spot. People from several towns began racing there. While on the subject of the Braintree quarter mile, I need to jump ahead to a most memorable experience, which took place there.

My friend Chippa owned a black Buick Wildcat that was pretty powerful. After the two of us had spent a few hours enjoying cocktails at the Nii Hau restaurant lounge, he began to express the opinion that his car would give my Dodge Challenger a good run for its money. Not being one who normally backed away from a challenge, I agreed to let him show me. We left the bar and drove to the quarter mile. It was late at night and extremely dark at the tree-draped drag strip. It wasn't the ideal time to be racing on an unlit desolate roadway. Add to the equation the liquid courage, which was in our veins, and we had all the ingredients of a possible disaster.

The race started with little discussion. I began to pull away from Chippa's heavy Buick at first, but I was nervous about judging the end of the track, which we could not see. I started to let off the gas.

Chippa and I were now neck and neck, staring back and forth at each other to see who would shut down first. It became obvious that it wasn't going to be Chippa, and there was no doubt that we were out of time. I locked up my brakes, but Chippa just kept going! Apparently, he was trying to stop, but it was too late. As my car skidded sideways and came to rest at the base of the barrier, I watched the bright red stoplights of Chippa's Buick fly up the side of the dirt mound and into the air. His car disappeared over the barrier, into the darkness!

I jumped out of my car and scrambled to the top of the berm, scared at what I might find on the other side. I was relieved to find that his car had landed on its wheels and Chippa was not hurt badly. He was just shaken up, but the Wildcat was not going anywhere without some careful and time-consuming maneuvering. I asked Chippa, "What do you want to do about the car?" He said, "I don't know. Let's get out of here!" We jumped into my car and quickly left. Chippa wasn't anxious to be questioned by police as the driver of that car with alcohol on his breath. A while later, as we sat drinking coffee in my car at the Braintree Five Corners doughnut shop, we heard a call over the police scanner that I kept in my car. Some lovebirds that were parked in the woods at the drag strip had reported that a car had gone over the embankment at the end of the quarter mile. The police dispatcher put out a call for an officer to go investigate. Chippa and I waited at least ten minutes after hearing that call, and then we headed back to the drag strip. We wanted to get there after the cops arrived, but before they could order the car towed. As we entered the long and lonely quarter mile, we realized that it was still dark down at the end where his car was. Nobody else had arrived yet. We had beaten the cops to the car. I looked in the rearview mirror and realized that it was too late to turn back.

There were multiple blue lights entering the roadway behind us at a high rate of speed. There was only one way in and one way out, so I thought to myself, "This is gonna be fun, explaining how we got here before the police."

When we reached the dead end of the drag strip, two cruisers pulled up and blocked my Challenger in. The officers shined their spotlights on us and approached with their hands on their guns. They asked, "What are you guys doing here?" Chippa was extremely quick thinking. He immediately announced that his car was on the other side of the berm. He told them that earlier in the evening, he had taken a wrong turn into this unlit road, and by the time he noticed that the road dead-ended, he was unable to stop. He said he lost his brakes and went right over the dirt mound. He told the officer that he was walking to five corners to get to a pay-phone when he ran into me. He said, "We came back to try to get the car out of there." They asked us if we had been drinking, and, of course, we said "No." None of the Braintree cops were strangers to us, and they knew our story was a load of crap. But it was a *good* story. They didn't even wait to see if we got the car out from behind the mound of earth. They just left us there, which was fine with us. We both had a good laugh as they drove away and out of sight. With some careful maneuvering through the woods, we were able to get the car out of there and back on the roadway. The exhaust system was missing, but that was *okay*. Everyone was all right and nobody got arrested. It was a good night!

As word spread, and the popularity of the drag strip increased, there were several other mishaps at the quarter mile. Cars were losing control, and we heard of people getting hurt. One Sunday morning, I observed a motorcyclist try to exhibit his riding skills by attempting to run the distance while sitting backward on his bike.

He didn't make it far at all before losing control and veering off into the woods. Thankfully, he hadn't gathered up too much speed.

The increasing number of accidents prompted the town to make several attempts to block off the drag strip in order to prevent its use. Using heavy equipment, they would line up huge boulders, the size of small cars, all the way across the entrance to the roadway. When that barrier mysteriously disappeared, they created a tall dirt and stone berm to keep cars out. As soon as the barriers went up, someone who had access to construction equipment would bring a front-end-loader up there and clear the massive debris out of the way. The following weekend, we would be racing as usual. Eventually the town resorted to installing asphalt speed bumps every so many feet, all the way down the quarter mile. The sight of wave after wave of large speed bumps over the entire length of the road was quite a thing to see. When I drove up and saw it for the first time, I remember that I couldn't help but smile with amazement at the sight. That drastic and expensive move finally deterred any further attempts to clear the obstructions.

As mentioned in the Authors Note, this is your book.
My hope is that you will use it to examine and
record important facts from your past.
You need never share the pages you personalize
with anyone, unless you so choose.
Have you ever felt like "the constant outsider?"
Write about it.

Reader's Notes

Reader's Notes

Reader's Notes

Reader's Notes

Chapter VII

Colorado: Bricks, Horses, and Cliffs

As soon as high school graduation day had passed, I felt it was time to grow up and make some changes. Working full time with my dad in Southie wasn't working out too well. I worked six days a week and wasn't getting paid a regular wage. When I would bring up my desire to be paid like everyone else at the shop, he would say, "If you need something, ask me." I was nineteen years old, and I wasn't allowed to buy a car of my own, and I couldn't come and go as I pleased with one of dad's cars. He couldn't understand why I hated living on such a short leash. In my eyes, I was an adult and should be treated as such. Mom was sympathetic but powerless to improve my situation. I had to find a way out. Ironically, it was another Mobil gas station, one at Braintree Five Corners that gave me that way out via a part time job. I would work there in secret a few nights per week after working at our own Mobil station in Southie during the day. I saved that money until I was able to buy a car of my own. Within a few weeks, I drove up to our house in my first car. It was a 1966, standard shift, Ford Falcon that cost me $300. Desperate to be treated as an adult, I gave my father an ultimatum. I told him I wanted to be paid like all the other guys at the garage, and I wanted to be free to come and go as I pleased. His reply was "As long as you're living under my roof, you'll do as I say." That was all I needed to hear.

I had already cleared it with my sister Fran and her husband Bill that if I couldn't work things out at home with Dad, I could go and live with them in Colorado for a while. So I loaded up my car and prepared to head west. It was hard to leave my mom because she was such a sweet person and loving mother, but it was time to take a stand. I called my sister from the pay-phone outside Dunkin' Donuts at Braintree Five Corners, telling her that I would see her in about four days. I estimated that it would take me that long to drive the 2,200 miles to her house, with just one driver. I got back in my car and headed out on the first leg of my exciting journey to an independent life. I imagined that it would be a scary experience to leave home that day, but it was just the opposite. It was the very first major thing I had ever done in my life that was entirely my decision, and it felt wonderful. Just thirty-six hours after making that phone call from Braintree, I was knocking on my sister's door in Castle Rock, Colorado. Having driven that same trip from Massachusetts herself several times, she was shocked that I had made it there in such a short time. I never told her that I had fallen asleep twice behind the wheel while doing ninety miles an hour through the state of Nebraska. Each time, I was awakened by the noise of the car going off the road. Thankfully, there were no trees on the side of those highways in Nebraska, just miles and miles of cornfields. I did tell Fran about a naked shower I took on the highway during a tremendous thunderstorm. I had to do something to wake myself up. It was such a downpour that no cars or trucks were able to drive by. With zero visibility, it was the perfect opportunity for me to revive myself.

Two drifters that I had picked up thumbing a few hundred miles back thought I was nuts as I stripped down, grabbed a bar of soap, and lathered up in front of my car. It was the best shower I've ever taken.

Colorado was not only beautiful, it was also a blast! My time there would evolve into a wonderful adventure and my first real taste of freedom from the overbearing control of my father. It was also an education, which no school could possibly have provided.

The view of the Rocky Mountains was mesmerizing, and I was anxious to explore my new surroundings. A day or so after arriving in Colorado, I informed my sister that I was headed to the mountains for the day. The Falcon was in need of some "TLC" after the non-stop and grueling trip across the country. I didn't feel that she was up to going mountain climbing, so I headed out on foot. When I made it to the main road, I stuck out my thumb. Almost immediately, a blue Monte Carlo pulled up. I jumped in, and to my delight, the driver was an extremely beautiful young lady, a year or two older than I was. Though professionally dressed, she would certainly spice up any lucky office she was headed to with her very short, 1970's style mini-skirt. She asked, "Where are you headed?" I pointed way off in the distance and said, "See those mountains? That's where I'm going." She seemed surprised by my answer. I went on to explain that I was new to the area and I just wanted to experience being in the mountains. Smiling at me, she said, "That sounds wonderful! I'm on my way to work in Denver and I can drop you off at the base of the hills near there." I suggested that if she could skip work she was certainly welcome to join me. I could tell she was actually very tempted, but duty called. During the ride toward Denver we had a great conversation. When we arrived at the foot of the mountains she warmly wished me a great adventure, and away she went. My day was off to a great start.

It wasn't long before a shiny new motor home pulled up. It was one of the nicest ones I had ever seen. The door swung opened and a deep voice asked, "Where are you headed?" I responded, "Up in the mountains." The driver said, "That's where we're going. Hop in!" Behind the wheel was a huge man who strongly resembled "Hoss Cartwright" of the TV show, Bonanza. The similarity was striking and he had a Dan Blocker type voice to match. Both the driver and his female companion were wearing bright red jump suits. I thought that was strange. It was something that people would wear if they *wanted* to draw attention to themselves.

Behind the drivers seat was a case of gin. The box was opened and only a couple of bottles were missing. The driver and his lady friend were occasionally passing an opened bottle of gin back and forth, just swigging away as we motored along. I was asked if I would like to try some, and they passed the bottle back to me. I had never tasted gin before, but not to be anti-social, I started taking small sips whenever it was offered. It wasn't long before I felt *comfortable* enough to ask if I could call him "Hoss." He said, "Sure, young fella. Lots of people do." We leisurely cruised through the mountains for hours, often stopping to enjoy the breathtaking views. More than once, we stopped in small mountain towns for food and drinks, all of which they insisted on paying for. The gin, even though it was straight, started going down rather easily. It didn't seem to have any effect on my hosts, but I was getting quite looped and feeling no pain. Suddenly, they asked if I wanted to see Buffalo Bill's grave! Being a city boy, I had only heard of Buffalo Bill from history and in cowboy movies. I was thrilled to have this opportunity to see the resting place of an icon from America's past. We exited the motor home and I was spellbound. I felt bad for Buffalo Bill because this seemed like such a lonely and isolated grave site.

It was surrounded by what I remember as being a six foot wrought iron fence. Obviously, the fence was meant to keep people out, but I had an idea. I knew of Buffalo Bill's wild reputation, so I suggested, "We should give Buffalo Bill a drink!" I asked Hoss if that would be okay with him. He whole-heartedly agreed. I climbed over the tall fence and they passed me a quart of gin. I exclaimed, "This is for you Buffalo Bill," as I poured a good portion of that bottle over his grave.

By now I was almost seeing triple from the gin. When we left the gravesite, the kind strangers asked me where I lived. I was glad they weren't going to just drop me off in the hills. I'm sure I never would have made it home. Remembering exactly how to get back to my sister's house proved to be quite puzzling to me. I couldn't remember any street names and Castle Rock was probably forty miles away. My hosts were very understanding and patient. Finally, I recognized an area we were driving through and knew I was close to home.

Not wanting to claim responsibility for my present condition, my new friends let me out of the camper pretty far from the house. They motored away as soon as I was safely near the door. My sister happened to be entertaining guests just a few feet away from the entrance, in her living room. As soon as I staggered through the doorway she noticed I was loaded, and loudly said, "Tommy! Where were you?" She says I announced that "I was out with Hoss Cartwright," and then fell flat on the floor in front of her quests. Fran told me I had a watermelon in my arms when I arrived. I can't remember how I came to be in possession of that, but she tells me it made quite a mess when it hit the floor. I made a great first impression on my sisters friends that day. Since then, I still can not stomach the smell of gin.

Even though I went way overboard that day, it just shows that sometimes when you just let things happen and have no special plans, life-long memories are formed and adventures can be found. You just have to go out and find them.

Following in my father's footsteps, I had an interest in firearms. I loved to shoot, and I wanted to have a gun of my own. I was now living in an area where I could target-practice at will, right outside my back door. Soon after arriving in Colorado, my sister's husband agreed to accompany me to the store and buy a pistol for me because I was under the required age. Arriving back at the house with my new .22 caliber, eight shot revolver, I immediately went out in the yard with my little nephews, Sean, Brian, and Danny to test it out. While I was shooting at some tin cans, the boys spotted a chipmunk scurrying around about 100 feet away in some bushes. They yelled, "Uncle Tommy! There's a chipmunk! Try and shoot it!" I looked over and thought there was no way I would actually hit that tiny thing from this distance, but I aimed and fired. One shot and the chipmunk was dead! I couldn't believe it. I felt like Clint Eastwood, and the boys were really impressed with my shooting skill. We went over and admired this beautiful little creature with its colorfully patterned fur. Then we respectfully buried it in the yard. The pride I felt upon showing the boys what a great shot their Uncle Tommy was turned out to be short-lived. A couple of days later, as the entire family sat eating one of my sister's great breakfasts at the table in front of a sliding glass door, one of the family dogs came up and stood directly outside the glass, begging to show the family the prize it had found. It stood there wagging its tail, holding something black and disgusting looking in its jaws. After looking closely, we discovered that the dog had dug up the chipmunk that I had needlessly killed. I had transformed an absolutely beautiful and harmless living creature into a grotesque and decaying black blob.

That sight did not make me feel good about myself. I decided there and then that I would never shoot another innocent animal again, and I never have.

The ranch owners in the neighborhood where I now lived were having a terrible problem with rattlesnakes. When outside, everyone had to be extremely careful and watch out for the poisonous snakes. When a rattler bit a neighbor's horse, people became fearful for their family's safety. The sheer numbers of these dangerous snakes indicated that there had to be snake dens somewhere close by. Something had to be done. Banding together, about twenty of us from the surrounding homes journeyed to the top of a nearby hill. It resembled a flat and rocky plateau on top, and it was the most likely location for the dens. Everyone had a shovel and a gun. Some carried gallon cans of gasoline which would be used to douse and burn the dens when they were found. Once we arrived at the crest, everyone separated to search his or her assigned areas.

I was standing in some bushes digging into an opening I had found, to see if it was the entrance to a den. All alone, and about fifty feet from the nearest person, I suddenly heard the one sound that I didn't want to hear. It was the rattle of a snake, warning me that I had invaded its comfort zone. I figured that it would be unwise to call out for help. I didn't want to agitate or frighten the snake which, from the sound of it, was very close. I froze, just as I was instructed to do in this situation. Turning my head slightly to see where the snake was, I saw that he was just two feet from my right wrist. With my short sleeved shirt, I made a tempting target. He was coiled back and ready to strike if he felt the need. Being left handed, I was wearing my pistol in a holster on my left side. I slowly reached with my hidden hand toward my gun. There were two clasps. One was on the leather strap that secured the pistol in its holster.

The other snap held the holster onto my belt. Without turning to look, I felt for the clasp and unsnapped it. Instantly, my gun, holster and all, fell to the ground. I thought, "Oh, shit! Now what do I do?" The snake continued to stare at me, rattling its tail ever louder after hearing the noise of my gun hitting the ground. The seconds ticked by until finally the snake decided to slither away. I was glad I had stayed completely still, and made no threatening or sudden movements. I don't remember any dens being found that day. An individual rattlesnake was shot at close range by my brother-in-law, Bill Malone, using his shotgun. He had shot it two inches behind its head, severing that part from the rest of the snake's body. When I went to reach down and pick up the snakes head, he grabbed my arm and stopped me, saying, "Let me show you something." He placed a stick against the snake's separated head and showed me what would have happened if I had gotten too close. The snake's jaws clamped onto the stick, and we could see the yellowish venom oozing out of its fangs. The head would live on for a while I was told, maybe until sundown.

Soon after settling in with my sister and her family, Billy landed me a job with a friend of his as a hod-carrier. It was my task to keep two masons in constant supply of mortar, bricks, and flue liners. I soon found out that my coworkers loved playing tricks on the "Yankee" from Boston. During my very first day on the job, we were to build the fireplaces and chimney for a beautiful new home that was under construction at the bottom of a very long and steep driveway. The supply truck couldn't make it down the hill to the house, so they unloaded thousands of bricks and other supplies up at the edge of the roadway. Still under construction, that long descending driveway was just gravel and hadn't been paved yet. That first workday was about to get interesting really fast.

The assignment issued to me by the boss was to move all of that material down to the house so they could get to work. We had a special dolly that was designed to move several hundred bricks at a time. I was told to hurry up. Being anxious to make a good impression, I loaded the dolly to the max. As I struggled to maneuver the brick-laden dolly to the start of the steep driveway, I thought it was a little strange that all the other workers were just quietly standing there, watching me. The moment I started down the hundred-foot driveway, I knew I was in trouble. The amount of bricks on the dolly far outweighed me. The gravitational force was pulling me faster and faster down the hill until I had a choice to make. I could let go of the dolly and have hundreds of bricks go all over the place and possibly smash into the house at the bottom of the hill, or I could hold on and try to slow down the load. I chose to hold on. The weight of the load soon pulled me forward off my feet and was dragging me faster and faster down the hill on my stomach. As the gravel from the driveway tore me up, the pain was intense, but I didn't let go. When everything came to rest at the bottom of the driveway, I just laid there for a quite a few seconds, unable to move. When I finally let go of the grips and stood up, there were holes through my jeans and my shirt with a little blood coming from too many scrapes to count, but the bricks were still neatly strapped together on the dolly.

I could hear the roar of uncontrollable laughter emanating from the top of the hill. These guys knew exactly what was going to happen to me, and they couldn't wait to watch the "Yankee Drag" as they later called it. I can't blame them for being paralyzed with laughter. It must have been quite a sight to see.

Hanging out with those guys, after getting to know them, was fun. The bricklayers would usually end their workday by stopping at the local liquor store to pick up some whiskey. I was always invited to join them. After sharing a pint or two, we would head out to our respective homes. I only had to drive three or four miles to get home from downtown Castle Rock, which, unlike today, was mostly wide-open space. One day, after sharing in those drinks, I was cranking right along down the dirt road leading to my sister's home, when I somehow failed to navigate my car past a cattle-guard. Those are heavy iron structures, which prevent cattle from crossing small bridges where dry creek beds go under the road. The spaces between the large pipes that cross the road fool cattle into thinking they could not cross over. On each side of the road at a cattle-guard, there is a heavy metal barrier sloped upward. Cars *usually* have no problem passing over these, but I slammed into one of the barriers. The old Falcon went up on two wheels, almost rolling over onto its side. When it came to rest, I was able to back down off the structure and proceeded on to my sister's house. Because it was such wide-open country, my little nephews and niece, along with my sister, were apparently watching all this from a distance. They said they heard my car's revving engine and saw me speeding along the dirt road with a huge cloud of dust following behind me. From more than a quarter mile away, they watched in awe as I smashed into the cattle-guard, backed up, and then just continued on home. That is one memory that they always bring up about their "wild" Uncle Tommy. Of course, being embarrassed because of my irresponsible driving, I made up a story about how the throttle got stuck on my car, and I couldn't control it. I did my best to make them believe my story, even going to the extreme of buying a can of spray throttle cleaner, and using it at the house as they watched. But seriously, I was just lucky that it wasn't another vehicle that I hit that day.

At around $2.50 an hour, I quickly realized that the hod-carrier job wasn't for me. It was extremely hard on my back, and every day, I had to use a rickety homemade ladder that was falling apart while carrying brick tongs in each hand. I would climb up on roofs without really being able to hold onto the ladder properly. It wasn't worth the risk. So, when another opportunity presented itself, I grabbed it.

I was offered a job with another of my brother-in-law's friends. He was a horse trainer named Lonny Barber. I worked with him at a fairgrounds-racetrack up in the mountains near Rifle, Colorado for a few weeks. There was adventure to be found there too. Our stable had several horses running at the small track. It was really small compared to the other tracks I had helped out at such as Suffolk Downs. One of the horses in our stable was a sweet old mare. I wish I remembered her name. There was something special about her, and I took a liking to her right away. Maybe it was because everyone else was constantly ranking her down. I knew how she felt. She was entered to race this particular day. Because she was the oldest horse at this track, she was the longest shot of the day. Nobody, not even the guys from our own stable had bet on her. I felt so bad for her that I decided I would bet my last $2 on her to win. Everyone laughed at me. She was going off at around sixty-to-one odds.

I gave her a big hug around her neck, whispering in her ear that I had bet all the money I had *on her* and wished her luck. I sent her off to the starting gate. Unbelievably, she somehow broke out of the gate first and had a several length lead at the first turn! That lead was slowly but surely fading as she entered the stretch. I don't think I have ever screamed as loud as I did during that race while cheering her on! There was a multitude of sighs heard from the crowd as she crossed the finish line first. I was the only guy that could be heard cheering. I collected an amazing return of $122 for my $2 bet, and I made sure there was a big celebration at the barn after the races. With some of my winnings, I bought beer for everyone at our stable.

As usual when the beer is free, everyone overdid it, me included. My cowboy coworkers started getting rowdy. We were sitting on the ground, leaning our backs against the wooden rail of the corral fence while drinking our beers, when one of the guys came up with a drunken plan. He wanted to lasso the young unbroken horse that was running wild in the corral next to ours. The horse belonged to an owner that nobody liked. They all started ranting that they would lasso that horse if somebody would agree to ride it. I was tired of being teased by those guys for being a "city slicker from back east," so I decided this was my chance to show them that Boston guys were not wimps. I accepted the challenge, saying, "I'll do it!" They never expected that.

Sure enough, they wasted no time as they grabbed their ropes. They chased that horse around the corral, and it took several of them with lassoes to subdue the wild thing. When I saw that they had it somewhat under control, I ran over. Those guys pretty much threw me up onto the horse because it would be impossible to control the animal for very long. With a rider on its back for the very first time, the horse was extremely upset to say the least. Its ears were straight back, its nostrils flared to twice their normal size, and its eyes were protruding wildly as she shook her head from side to side trying to escape the ropes. I wrapped my legs around her as tightly as I could. There was no bridle, no saddle, just me on her back with a handful of mane to hold on to. I remember yelling, "Let her go!" The horse neighed loudly as they quickly removed their ropes, and away I went. Because I had consumed plenty of liquid courage during our celebration, I felt no fear at all. I remember being really happy that the very first buck hadn't thrown me and I was surprised at how long I was able to stay on her back.

In reality, it wasn't long at all. I was on just long enough to make it from one side of the corral all the way to the other. Once we had made it to the far end of the enclosure, I remember the horse gave one last furious lurch upward toward the sky, and I was launched high into the air. When I came down, the horse was gone. There was a pile of broken fence pieces in the corner of the corral where I landed. My wrist got cut on a nail that was sticking out of a broken wooden post, but other than that, I was uninjured! I was the hero of the barn that day, and they could never rank me down as a city slicker or *outsider* again.

After the racing season ended at that track, I answered an ad and got a job at a Target department store in Littleton. I was happy when I was assigned to be in charge of sporting goods. I enjoyed the job until I left work that very first day. I walked out of the front door of the building, and to my surprise, it was storming very badly. There was heavy rain with thunder and lightning as I made it to my car. I can't explain the feeling that I experienced as I left there, but it was strong enough that I quit that job the next morning. I realized that I could not have a job where there were no windows, and where I was totally isolated from what was going on outside. I had always worked outdoors, and this felt so foreign to me.

There were many memorable experiences during those months in Colorado. I had made one great friend named Dave Case. As the newcomer in town, he took me under his wing. We partied at all the honky-tonks and nightclubs in the area. My sister Fran, known professionally as Peggy Malone, would often be entertaining with her guitar and singing at many of the nightspots Dave and I frequented, which made it even more fun. In 2006, she was inducted into the Colorado Country Music Hall of Fame.

There were also some not-so-fun evenings. Dave got punched out one night outside a bar just because he danced with this cowboy's girlfriend. I could never understand why he didn't raise one hand in his own defense. I had all I could do to hold myself back from intervening on his behalf. I was thinking, why should I jump in and fight when he won't even defend himself? Plus this other guy had four or five cowboy friends standing there with him. I couldn't possibly fight them all without Dave being willing to help. The guy hit Dave three or four times with several seconds between punches, but Dave's hands stayed right by his sides. Maybe he was just totally against violence. We never talked about it. The next day, Dave's assailant brought a few hundred bucks over to his apartment so Dave could fix his teeth. He also accompanied that money with an apology. Things were certainly different out here in the West.

On another evening, Dave and I were at somebody's house, playing drinking games with some of his friends. There were several cases of Rocky Mountain-brewed, ice-cold Coors beer. Streaking was the fad of the times and naked runners were constantly in the news. As the night progressed, and the beers disappeared, one of the drunken cowboys began daring people to go streaking. Once again, looking for a way to stand out and be accepted, I called his bluff saying, "If you'll do it with me, I'll do it." He took me up on it, so we stripped down within seconds. I was wearing only a borrowed cowboy hat and cowboy boots as we jogged out the front door. We were now in full view of a newly built residential subdivision, which was jammed with cookie-cutter homes. The deal was that we had to go all the way around the block with no turning back. As the two of us trotted past one house, an old lady was standing in her big bow window. I saw her expression when she spotted us under a streetlight in front of her house. We gave her a big wave as we passed.

She was pointing frantically and yelling to everybody in her house to come and see what she was seeing! It was the best!

Frequenting all the local nightspots with Dave required money. I didn't waste any time between jobs. The very last employment I secured in Colorado was with a real estate investment firm. It was my job to sell land in Arizona, sight unseen, with the promise of great appreciation of value. The office supplied appointments to each member of the sales team every day. Most of the appointments were set up to take place during evening hours, after people got home from work. I imagine those leads were probably generated through some boiler room full of phone solicitors. They even supplied maps and directions to the prospects' homes. The lots we were selling were priced at only $1,250 each, and we were encouraged to sell several lots to each customer as an investment. On my second night out on these appointments, I was assigned a lead that was way up in the mountains. I had to get there by way of a private dirt road that was very isolated. It was one of those extra-dark nights when there was no moonlight and there were no streetlights. As I negotiated the steep incline of this winding roadway with its several hairpin turns, I was very nervous. No, I was actually scared. Colorado mountain roads like this one have no guardrails. You could be driving on one of these narrow roadways and if you had the misfortune of going a little too far to the edge, you would be history. You could drop thousands of feet and not be found for months. In the daylight, it was intimidating enough, but being up there alone on a pitch-black night like this was downright spooky and terrifying.

I was so proud of myself for finding this desolate location once the dim light from their windows finally came into view. It was a very large and stately home. These folks definitely had loads of money to invest. I didn't want to impress my prospects too much by parking my $300 car in front of their million-dollar house. So in the darkness, I searched for a spot to park where my car would be out of sight. I spotted what looked like a nice opening, around fifty feet to the left side of the house. I pulled in and shut the trusty Falcon off. After grabbing my briefcase and exiting the car, I happened to glance over in front of the car. I stopped breathing and had to inch myself forward to confirm what I thought I was seeing. There was *nothing* in front of the wheels of my car! The front wheels were resting right on the edge of a vertical stone cliff! The yard *ended* right there, and from that point, it dropped off into thousands of feet of black oblivion! No markers, no flags, no line of stones to mark the edge; *no* warning of any kind! If I had not stopped at that exact point, I would have gone right over that cliff. Those folks would have never even known I had shown up! I got back in the car and backed it away from the edge.

Struggling to compose myself, I rang the doorbell, or in this case, pushed a button that set loose the ten-piece orchestra. The young couple cordially invited me in. Needless to say, they noticed that I appeared to be a little shaken up, so I told them what had just taken place outside. They explained that they had just finished building their dream home on this remote spot and apologized for not having marked the hazards in the yard as yet. After all was said and done, no property deals were made that night.

I quit that job the very next day, not just because of almost getting killed, but because I was having a hard time selling something that I wasn't sure I believed in. My heart just wasn't in it. On top of that, I was feeling a little homesick for Massachusetts. I was starting to miss and appreciate the people and situations I had walked away from back at home.

While in Colorado, I had stayed in contact with my family back in Braintree, calling home at least once a week. My mother would always answer the phone, and we would talk for a while. The calls usually ended with the news that nothing had changed in Dad's ways of thinking, and he still didn't want to talk to me. Then, something extraordinary happened that couldn't have been timed more perfectly. During a call I made soon after quitting my sales job, I was surprised to hear my mom say, "Dad wants you to come home." I was thrilled to hear those words, but kept calm, trying not to show too much enthusiasm until I found out his terms. I asked her, "If I come home, is he willing to pay me like everyone else at the gas station and not tell me what to do and where I can go?" She said, "Yes." This was music to my ears. After the jobs I had in Colorado, the repair shop back home started to look pretty good to me. I missed my family, my friends, the trees, the lakes, and the ocean. Fran and Bill were great to let me stay with them all that time and give me my first taste of independence, but now it was time to go home. To his credit, Dad kept his word and let me make my own decisions and my own mistakes from that time on.

Chapter VIII

Total Wrecks, 1 and 2

After returning to Massachusetts, it didn't take me long to get right back in the swing of things both at work in Southie and with the gang at the Colbert School. My old Falcon had served me well and supplied me with all the great memories that first cars earn. In Colorado, the Falcon almost got a chance to see if it could actually fly. But now that I was making decent money at the garage, it was time to move on to a nicer vehicle. I sold the Falcon for the same amount I had paid for it, $300, and I purchased a used 1971 Cadillac Eldorado. The Caddy was a beautiful shade of emerald green with a white leather interior and white vinyl roof. It had less than twenty-five thousand miles on it and possessed a powerful five-hundred-cubic-inch engine. It could smoke its front tires as well as anything "up the school." It was a wise move when I paid the dealer the extra $25 to transfer the remaining factory warranty into my name. Shortly after buying that car, I was racing down Pond Street in Braintree and manually downshifted at too high an RPM. The engine literally exploded with such ear shattering noise that a man came out of his house to ask if anyone in the car had been injured. The motor had a gaping hole in the side. This was one of the many times that owning a tow truck came in handy for me.

I got a ride into Southie, grabbed my truck, and towed the car to a Caddy dealer. Within a week or so, I had the car back with a brand new engine at no cost, and it was back to business as usual.

One night while hanging out at the Colbert School with the gang, I drank too much MD 20/20, which is a very potent wine. I was trying to drown the pain of the breakup I had just gone through with the girl I had been dating. Being both drunk and furious, driving that powerful Eldorado was the wrong choice to make that night. I remember leaving the schoolyard at full throttle. I must have kept the gas pedal floored because I only made it about an eighth of a mile down Pond Street when I felt a tremendous impact! Everything came to an abrupt standstill. I didn't see it coming or sense the impending accident at all. All I knew was that I had hit something *really hard*. I gazed out over the massive hood of the Eldorado and everything looked fine! There was no obstacle that I could see in front of the car, and I couldn't discern any damage at all, yet the car was sitting in somebody's front yard. I backed out into the street and headed back to the Colbert School, still not aware of any damage to the vehicle. I could hear a loud grinding noise coming from the rear wheels. I pulled up to where my friends were all gathered. They were shocked when they saw the car. I said, "I think I hit something." When I tried to open the driver's door to get out of the car, it wouldn't budge. My friends were quite excited as they pulled me out through the driver's window, which was missing. Someone yelled "Nick! You hit a pole!" They had watched me leave the school like a maniac, and they said, ten seconds later, all the streetlights in the neighborhood went out. How I ever stayed conscious and was able to drive that car back to the school after taking down a telephone pole with a direct driver's-side impact was one for the books. My friend Steve "owned" the pole just before the one I hit. The night he hit that pole and totaled his Shelby Mustang, I had to retrieve him at the police station.

My friends asked me what I wanted to do with the car. They knew the cops would be arriving at any second. As drunk as I was, and not thinking normally, I told my friend Ralph Riccardi, "Take the car to Braintree center and just leave it there." It was evident that I was delusional with alcohol when they said I mumbled, "I'll report it stolen." Ralph said, "Nick! You're crazy! Look at this car! It looks like a pyramid! It's driving sideways down the road! I'll take it home for you." With that, the guys helped Ralph get in through the broken window. I told him to park it all the way down at the end of the side driveway next to my house so my parents couldn't see it. My house was only a few hundred feet from where we were standing. I turned and stumbled back to the stairs of the school where my friends and I sat down. They were all laughing at the sight of my wrecked Cadillac, dragging its ass sideways as it attempted to leave the schoolyard.

Poor Ralph never made it out of the Colbert School driveway. Braintree Police cruisers from both directions surrounded my car and flashing blue lights lit up the entire area. The cops figured it *had* to be one of the Colbert guys responsible for the pole down the street, and they were right. As the officers approached the car, Ralph was yelling from inside the crumpled mess, "Nick! Nick! Get down here!" I got up from my seat on the steps and made my way toward the car. I remember almost falling to the ground a couple of times en route. As soon as I made it to where they were standing, a cop asked me, "Is this your car?" I said, "Yes." Then he asked me what happened. I don't know where this tall tale came from, but out of nowhere came my story that, "My friends and I were sitting up at the school and a stranger walked up to us and was all upset.

The guy told us he had a family emergency and needed a ride to the hospital right away. I wanted to help him, but because I had been drinking, I couldn't drive him, so I lent him my car. This is the way he brought it back to me, and then he ran away!" I told them that Ralph was just driving the car home for me, and I pointed down to my house. After hearing my explanation, one of the cops started yelling from behind me, "Lock him up! Lock him up!" They put me in the back of one of the cruisers and were ready to transport me to the station when *another* cruiser pulled up with its lights flashing.

As luck would have it, the very last police officer to arrive happened to be a pretty good friend of mine. He had just recently joined the force after growing up in this part of Braintree. I had met him though the gang at the Colbert School. You could say he was a senior member of our group. His brothers and cousin still spent time there with us at the Colbert quite often. Now I had several police officers gathered outside of the cruiser discussing my fate as I sat inside listening. I kept hearing one particular cop repeat the same words every couple of minutes. "Lock him up! Lock him up!" I guess because I showed no signs of visible injuries, and they never actually saw me driving the car, or even sitting in it for that matter, it might have been a tough case to prove in court. My story was hard to believe yet not an impossible scenario. When the talking subsided, the officers started returning to their cruisers one by one, and began pulling away. I think my friend may have saved my neck. The remaining cop told me, "Get out of the cruiser and let Ralph drive the car to your house." Ralph put the car right where I had asked him to, at the very end of the side driveway. I ended up paying for the telephone pole and the car was obviously totaled. Goldie's junkyard gave me $600 for the car, due to the new engine and perfect front-end parts. They could sell those parts for a nice profit.

The very next morning, my parents were scheduled to fly out to Colorado to visit my sister Fran and her family. I hadn't mentioned anything about the accident to them, so when it came time to drive them to the airport, I said I would have to take them in Dad's car. "My car isn't running right," I said. We got into his car, which was in the garage, and backed out into the street. As we drove past the side driveway where my car was, my fingers were crossed that they would not look to the right and see the roof of my car pointing up to the sky. Dad *did* glance to the right, as if he smelled a rat. I don't think he believed his eyes because his face turned red as he turned back and glared at me. I smiled at him, and he never uttered a word that morning. I think he understood that I didn't want to upset my mother by having her see what was left of my vehicle. There would be plenty of time for him to rub my nose in my stupidity when they returned from their trip. At least by then, my hangover would be gone.

When I returned from the airport, I went to check out the damage at the crash site. A new pole had already been installed, but part of the old one was still there. The telephone pole had snapped off six feet up from the ground, and the stump was still standing there. It had moved a few inches sideways in the surrounding earth. The sight of the damage and the thought of how things could have turned out gave me pause. As I stood there gazing at the marks on the pole where it had impacted my car, something caught my eye. There was a piece of chrome stuck in the pole around four feet up from the bottom. It looked oddly familiar but I couldn't figure out exactly what it was at first. Then I recognized it, and it was a shock! A few months prior to the accident, I found a set of chrome initials on the street that said "*TC*." I thought having my initials on the car would look cool, so I installed them behind the driver's door on the white vinyl roof where it angled down to the fender.

It personalized the car nicely. Right where my car made contact with the pole, there was that set of chrome initials *"TC" embedded* right in the wood! The letters were inverted of course, because of how they were situated when they came in contact with the pole. That reversed appearance is why I didn't immediately recognize what they were. I remember getting flushed when I realized that this was my indisputable signature of irresponsibility. Talk about leaving evidence!

The Eldorado was a two-door car, and the pole made contact directly behind the driver's head with an impact so great that you could stand straight up with your feet on the ground and look out through the windshield over where the driver's head would be. The frame, along with the rest of the car, had wrapped around the perfect impression of the pole like a horseshoe. The center of the roof was now about two feet higher than it used to be. It took a tremendous impact to do that kind of damage and it was a miracle that I walked away without a scratch, or any injury whatsoever. If that pole had hit just six *inches* farther forward, my head would have been smashed, killing me instantly. If it had hit six *inches* further back, it would not have held the driver's door shut. I would have been ejected from the vehicle at a high rate of speed. I know, after reading this, you would be fair in saying that I would have deserved it if it *had* happened that way.

The most disturbing fact is, if there had been a car coming in the opposite direction at the time I crossed the oncoming lane, there would have been a horrific ending to this story. Lives would have been ended and families ruined. Unfortunately, many young people, such as I was back then, don't stop to consider the consequences of their actions. If just one person stops and thinks before drinking and driving after reading what happened to me, then writing this book will have been worthwhile.

Months after that night, I was out partying with friends, wearing the same suede jacket for the first time since I had worn it the night of the accident. I happened to reach into the jacket's left side pocket and felt something strange. I grabbed a handful of what was in there to see what it was. To my astonishment, it was broken glass. A large amount of glass shards had found their way into that pocket during the accident. If the police had checked my pockets that night, they would have had the evidence they needed in order to prove I had been in the car when it crashed. To my friends, it was hilarious. To me, it was a grim reminder of an awful night.

A couple of years after the Eldorado accident, a few of us from the Colbert were hanging out in the lounge at the Nii Hau Chinese restaurant. Somebody brought up "the night Nick took down the pole on Pond Street and drove his car back to the school." The guys occasionally liked to relive that night and repeat the amazing story. A man that was sitting with friends at a table close by interrupted our conversation and asked, "Where on Pond Street did that happen?" When I told him, he exclaimed, "I can't believe it! That was you?" He continued, "My family and I were sitting in our living room watching TV, and all of the sudden we heard this tremendous crash, and the whole house shook! All the lights went out. We went to the front window to see what had happened, and there was a pole lying in our front yard, but there was no vehicle there! We couldn't figure out what had hit that pole and then just disappeared." The man wasn't angry. He was amazed at the coincidence of meeting the mystery driver after all this time had passed.

There were also many other minor crashes over those years. Usually they were the direct result of going too fast or using bad judgment. I didn't need to have been drinking in order to smash up a car.

The most upsetting automotive loss I ever endured was that of my 1974 Dodge Challenger. It still bothers me, especially when I see that those cars are going for up to, and sometimes over, $100,000 to collectors today. That car was waxed and cleaned at least once per week. The day it bit the dust, it still looked brand new inside, outside, and even underneath. I always had it up on the lift at work when things were slow, adjusting this and cleaning that. It was my first brand-new car. The first time I saw that black beauty, it was literally *love at first sight.* When I'm occasionally in the area of that Braintree dealership, I still look to the exact spot where I first saw that car, hoping in vain that history could somehow repeat itself. Late one night, the Challenger was parked along the unlit side of the car dealer's building, in the fog. I saw just the silhouette of that car in the dim light of a distant streetlamp. I knew I had to have her, and I bought it the very next day. I paid $4,600 for the car and kept it fully insured with collision, fire, and theft coverage for five straight years. The sixth year, I started thinking, "Why am I spending all this money on insurance when I've never had an accident with this car?" I decided to drop the coverage down to the compulsory levels and save a couple of hundred bucks. That was the year the car met its fate.

I could fill chapters just with stories involving this car, but I will just highlight a couple. Everyone has heard the standard car dealer advice, which is, "Keep it under sixty for the first five hundred miles." Well, I had to replace the tires on this car after just 475 miles. I broke her in at 135 mph, and she loved it. At times, I was tempted to see if she would actually close in on the 160 mile-per-hour mark that was stated on the speedometer, but that would have put her way over the red line on the tachometer. That wouldn't be a good thing while still breaking her in. I cruised from home to Maine and back in just a few hours. While on the Maine turnpike I spotted, and began racing, an *identical twin* to my Challenger. It was the same year and model, and the same black color. It even had the exact same mag wheels and strobe pin striping. Before long, the two of us were taking turns, purposely passing each other at tremendous speeds. I would zoom past the other car at twice its speed, and then slow down so the other guy could do the same thing. I'm sure the other driver was enjoying the sight and sound of my car screaming past him just as much as I was enjoying seeing and hearing his fly past me. It was like seeing what our own car looked and sounded like at those speeds.

The one dangerous characteristic of the Challenger was its *true* possitraction rear end. You could not spin one rear wheel independently of the other. Both rear tires would always spin with equal power. It was a great feature to have on straight-aways, such as the quarter mile, but that characteristic also made the car extremely unstable and hard to control under certain conditions. If I happened to be on a damp and curvy road and goosed the gas pedal a little too much, the back end of the car would just swing right out from under me, putting the car into an uncontrolled skid or a spin. It would even do that on dry pavement if you wanted to do doughnuts. I was getting so many traffic tickets with this car that after paying and throwing several of them away, I decided I should start saving some as mementos. One night in Braintree, I got two tickets within minutes of each other, from the same cop. He had written me up after "clocking" me at sixty in a thirty-mile-per-hour zone. Thinking he had already driven away, I put my papers back in the glove compartment, started my car, and then I proceeded to do a 180-degree spin, smoking the tires down Washington Street toward Braintree center. The blue lights went on all over again.

I couldn't believe it. I was totally unaware that the cop had been sitting there, still watching me. He was probably shaking his head in disbelief, or laughing out loud as he witnessed this. Thank goodness, this happened before the point system which raises your insurance premium drastically with each ticket you get.

In Southie one day, while on my lunch hour, I headed down to Castle Island to sit by the waterfront. The parking spots along that roadway are diagonal to the curb, so people can look out over the bay while parked. As I cruised down that road, looking for a good place to park, I spotted a friend walking along the sidewalk. Without giving thought to the fact that the road was still damp from an earlier shower, I stomped on the gas to show off the sound and power of my engine, and I instantly lost control. There was a slight curve in the roadway, and the rear wheels lost traction, putting me into an uncontrollable spin. I pretty much just let off the gas and held onto the steering wheel, waiting for the crash as the car spun completely around doing a full 360 as it headed toward the parked cars along the road. To my amazement, and to the amazement of all those who happened to witness this, the car came to a stop, perfectly parked, facing the water! The Challenger was within the white parking space lines, about three feet away from the cars on each side. I glanced over at the guys sitting in the cars next to mine with a look on my face that indicated the maneuver was planned. One of the drivers had cold cuts hanging out of his mouth from the sandwich he was eating. Neither driver said a word to me. The friend I had tried to impress came over and said, "That was amazing! How did you learn how to do that?" I said to him, "Lots of practice." The fact was that I could never do that again in a million years!

Prior to buying a house in Weymouth and while still living with my parents, I bought a thirty-five-foot long, 1953 Ford bus. It had been partially converted into a camper. I customized it further and installed a full-size refrigerator and insulated it for winter. I only paid $1,000 for it because it had a blown engine, which I later replaced. It was very comfortable and had a gas stove, two bedrooms, a kitchen, and a bathroom. I kept it in East Bridgewater at Robin's Pond. There was a small campground there that was run by an eccentric old lady, named Evelyn. The campground supplied water and an electric hookup, which I used year-round, even in the dead of winter, which was against the rules. Everything was included for only $300 per year. It was wonderful having this getaway at my disposal. Most weekends after work, I would head straight down to the camper and usually wouldn't return until Sunday afternoon or evening. Even though I was still living with my parents, it was like having an apartment of my own at the same time. I never had to extend an invitation to my friends, as they all knew where I was and that everyone was welcome. My guests could get as plastered as they wanted, and there was very little chance of them getting into trouble. I am forcing myself to *not* write chapters and chapters just about the fun times at the bus.

Late one evening, I arrived at my parent's Braintree home after a few hours of drinking at the Nii Hau. I received an unexpected phone call from my friend Jim Hunnefield, who was a fellow camper down at Robin's Pond. He informed me that somebody had broken into my bus and stolen all my stereo equipment. I was furious! I got out of bed, got dressed, stuck a loaded pistol in my waistband, and jumped on my motorcycle to head to the campground. The combination of alcohol, anger, and firearms is never a wise mix. I remember that I was driving at a very high rate of speed down Route 18 on my way to the campground. It was a thirty-or-so mile ride.

When I got there, I made sure everybody saw my gun as I terrorized the campground, stating that whoever stole my stuff had twenty-four hours to return it, or I would find out who did it and come after them. I secured the forced-open door to the bus, jumped on the bike and headed back home. Jim called me at work the next morning to say my stereo system had mysteriously turned up on the picnic table outside the bus during the night. He was going to keep it for me until I came back down.

Being young and having a getaway such as a large camper in the woods, situated by a lake, tends to make a person very popular. I never knew who would be showing up. One particular Sunday, a girl I had been dating for a while drove herself down to the camp for a visit. Things hadn't been going well between us, and it was obvious that something had changed. I could tell that our relationship was over. After enduring a long weekend of partying, I was not in the greatest of moods to begin with, and I became quite emotional while trying not to show it on the outside. Because it was a Sunday afternoon, I told her I was closing up the camper and heading back to Braintree. I know from the police report that the date was May 13, 1979. Both of us left the camper at the same time, with her driving off ahead of me. A couple of miles from the campground, we approached a traffic light that had just turned yellow. The two or three cars in front of me slowed down to stop at the red light. I was agitated and upset and decided I didn't feel like stopping for that light. Instead, I pulled into the oncoming traffic lane in order to pass all the cars that had stopped, including the girl that had left the camper before me. I quickly sped past those cars at the light. Stepping on the gas, I flew into the intersection. Once again, the roads were damp from an earlier rain and I misjudged the power of the car I was driving. The rear wheels spun right out from under me. The car went into a slow-motion skid, with the Challenger sliding directly sideways. I could see the telephone pole coming right at my driver's door. There was absolutely nothing I could do but just watch as the pole honed in. **BANG!** I actually felt and heard the tremendous impact of the crash before everything went black. I had been knocked unconscious. When I came to, the girl that I had passed at the traffic light was yelling through the splintered windshield, trying to wake me up. She told me that she was afraid the car was going to catch on fire, and they couldn't open the driver's door. The pole had hit the door just in front of my seat. It had smashed the dashboard right in front of my face. Once again, just like with the Eldorado, I was being helped out of a car's shattered driver's window opening. Even though I had been knocked out, the only injury I could visibly find was a cut on my baby finger.

Police arrived and questioned me. They wrote me up for "driving-to-endanger and running a mechanical signal," (a red light). I guess the officer deduced all this from talking to the people at the scene, but since no witness names were mentioned in any of the paper work, I decided to take a chance and contest the charges in court. I didn't want a driving-to-endanger conviction on my record if I could avoid it. Plus, I wanted to know what the police officer had based the charges on because he wasn't there to actually see what happened. When I went to court, nobody else showed up. There were no witnesses and no police officer. When my case was called, and I was the only participant present, I was never placed under oath. I voluntarily explained to the judge that I had lost my brakes as I was approaching that intersection, and I had two choices. Either I could slam into the cars that had stopped for the light, or I could step on the gas and try to get through the intersection before traffic had time to resume from the other directions. I told him I chose the latter option and lost control due to the wet road.

With nobody to testify against me, the charges were dropped. I finally did learn from my mistakes of that awful day. Since that accident, I have been extremely cautious when driving on wet roads, especially at night. I gained a healthy respect of such driving conditions. Something finally clicked, and my driving changed forever. It wasn't really due to the fact I took a total loss on that car with no collision insurance, but more so because of the old saying, "the third time never fails." I had been extremely lucky to live through two total wrecks, which were entirely due to my own choices and bad judgment. I'm not about to tempt fate a third time. Now I'm constantly watching out for "the other guy," the kind of driver that *I* used to be.

Good friend Lyle Lindberg took this photo of my 71 Eldorado
along the roadway leading to Castle Island. We would eat lunch
as we watched the jets glide overhead into Logan Airport.

The 74 Challenger ended up in the auto graveyard after yet another
irresponsible decision to drive while both impaired and upset.
"Shine-Em-Up, Smash-Em-Up" became my assigned motto.

The impact snapped the telephone pole and knocked me unconscious.
It crushed the windshield and the dashboard directly in front of me.
I now owned telephone poles in two towns.

After tossing numerous speeding tickets away, I decided it might
be fun to start saving them. I regret the top ticket the most,
It is dated 5/13/1979, the day I totaled the Challenger.
I was cited for driving-to-endanger and failing to stop for a red light.

The bus at Robins Pond, in East Bridgewater,
was a wonderful place to unwind.

My friend "Pudgy" was one of the many friends that would just show up and party on the weekends. We had all the comforts of home, with none of the hassles.

A good friend, Mary Ellen "Pill" Pilling, patiently waits for her clothes to dry after a dip in Robin's Pond.

The bus had a blown engine when I bought it, so I towed it to
the camp. After finding an old flat-head 6 lying on the ground
at "Goldie's" junk yard, I rebuilt it at the shop and made engine
mounts from angle iron to make it fit. I installed the engine while
at the camp site. It was quite a thrill to turn that key and drive the
camper out of the woods and to Southie for the first time.

Chapter IX

A Case Of Mistaken Identity

The Nii Hau became our regular hangout when it was too cold or too rainy to spend time at the Colbert School. We treated the Nii Hau's lounge as if it were our own private club. At times, we may have acted up a little too much, but we were never permanently banned from the bar. The fact that we were never expelled was either due to the owner's fear of our reaction or the fact we spent tons on money on White-Russians, Mai Tais, and appetizers. There were also times when we bailed the bartender out of trouble when a strange group of people would come in drunk and give him a bad time. That happened more often than you might expect.

When you came into the Nii Hau from outside, the entrance to the bar was directly to your left. Nobody could enter or leave the restaurant without walking past that doorway. There were *two steps* leading down into the lounge, and the entire area was always kept very dimly lit. When coming in from the bright sun or the bright parking lot lights outside, you were almost blind until your eyes adjusted to the low light level inside. We could always tell if somebody had never been to the bar before because they would not see the two steps.

Watching guys pause at the entrance, survey the bar, and then attempt to make a cool entrance was always lots of fun. They would *always* miss the first step and come stumbling down the stairs! With the dim lighting, no windows, and dark stone walls, it was always like nighttime in the Nii Hau, very much like a dungeon. Usually, on Sunday mornings, the owners would allow us into the bar early, when they arrived to do their daily prep-work. I would enjoy a vodka and grapefruit juice at the bar along with a fried-egg sandwich that had been specially prepared for me. The restaurant officially opened at noon. Walking out of the front door a few hours later was quite a shock when the bright sunlight hit your eyes and you were reminded that it was the middle of the day.

The senior owner of the Nii Hau was named Arthur. He truly resembled the character from the James Bond movie called Oddjob. He had the same hat, physical build, and personality as that character. On one occasion, there were probably fifteen of us from the Colbert Gang enjoying ourselves at the bar. Some in our group were pretty lit and getting rather rowdy. Arthur came to the lounge entrance, stood at the top of the stairs *glaring* down at us, and announced, "Nick! Your friends cause bad atmosphere! Bar Closed!" There was immediate silence. This had never happened before, so we glanced around at each other for a few seconds, wondering how to respond. I happened to be seated at the center of the bar, closest to Arthur. I slowly turned on my barstool. Facing him squarely, I said, "Arthur! You close bar, we bust place up!" Arthur looked at me, scanned the group for a few seconds, and announced "Bar Open!" He turned around and walked away, shaking his head. It was the funniest thing we had ever seen. From that day forward, "You cause bad atmosphere" became Arthur's signature statement. He used it often as a warning to bar patrons to calm down.

One late afternoon, a few of us were playing a board game called Risk at the corner booth of the lounge. The object of the game is to conquer all of the opposing players' armies and eventually take over the world. Things got out of hand when our Irish contractor friend drank too much while playing the game. He was acting as if he was on the verge of taking over the world for real. By nature, "Mike" was very excitable and had a naturally loud voice, but after drinking, he got disturbingly louder and more out of control with each country he conquered. People eating in every section of the large restaurant could certainly hear every word and curse he yelled out. Arthur put up with him for the longest time, but finally had to put his foot down. He came to the booth and said to our friend, *"Mike, No more play game! You cause bad atmosphere!"* Mike responded to Arthur's outburst by telling him where to go, in no uncertain terms. We all tried to calm our friend down, but that only agitated him even more. Understanding Arthur's concern, we all agreed that we should quit the game, with the exception of Mike. He stood up and started yelling, "Nobody's quitting! We're finishing this F—n game!" Arthur signaled the reception desk to call the police, and they quickly arrived. With his hands cuffed behind his back, the police dragged our friend backwards up the stairs and out of the bar as he continued yelling as loud as he could, *"I was about to take over the world! Leave me alone! One more country and I've got the world!"* Soon after that incident, our friend began attending AA meetings, and surprisingly, he stuck with it. It was an amazing transformation both personally and professionally for him. His business went from being one guy driving an old broken-down dump truck, with a pint under the seat, to a thriving business with new equipment, employees, and plenty of work lined up.

There were a few good fights in the Nii Hau over the years. I had a couple of altercations myself that happened to be with members of my own group, guys from the Colbert. After one such scuffle that took place at the bar, Arthur told me that I was not allowed back in the lounge until I repaired the barstools that we damaged. I went right to work on doing the repairs. After seeing what a great job I did on those pieces of furniture, Arthur hired me to repair all the other tables and chairs throughout the restaurant that needed to be dismantled and re-glued.

On another occasion I was involved in a far more destructive altercation at the Nii Hau. I was sitting at a table near the bar with a few friends from South Boston. They had never been to Braintree with me before. Two guys that I knew very well were sitting ten feet away from us, at the corner booth. They were older members of the Colbert Gang, and both of them had been drinking for quite a while. They were having fun making wise remarks about several people in the lounge. I had invited my Southie friends to the bar so I could introduce them to my suburban hangout, and the evening was being ruined by these local guys who were in the process of embarrassing me. They knew from the looks that I was giving them that I was getting irritated. Feeding on my emotions, as bullies love to do, they began whispering comments about the people sitting at my table, just loud enough so that I could hear every word they said. I heard them say, *"Nick's friend has a big nose. Look at the size of that thing!"* That really pissed me off, and my blood started to boil. They were referring to Lyle, a friend who had bailed me out of so many situations. The people sitting at my table were oblivious to the comments coming from the corner. They didn't know me as "Nick" because they were friends from Southie, so they didn't associate the comments as being directed at us.

Only Colbert guys knew me by that nick-name. I couldn't tune out what the two guys sitting in the corner were saying any longer. I had heard enough. Without saying a word to my guests, I simply got up from the table and walked over to the corner where the two men were seated. I certainly wasn't looking for trouble, because they were my friends, and they were both pretty tough guys. I calmly and quietly said to them, "Hey guys, I'm with some nice people here, so could you please knock off the wisecracks?" As soon as I said that, one of them filled his mouth with beer and expelled a stream of it at me, but I stepped to the side and he missed his target. I reacted by reaching over the table and tipping the remaining beer that was in his glass over into his lap. Then, all hell broke loose. He jumped to his feet to retaliate, and I threw a punch at him that caught him square in his face. He was a very strong guy, and he immediately leaped over the table at me. Over time, the fight encompassed the entire bar. We were fighting on tables, on the floor, and standing up. People scattered to get out of the way as we knocked furniture over. Eventually, I got him in a headlock, and as I was trying to bang his head against the bar, he tried very hard to gouge my eye out. It was awful. I had to let him go or lose an eye. I was bleeding from the fingernail scrapes over my eye. The eye gouging was probably a tactic he had learned while in the armed forces, and it worked well. Toward the end of the fight, we were both exhausted on the floor, immobilized in each other's strangle holds. I saw my friend Lyle get up from our table. He came over and knelt down next to me on the floor. Leaning over, he whispered in my ear, "Should I plug him? Should I plug him?" I emphatically said, "NO! He's a friend of mine!" Lyle got up off his knee and went back to his seat. I knew he always carried his gun with him, but I couldn't believe my ears when he offered to shoot my opponent! The struggle went on and on. When the cops finally arrived, we were still rolling around on the floor, choking each other.

Then the greatest thing happened! Two cops grabbed the guy I was fighting with by the arms to lift him up. As soon as his arms were immobilized, I took advantage of the opportunity and hit him with two hard shots, one to each eye. Each punch hit its target perfectly with an audible smack. That was payback for his trying to gouge my eyes out. My opponent was taken away by the police and I got up and rejoined my party. Arthur must have told the police that I was not at fault in the altercation. The officers never spoke a word to me. After the fight, I was very surprised when Arthur sent a round of drinks over to my table. I guess he was just as fed up with the antagonistic wisecracks coming from the corner table as I was.

As our free drinks arrived, I was cleaning the blood off my face with wet napkins supplied by my friends. They were all looking at me strangely when Lyle asked, "What the hell was that all about? One minute we're all sitting at the table talking, and the next minute you're in a big brawl with some guy!" I said, "Didn't you hear the wise remarks coming from the corner?" My guests said they hadn't heard anything.

A day or so later, my opponent's equally intimidating brother spotted me sitting alone in my car at the Colbert School. Driving a menacing looking front-end-loader, he pulled up right next to me. I thought he might crush my car with the heavy shovel that was mounted on the front of the machine. To my relief, he wasn't angry about his brother. Instead, he yelled over the loud noise of the diesel engine "Hey Nicky! What did you do to my brother? He looks like a panda bear, and he won't leave the house!" I just replied that we had a little disagreement down at the Nii Hau. He laughed and said something like, "Good work!" He drove away, laughing and shaking his head. A few weeks later while out on a date, I ran into the guy I had fought. It was at a different Chinese restaurant that was located at Braintree Five Corners. I expected he might be looking for revenge, and we might go at it again, so I was on my guard. Instead of taking a swing at me, the guy reached out to shake my hand. He smiled and said, "Nice fight, Nicky."

On another evening while socializing at the Nii Hau, somebody came rushing into the bar very excitedly and announced that there had just been a robbery up at the drugstore at Five Corners. They said a Braintree cop had been shot in the face, and that there were helicopters, state troopers, and Braintree cops searching the entire area for the suspect who had gotten away. There was a group of us sitting in the corner booth in the bar when this took place, and I was ready to go home and call it a night. As I stood up to leave, a friend named "Trisha" asked me if I would stop at her dad's house to check on him before going home. She was worried about him because his house was just a couple of hundred feet away from Five Corners where the search was under way. Her father had a habit of leaving his front and back doors wide open while he might be drinking in the living room. "Dan" was a real Irishman, and he was always happy to see me. I visited him quite often. I told Trisha I would stop by and check on him before going home. When I got to his house, I parked out in front along the road. I could hear the police helicopters searching the area from up above, and I could see the distant reflections of the blue police lights in both directions from the house. Cops don't fool around when one of their own gets shot. Police from all the surrounding towns had also joined in the search.

I was very surprised to see Dan's front door closed, and all the shades were drawn. I approached the front door and tried to open it. It was locked. This had never happened before. I would always just walk right in and be welcomed by Dan with a drink whenever I had visited. When there was no response to my loud knocking or to my calling out Dan's name at the door, I got very nervous.

My adrenaline started to pump from this strange situation and from all the activity I could sense in the area. As I stepped back away from the house, I saw something that really disturbed me. It was the shadow on the window shade of a man moving around within the house. If everything was okay inside, I figured Dan certainly would have answered my calls. It looked like Trisha's worst fears had actually come to pass. I believed that the assailant/robber must have run from Five Corners and entered Dan's wide open house and taken him hostage. Because I'd had a few drinks, I probably didn't use the greatest judgment that night. I should have run down to Five Corners and got the cops, and had them check Dan's house. But instead, I decided I would sneak around to the back door and enter that way. I would surprise whoever was in there because I had seen the shadow, and I knew they were in the front room. I happened to be carrying my .32 caliber Beretta that night. I was licensed to carry a concealed weapon, but usually didn't have a gun on me. Why I decided to carry it that night, I don't remember.

So, wearing my dark brown leather jacket and with my gun in hand, I snuck around to the back of Dan's house under the shroud of darkness. It was unusual that there were no lights on at his back door. I crept up the stairs in the dark, and quietly tried the door. It was locked. I decided to try and force the door open by slamming into it with my shoulder. Behind Dan's house was a wooded area, which I didn't realize was being actively searched by police. At the exact moment my shoulder made contact with the door, I heard a loud voice scream, "Freeze, or I'll shoot! Don't move!" The voice scared the hell out of me! It came from only about ten feet away. I immediately placed my hands high on the door. All I could make out in the blackness of the night was the faint vision of a white helmet approaching me quickly up the stairs. It was a state trooper of the really large variety.

He grabbed my gun and pulled me quickly down the back stairs and away from the house.

Here I was, looking like a common hood, armed with a gun and wearing a leather motorcycle jacket. On top of that, I was caught breaking into a house within an area being actively searched for a possible cop killer. This did not look good at all. I remember what happened next as if it was last night. When he got me over to the edge of the wooded area, the state trooper pressed the long barrel of his revolver against the side of my head, right to my temple, and I heard the hammer being cocked back. His exact words to me were, *"You're never gonna make it to court, mother f—r!"* I knew I only had a split second to live, so as quickly as I could, I yelled, "Wait! A friend sent me here to check on her father because of the robbery! Just check out my story before you shoot! I think the robber is in this house!" After what seemed to be a long hesitation, the officer reached for a button near his throat and said "This is so and so. I have a possible suspect in custody." Wow! What a relief! Within a minute, there were all kinds of cops at the house. I pleaded with the officers to just take me to the Nii Hau, right down the street, and check out my story. I was cuffed, put in a cruiser, and taken to the Nii Hau. Two cops led me into the restaurant telling me not to speak. They stood me at the top of the stairs leading to the bar for all to see and then walked me right back outside. Officers went in and questioned the patrons. Thankfully, my friends were all still there, and Trisha explained to the police that she had sent me to check on her father after we heard about the shooting.

Because I had explained my concerns about what might be going on at Dan's house, the police, Trisha, and I drove back there. I told them that I had seen movement in the house, but got no response at the door. The police also tried to get a response to no avail. I'll never forget the courage one officer displayed that night. Everyone believed that there was a very good chance that an armed cop shooter had taken a hostage and was in that house. One fearless officer went to a front window, reached up and pried it open with a crow bar. He tugged on the shade and it flew all the way up so we could now see inside the house. Then with the help of two other cops, he was hoisted up and into the window. As he was climbing in, we saw a man inside the house walking toward the window. The man was wielding a baseball bat high in the air as he approached the cop! We recognized that it was Trisha's father, and we all yelled that it was the police coming in the window. Thankfully, the cops didn't shoot Dan, and Dan didn't swing the bat.

As it turned out, Dan had heard a news report about the robbery and the shooting. He saw that they were searching his neighborhood, so he locked all his doors and windows and pulled all his shades. I will never understand why he hadn't responded to me, the voices of the police, or all the blue lights flashing outside his house. He had unwittingly put himself, as well as several other people in a tremendous amount of danger. I was especially upset that his refusal to open his door almost got me killed at the hands of a vigilante-minded state trooper.

Chapter X

Where's My Car?

Occasionally on weekends, a few of us would start out drinking at the Nii Hau and then move on to a nightclub somewhere else. One Friday night, three of my friends and I did just that. We rode together to a club in Avon, several miles from Braintree. As the night wore on, we socialized separately, and I ended up meeting someone nice. She had offered me a ride home in her new Cadillac convertible. The top was down, and it was a beautiful night, so it sounded like a great idea to me. Thinking that one of the other guys had driven us all to the Avon nightclub from the Nii Hau, I accepted her offer of a ride. I looked around to find my friends and tell them I was leaving, but they were nowhere in sight. After searching for a few minutes, I left the club figuring they would be fine without me.

The next morning, I had to open up the gas station in Southie, but I saw that my car wasn't in the driveway when I woke up. I figured that I had left my car at the Nii Hau the night before, when I rode to the club with my friends. I asked my dad to drive me to the Nii Hau to pick up my car on the way in to work. To my dismay, my car was not there. I was adamant with my father that my car had been stolen, pointing to the exact parking spot where I swore I had left it the night before. I walked over to a nearby pay-phone, which was outside of the Nii Hau, and called the Braintree Police. I reported that my black Dodge Challenger had been stolen. The police took the report over the phone when I explained that I had a ride waiting for me, and I had to get to work.

When I got back into Dad's car, he asked, "Where else did you go last night?" I replied that it didn't matter where we went because I had not driven to the other place. Again he asked the same question, which I answered. He insisted that we drive over to the club in Avon. I told him he was wasting our time, but off we went to Avon. As we entered the parking lot, lo and behold, I saw my shiny car sitting there. It was the only car in the huge lot.

I felt quite stupid, and then I thought to myself, "Oh my god! I had abandoned my friends at that club the night before, leaving them no way to get home!" They were not going to be happy campers the next time I saw them. My dad said, "You should call the police back and let them know you found your car so they can cancel the stolen car report." I looked around, and there were no pay-phones in sight. (This took place BC—before cell phones). I told him, "I'll just call them back after we get to work. We're running late." Off to Southie we went.

It was good that it was early on a Saturday morning and there was practically no traffic on the highway into Boston that day. Because I was running late, and in a rush to get to work, I was cranking along the South East Expressway at about ninety miles an hour in the passing lane. I came upon a Ford LTD that was cruising at exactly 55 mph, in the same lane! That was the speed limit at the time, because of the gas shortages. I was a firm believer that slower drivers should stay out of my way and pull into the right lanes where they belonged.

Thus, instead of just going around this "jerk" I got *right on his ass*, blowing the horn, and flashing my lights. Still, he *refused* to pull over to the right. When my prodding had no effect on him, I zoomed into the middle lane, glanced quickly to my left and gave that driver the finger as I blasted past him like a bat out of hell. Simultaneously, as I shot him the bird, I caught a glimpse of a patch on his shoulder that read "Massachusetts State Police!" I said out loud, "Oh shit!" On went his lights and siren. The invitation to pull over was issued, and I began to slow down and comply. Then I remembered something. *"I am driving a stolen car!"* This was the perfect opportunity to do something I had always wanted to do. Outrun the cops!

I knew my car was fast, and it was as if an alien force instantly took over my body without my permission. I *nailed* the gas pedal, and the adrenaline instantly started pumping. That slow poke from the passing lane suddenly turned into a speed demon. Soon we were hitting speeds of *110-120 miles per hour*. The road resembled ribbon candy to me at those speeds, and I was through the curves before I even realized it. It is hard to describe, but it was as if I was actually part of the road. It was amazing to experience that feeling at least once in my life. To my surprise, this cop was keeping right up with me, staying to within 75-100 feet of my bumper. At these speeds, South Boston was coming up on us really fast, but thankfully, my pursuer had no idea where I intended to go. If I wasn't going to be able to leave him in the dust by pure speed, I would have to outmaneuver him. My Morrissey Boulevard exit was coming up in a mile or two as we played chess from the passing lane to the breakdown lane. I had to make sure that as we approached that exit, he would not know my intentions. Thanks to a couple of cars that were strategically at just the right place and speed to benefit me, I was able to maneuver us both into the passing lane. At the very last possible second, I veered right and was able to take that exit! I did it all the way from the passing lane at a tremendous rate of speed, just clearing the guardrail by inches! Because of two cars traveling in the middle lane, it was impossible for that Statie to make that exit! I got around those cars just in time, and they ran block for me. I had ditched him! I was certain that I'd better get to where I needed to be and do it as fast as possible. The MDC (Metropolitan District Commission police), state police, and the Boston Police had surely all been notified to be on the lookout for a *stolen* black 360/thermoquad Challenger that had just been involved in a high-speed chase. It wasn't hard to spot my car. After leaving the highway, I drove right past the MDC police station at double the speed limit, and took a left as soon as I could, in order to disappear into the maze of side streets that make up South Boston. Within two or three minutes of taking that highway exit, my car was safely tucked away in a repair shop bay at the gas station, with the door closed. My dad would not arrive for another twenty minutes as I had left him in the dust way back in Avon.

By the time my father made it to the shop, I had already called the Braintree Police Department and informed them that "unbelievably, I was on my way to work, and I spotted *my car* parked on a side street in South Boston!" I told them that the thieves must have had a key that worked because the ignition was not broken, and I was able to start it up and drive it to my workplace. Now that I had reported the car as being found, I was safe! The officer on the phone thought that this was just "amazing!" I had quite an exciting morning thus far and an interesting story to tell my dad when he arrived at work. He always seemed to glow with pride and brag to his friends whenever I would tell him of some mischief I had gotten away with. It made for great conversation with my friends at the Colbert as well.

Even the guys that I had abandoned at the Avon nightclub forgave me after hearing my account of what took place.

There was only one other time when I outran the cops. Four or five of us were on our motorcycles heading north to our friend's lodge up near Conway, New Hampshire. It was a fun trip from Massachusetts as we all horsed around with each other while cruising along the highway. My buddy Mark would drive up next to me, reach out, and grab my clutch handle as he went by, being a wise guy. We took turns flying past each other on the highway, missing each other by only inches.

At one point, after messing around with me several times, Mark pulled up next to me as we cruised at approximately eighty miles an hour. He was grinning at me from ear to ear looking for forgiveness. He knew I was getting upset with his antics, so not to be a party pooper; I gave him a big accentuated smile as we rode side by side. With perfect timing, the moment I broke into that big teeth grin, I was hit hard, directly in the mouth with a huge seagull crap from above! *SMACK*! At this speed, it felt exactly like getting punched in the mouth, only with a horrific fishy aftertaste. Mark was staring right at me at the instant it hit. I immediately had to pull over to the side of the highway for obvious reasons, and my companions could hardly control their machines, they were laughing so hard. After dismounting their bikes, they were rolling around on the ground, laughing hysterically. I, of course, was bent over, spitting and trying to clean myself up. It took a while, but we recomposed ourselves and resumed our journey.

As we were approaching the town of Conway, I yelled to my companions to drive at normal speed and not draw attention to us because I didn't have a motorcycle license yet. I was still driving with a learner's permit that was not valid outside of Massachusetts.

I didn't want to get stopped by the cops and have my bike towed to impoundment. Like the fools they were, they decided to ignore my request. They all started popping wheelies and racing down the main street of Conway.

To my dismay, within seconds we heard a siren and we looked back to see two police cars coming up on our tails. My idiot friends couldn't have picked a worse place to show off. As they slowed down getting ready to pull over, I screamed to them, "I can't stop! *I told you,* I don't have a license! Block those cops for a few seconds to give me a head start!" I immediately took off and left them behind. Of the two cruisers behind us, one stayed with my friends, and the other took off after me once my pals got out of the way. I made it to the Kangamagus Highway, which is a winding road through the White Mountains. Because of the superior cornering ability and rapid acceleration characteristics of my bike, on that curvy road I was able to put some distance between the pursuing officer and myself. I went around a left-hand turn in the highway as fast as I possibly could, leaning over so far that my foot peg was scraping the roadway. I knew I had to figure out something quickly if I was to avoid capture. I'm sure there were probably more cruisers joining the chase, possibly from the other direction. Just as I was coming out of that hard left curve in the road, I spotted a trail leading off to the right. I slowed as quickly as I could, but still entered that dirt trail at a high rate of speed. As soon as I could, I pulled into the bushes beside the trail and laid the bike over onto a stump so it wasn't completely laid down. I hugged the ground as I heard the cruiser quickly accelerate past my location with the siren screaming. I stayed there for the longest time. Every few minutes a cruiser or two would go racing by within a few hundred feet of me. I watched and listened as my heart raced. They went back and forth for what seemed like forever.

I didn't dare try to leave my hiding spot till the sun was going down. While there in the woods, I stowed my leather and dressed myself in totally different clothes than I had on during the chase. Reluctantly, I left the safety of the woods and I got back out onto the road. I couldn't stay where I was forever. When I got close to the lodge, I was surprised to see that there was a cruiser still parked in the driveway waiting, so I decided I better take a long ride and eat at a restaurant. It was almost midnight when I returned. The coast was finally clear, so I parked the bike around back, out of sight, and went in. I guess the cops didn't believe my friends when they told them the rider that got away was just somebody that started riding along with them that day and that they didn't know me. The officer told my friends, "If you run into that guy again, tell him he better take it easy going through Conway because we'll be watching for him."

My attempts to outrun the police on two occasions were extremely unwise choices. Today, when I look back, I can't believe I was stupid enough to try it. My bad judgment could have ruined my life, the lives of those police officers who were just doing their jobs, or many other innocent people. We see the tragic results of these bad youthful decisions on the evening news way too often. Somebody up there was watching over me, and thankfully, nothing tragic happened. I was just extremely lucky because those situations very rarely end well.

*Have you ever had a time in your life
when poor judgment ruled?
What youthful memories did you create with good friends?*

Reader's Notes

Reader's Notes

Reader's Notes

Reader's Notes

Chapter XI

"It Wasn't Me That Shot Those Guys"

Because of the nature of my work, I met all kinds of interesting characters in Southie. One rugged-looking Irishman, named Ken, would come into the gas station quite often. He had spotted a boat that I was selling at the shop. It was an old wooden boat and motor, which wasn't worth very much. As he checked it out with great interest, he mentioned that he had a motorcycle, and he was willing to trade even-steven with me if I was interested. By him making that offer, I can thank Ken for spurring my original interest in motorcycles, which eventually would lead to much enjoyment as well as incidents such as the one mentioned in the previous chapter. Up to that time, I had never given much thought to owning a bike, but it sounded like a good idea. I said, "Sure! Let's do it!" The bike was an old BSA 250cc, but it was in good shape, and it ran really well. After consummating the trade and riding the bike for a while, I discovered that it had a top speed of exactly eighty miles per hour.

My friendship with Ken, along with my newly acquired interest in motorcycles, made life very interesting. I had a terrifyingly close call on that bike one day while driving into work. I had spotted a

Mobil Oil Corporation gasoline truck way up ahead of me on the expressway. We were a Mobil distributor at that time, and I knew all the drivers. Whoever was piloting that truck was really flying! In order to catch up so I could see who was driving, I had to hold the bike at full speed for the longest time. Once I finally caught up with the truck, I still had to maintain my speed at close to 80 mph. I was directly below the driver's window as I kept waving and yelling, trying to get his attention. It happened to be one of my favorite drivers who often delivered to our station. He was a big black man who was built like Kenny Norton, the heavyweight boxer. We didn't get to see many black people in South Boston, so he was kind of a novelty to us. Anyway, no matter what I did to try getting his attention, he kept his eyes straight ahead and on the road. I should have done the same. I had looked away from the road for several seconds and failed to see that the highway was curving to the right. When I finally looked forward, it was too late. I couldn't negotiate the turn and saw my front wheel going up over the slanted curbing. I was then on the dirt-and-gravel median strip heading toward the guardrail. I couldn't turn sharply or brake at all on this surface. I had to keep my speed rather constant and try to keep control of the bike to get back onto the pavement. All this time, I was praying that I wouldn't run into any of those stray metal posts that happened to be sticking up in the median strip every few hundred feet for no apparent reason. Unable to avoid the guardrail any longer, I hit it with a hard-glancing blow, which ripped the foot peg off the bike. I had tucked my leg in tight to the hot motor, and it was getting burnt, but it was still in one piece. Keeping my speed as steady as possible and steering to the right ever so slightly, I somehow managed to get back onto the paved highway after being in the median for quite a distance.

Drivers behind me who were witnessing this were most assuredly holding their breath, just as I was.

Taking the very next available exit, I stopped and got off the bike, shaking like a leaf. I remember just walking around, circling the bike, as my heart beat much faster than usual. I thought to myself, "Wow. You just started your *second life* right now, Tom." While I was in that median strip, struggling to stay on my wheels, I pictured in my mind the instant and gruesome death that was inevitable if I were to go over that guardrail and into the oncoming traffic. Somehow, that didn't happen. That day, I learned the hard way to *never* take my eyes off the road again, for *any* reason. During that period, crazy things were always happening in Southie, but it seemed that getting there was always half the fun.

As my friendship with Ken evolved, he introduced me to the bars where he was accustomed to drinking. It wasn't long before I came to the realization that the same tactic I had used to initiate myself and bond with the Colbert Gang in Braintree would most likely work in South Boston as well. The people I knew in Southie were not opposed to putting down a few cold ones. Just about every street-corner had a bar. The taverns were a neighborhood gathering place with activities of all kinds. It seemed to me that if I became a regular at a tavern in Southie, I would be considered part of the community and accepted as "okay." I started going out of my way to deliver cars to my customers at the bars where they hung out. Of course, while I was there, I would be invited to have a beer or two before heading back to the shop. My experiment proved me right. In fact, it seemed the more intoxicated I got, the more accepted I became. I guess being loaded showed everyone that I was no better and no worse than anybody else. I was just as vulnerable and human as the next guy.

Over the next few years after Ken traded me his bike for my old boat, I kept in touch with him. He was fun to hang out with at bars, plus he always had a "good deal" to offer on one thing or another. One day he called to ask if I would be interested in buying some nice suits and dress coats "really cheap." When I said I wanted to see what he had, he invited me over to his apartment to take a look. I was impressed to find that his apartment was set up as if it was an actual clothing store. There were racks and racks of suits and jackets arranged by size and style. I bought a couple of sport jackets for a total of around twenty or thirty dollars. I never asked where all the clothing came from. The jackets were just another of Ken's great deals.

Some months went by during which I hadn't heard from Ken. He called me out of the blue one day and suggested we should get together for a drink at a bar on the west side of Southie. I didn't like going to that area, and for good reasons. The bars on that side of town were much less friendly to strangers, and also, that was Whitey Bulger's territory. Whitey headed up one of the most violent and ruthless organized crime families in the country. From reputation and stories on the street, I knew that some really nasty guys hung out in these bars. On the other hand, I always liked these challenging situations of testing out new and maybe forbidden territory. I agreed to meet Ken at a bar I had never been to before. I showed up at the bar on time, but Ken had not arrived yet. That particular day, I was riding my new motorcycle, which was much larger and more impressive than the BSA.

I pulled up in front of the bar, which was nothing more than a big rat hole, and parked the bike right on the sidewalk at the entrance where I could watch it through the open door. The place smelled awful, like a combination of stale beer and an un-flushed urinal. There were five or six scruffy, mean-looking patrons on barstools that stopped talking and stared at me the moment I walked in.

Ignoring that fact, I sat down and ordered a beer. After ten minutes, still no Kenny. I could sense that I was about to wear out my welcome as a stranger in this place, so I walked out with the silence and stares following me. I jumped on my bike and wasted no time getting back to the relative safety of the gas station.

I was back at the garage for less than an hour when a blue Impala pulled up near the office. Two men in suits got out. They walked up to me where I was standing by the pumps. They were Boston Police detectives. They asked me my name, and then asked if I had been at this particular bar that day. I said, "Yes, I was supposed to meet a friend there for a beer, but he didn't show up." They asked my friend's name, but I could only give his first name and no address. I couldn't remember what Kenny's last name was, and he no longer lived at the apartment I had seen just one time. I asked why they were asking me all those questions. They explained that five minutes after I left that bar, a guy on a motorcycle just like mine drove up and parked in the doorway right where I had been parked. The guy got off the bike, walked in wearing a ski mask, and shot three people at the bar. He then walked out, got back on his bike, and left. The detectives said *somebody* at the bar identified *me* as having been there just minutes before on a bike just like the one ridden by the shooter. That was very strange to hear because I didn't recognize anybody in that place. I didn't know anybody in there! I suppose it's possible that Ken showed up after I left and told the police I was supposed to meet him there on my bike. All I could tell them was, "It wasn't me that shot those guys! When I left that bar, everything was just fine there!" They said they would probably be back to talk to me again later and asked if I would be at the shop for a while. They never came back again, and I never saw or heard from my "friend" Ken again either.

Moe, a regular at the Nii Hau, enjoyed hanging out with our rowdy young group. We could always tell a newcomer to the bar by the way they would stumble down the stairs. Not evident because of the camera's flash, the entrance was dimly lit, making the stairs virtually invisible.

Enjoying a cool fall day at the Colbert School
This bike was mistakenly identified in a barroom shooting.

The neighborhood kids liked my first bike "better than the old boat."
This is the bike that glanced off a guardrail at 80 mph.

Master mechanics Ken and Bucky, relaxing on the hood of my
interim vehicle between total wrecks

Friend Steve Natali and I prepare for a day on the water
on my poor man's yacht, the "Nii Hau."

What experiences and people have helped shape who you are?
Have you had some close calls?
What are the riskiest things you've ever done?
Who inspired you? Who betrayed you?

Reader's Notes

Reader's Notes

Reader's Notes

Reader's Notes

Chapter XII

Fitting In More And More

Becoming more and more comfortable in South Boston was a wonderful feeling. There is so much to talk about! The events and the people, although still vividly etched in memory, tend to blend together with regard to time. There were so many interesting people that came in and out of my life during those years, it would be impossible to give each individual the attention and detail he or she deserves.

Kenneth Saunders, not to be confused with the Ken in the previous chapter, was the seasoned mechanic at our shop. He had worked for our family business for many years. Ken had grown up and lived in Connecticut for many years before moving to Boston. He was a widower. Ken never had children, but if he had, he would have been a great father. As I was growing up, Ken taught me many valuable lessons. He was even-tempered and extremely patient. In those two respects, he was the opposite of my dad, so his influence on me was invaluable. As a young mechanic, I would often find myself in the middle of a very tough job and reach a roadblock, such as a broken stud or rusted and frozen bolts. Things would just keep going wrong and I would struggle and struggle, sometimes having painful cuts all over my hands.

Ready to give up, I would slam a tool down in frustration, saying, "I can't do this! There's no way!" Ken would look at me with a kind smile and say, "You *have* to do it. You're getting *paid* to do it." After his encouragement, a few words of wisdom, and maybe a suggestion or two, I somehow always found a way to finish those jobs. He would not jump in and do it for me. Having an "impossible" job successfully completed was quite rewarding. I learned from Ken that no matter what obstacle or difficulty I ran into, there was *always* a solution. I just had to take the time to figure it out. My wife Diane and I were honored to name our son Kenneth after this wonderful man. He was a great companion and role model to me for many years. It was Ken who had played a major role in building those homemade cars for me at the shop when I was just a child, and now, years later, I would end up being his employer and drinking buddy. He was a man who was not driven by material things, and everybody liked and respected him.

After Ken's wife passed away, he and I socialized quite a bit together. Even though I was in my twenties, and he was in his sixties, he would join me quite often in activities after work, never complaining of being tired. In his latter years, he would sometimes stop in the middle of what he was doing and pound on the middle of his chest when his ticker, as he called it, would act up. I guess that would somehow ease his chest pain or reset his heartbeat. He would pop a nitroglycerine tablet every once in a while and then just keep on doing whatever we were doing. One night while bowling at the alleys up on Broadway, he was popping those nitro pills every few minutes. Finally I asked him what they did for him. He said, "Here, try one." I popped it under my tongue as he instructed, and everything immediately went white! My chest felt like it was going to explode, and I came very close to passing out. I was pretty scared as I sat down, hoping I hadn't killed myself and that the feeling would pass. Finally it did. Ken was surprised that I had such a severe reaction to the pill, because they made him feel *better*. I learned to be more cautious about other people's medications after that experience.

One evening when Ken and I were out together with our dates, we decided to try a new restaurant. He suggested The Farragut House, which was located in the City Point section of town. It was a historic-looking building and one of the fancier more expensive restaurants in Southie. Ken mentioned that years ago, the place had been known as a Mullens Gang hangout. I had no idea who or what the Mullens Gang was. I found out later that they were a group with a long violent history. They had a reputation for controlling the criminal activity in this part of Southie and also down by the docks where cargo from all over the world was unloaded. Over the years, they had apparently made out very well by way of extortion, hijacking, and intimidation.

When we entered the restaurant, I immediately felt that it had a wonderful old time atmosphere to it with its massive bar and intricate century-old woodwork. We were seated at a table pretty far from the bar, but close enough that I could enjoy gazing at the detailed woodworking that went into it. The four of us enjoyed truly outstanding steak dinners. Our server seemed to be going out of her way to make us feel very welcome, like VIPs.

After dinner, we took our time and enjoyed the evening, sitting around and talking over cocktails. When it was time to leave, I told Ken it was my turn to take care of the bill, so I signaled to our waitress. She immediately came to the table as she had done all night. I told her everything had been great and I asked for our check. She smiled at me and said, "You're all set. It's been taken care of."

I had never heard those words in a restaurant before. I was confused and asked, "What do you mean it's been taken care of?" I didn't see anyone there that I knew, so I wondered who took care of our bill. She said, "The man at the bar took care of it." I looked over, and I didn't recognize the gentleman. I asked Ken and the others at our table if they knew him. They said they didn't know him either. There was only one man standing at the bar. He was tall with very dark hair slicked back, well groomed, and rather dapper looking. He was wearing expensive-looking shoes and a suit jacket with no tie. Nobody that I personally knew in Southie dressed or looked like that. He wasn't paying any attention to our table at all. I had to find out why he had paid for our night out, so I got up and walked over to him. I cordially said, "Hi. The waitress said you took care of the bill for our table. Do I know you?" There was no smile of cordiality on his face when he looked down at me and responded, "No. But I know who you are." I asked, "How do you know me?" He said, "One day, you stopped with your tow truck, during a blizzard, and pulled my mother's car out of a snow bank when you saw that she was having trouble. She told me she asked you how much she owed you, and you said, 'Nothing.' She said you just got back in your truck and drove off. I was just thanking you." I vaguely remembered the incident. Occasionally I would stop and assist someone if they really looked like they could use some help and I was not in a rush. They would sometimes look at me suspiciously, thinking I was going to ask them for money, which I wouldn't. I told him that I appreciated the gesture, but I didn't feel right about him paying our bill. I told him I would rather pay it because I knew it had to be over a hundred dollars with the meals and all the drinks we had. The man obviously started getting upset that I was discussing this with him. I sensed that he was the type of guy that was used to being listened to, not talked to.

Still with no smile, he reached down and pulled a large roll of money out of his pants pocket and showed it to me. It was about three inches thick and had a $50 bill on the outside. He looked me in the eyes, and said, "Don't worry about it. Did you ever *kill* anybody?" Hoping he was joking, I replied "Not today." When once again I got no smile, or response of any kind, I decided that he could pay if he wanted to. I thanked him and went back to my table. Later that night, as I was about to go to bed, I remember chuckling as I thought to myself, "Where else but in Southie would you ever have somebody say such a thing to you?" I was really glad I had treated that guy's mother the right way. If I hadn't, who knows what kind of night we would have had at that restaurant.

Illegal activity was an accepted way of life with many of the folks I happened to know through the garage. Those who weren't directly involved with some sort of criminal activity in one way or another were certainly aware of the goings-on in the neighborhood, and tolerated it. Of course, there was also the code of silence, which dictated that the streets would dish out their own form of justice amongst those who needed it. That same code is still a persistent cancer in many city neighborhoods today.

Several of my friends were bookies. It was just their job. We were friends to the point that I even vacationed with a few of them in Florida on occasion. They provided a service that lots of people wanted access to. They were just regular nice guys.

At times, I was the mechanic for bartenders and owners of some of the toughest bars in town. Bouncers and enforcers were my regular customers. Those guys treated me just fine. Certainly, there were the other kind of bad guys. You could tell which ones were just plain rotten to the core. They were the type I sensed had no scruples whatsoever. That kind of person doesn't take too long to show his or her true colors.

When my gut told me to stay away from certain people and keep my distance, I always listened. I was proven right many times.

Once in a while there would be an opportunity offered to me which would involve easy money if I wanted it. One such offer came to me through a man I'll call "Buddy." He was a six-foot-four, three-hundred-pound, regular customer. I also considered him to be a friend. Over time, I came to realize that he was connected in some capacity to the Mob. I had deduced that from things he would say and the fact he always had a very nice car, lots of money, and no discernable job. He also knew all the bookies, bartenders, and tavern owners on the west side. He sent many a tough-looking customer my way, but they always treated me with respect. Buddy had a soft-spoken, unintimidating voice, at least when he talked with me. Always well dressed, he was usually wearing an expensive leather jacket that, in his case, took the hide of an entire cow to make. As I was giving Buddy's car a tune-up one day, he leaned over the opposite fender and asked me something out of the blue. "Would you consider holding some high-stakes poker games in your back room, for some heavy hitters?" He said he had been told to ask me. He went on to explain that there would be a game approximately once a month, and if I agreed, I would get ten percent of every pot. That money would be mine no matter who won or lost. All I would have to provide was the space, that being the large secluded rear bay of the shop, some tables and chairs, and refreshments. I was assured that the only participants would be well-connected big-time gamblers that he personally knew, and there would be no trouble at the games. As I leaned over Buddy's engine, installing his spark plugs, I almost blurted out, "Yeah! That sounds great!" but my gut stepped in and spoke for me, saying, "I don't know, Buddy." Sensing my hesitation, he said, "It would be a lot of money. You should think about it and let me know." I told him I would sleep on it and let him know the next day. This was really enticing, because it was a bona fide offer from a connected enforcer. But sometimes, not making quick decisions is a good thing. My philosophy has always been that if I have trouble getting to sleep while trying to decide whether or not to do something, it's probably better not to do it. When Buddy came back the next day for my answer, I declined. That was okay with him. He didn't try to influence me, and I didn't have to explain my reasons. I hadn't played ball with them in the past, so I still owed them nothing except to do a good job on their cars, and that was the way I liked it. In other instances, I had also been approached and asked to store an occasional truck or some other item in my shop for a substantial fee. Not asking any of the details, I declined each and every one of those offers as well. I wanted to be able to sleep at night. Certain people would have loved to have my shop at their disposal. Enough said about that.

By 1975, I had endured my fill of fighting traffic every day, commuting to and from Braintree. Each morning and evening I was being held captive by gridlocked cars, breathing exhaust fumes, and listening to irate drivers blast their horns at each other. I had even gotten into confrontations at times while in traffic. One morning after arguing back and forth with some guy and cutting each other off a few times, he tried to purposely hit the side of my car with his. That was the last straw for me. Although the term "road rage" was still decades from being coined, I took the oak axe handle out from under my seat and when properly positioned next to his Mercedes, I proceeded to reach out of my window and smash his headlight with the club. Then I yelled to him to see if he wanted to continue playing with me. I guess I was spending too much time in Southie, and I was picking up some bad habits. He faded back, holding up traffic in his lane.

I expected to get a call from the police later that day, but I never heard from anybody. One day, I used that time sitting in traffic to figure something out. Commuting from Braintree was consuming *one-twentieth of my life* as I sat, stressed out in bumper-to-bumper traffic on the Southeast Expressway. When you think of it in those terms, that's a large chunk of your life to needlessly waste! By this time, I had become very comfortable with being in Southie, so I decided that I should rent an apartment close to the shop.

The very next day, as I was changing the oil in a regular customer's car, I mentioned to him that I would be looking at apartments after work. He perked right up and said he had one for rent, which was available right away. His tenant had just moved out. I looked at it right after work that day and immediately fell in love with the place. It had a fantastic location at the very top of G Street hill, with South Boston High School situated directly across the street. It was an incredible stroke of luck that this man was in for service on that particular day, and I mentioned apartment hunting to him. The landlord's only stipulation was that I not have any parties in the apartment. Later, I found out that his definition of a party was having another couple over for pizza on a Friday night. I cooperated and kept the noise down whenever I had friends over. It was a wonderful third-floor flat with a spiral staircase that led up to a small glassed-in room on the roof, called a widow's watch. I had a fantastic view of Boston Harbor from the highest perch in town. The 747s and other assorted planes arriving at Logan Airport would glide directly over my apartment. When up in the widow's watch, I sometimes got nervous that they might not make it over the house. It felt as if I could reach out and touch the planes as they passed overhead. All this was mine for just $80 per month!

Entering the owner's flat on the first floor was like stepping back into Boston history. There was an ornate marble fireplace in one room. The dining room had a beautiful *hand-painted* mural of Boston Public Gardens covering the walls, just as it looked a century or so ago. Most of these homes on the hill had been built for sea captains in the 1800s. From this high and desirable location, the captains' wives could watch for their husbands' anticipated return from months at sea.

Being in a nice location did not exempt me from the occasional craziness that goes hand in hand with inner city life. While living at the top of G Street hill, I was awakened late one night by loud bashing noises off in the distance. It must have been two or three in the morning. When I got to my front window, which was three stories up off the street, I could see way down the hill that there were five or six guys walking slowly up G Street. They all had baseball bats and they were strolling along the side of the street on which my Challenger was parked. These were not young kids. They were big guys in their late teens or early twenties, and most likely drunk. As they walked, they were smashing every car along the way with their bats, without exception. I couldn't believe my eyes! They would hit the hood, the headlights, the windshield, or whatever else they felt like destroying as they walked along. Each car was getting hit at least twice. I ran to my closet and grabbed the pellet rifle that I kept there. It was a warm summer night, so my windows were already opened. I raised the screen a couple of inches and rested the barrel of the gun on the windowsill. This was a very powerful air rifle, and it would do serious damage if I hit someone in the right place. It was quiet enough when it fired that I knew they would never be able to tell where the shots came from, especially over the sounds that they were producing with their voices and bats.

It was the perfect situation to teach these guys a lesson. I had the lead guy's head in my sights as they approached my car—the car that was my pride and joy. Not a scratch was on that baby, and I wanted to keep it that way. The first one to raise his bat to hit my car was going to be in for a big surprise. I had my finger on the trigger. They had not skipped over any vehicles along their destructive path. I watched silently as they hit the car behind mine a few times, taking out the headlights and smashing the hood. Then, as they surrounded my car, they all paused! To my total amazement, they walked around my car just looking at it and not laying a finger on it. Upon reaching the car in front of mine, they continued the infliction of damage. Why was my car spared? I can only guess that they were car enthusiasts and liked my car, or possibly one of them knew me. Anyway, they were spared a lot of pain, and I was spared the awful task of having to shoot them. I was surprised that nobody came outside and no police showed up. The people on G Street were either really heavy sleepers or they knew better than to go out there in the middle of the night and confront those guys.

On another evening, I was not as lucky in avoiding conflict out on the street in front of my apartment. I had spent an evening in Braintree with a date. We had enjoyed dinner, and quite a few Black-Russians at the Nii Hau before heading home to South Boston. On the way back in, I was feeling my oats, so to speak. I was burning rubber around corners and goosing the gas pedal whenever I could. I was just really having a great time. As I came up from Day Boulevard into Thomas Park, the car ahead of me apparently became annoyed with my driving antics. He slowed to a crawl in front of me to show his disapproval. The street was too narrow to pass him. As we got to the corner at G Street, there was a parking space open directly to the left side of where he had stopped to block my progress.

He didn't know that I lived right there and didn't need to get past him. I sped into the parking spot and was within inches of the side of this guy's car. When I backed up to straighten out, my front bumper clipped his rear fender. The guy jumped out of his car and approached my driver's door. In a flash, all I could see was his belt buckle waiting for me as he stood there outside my window. He was quite a bit taller than I was, but I wasn't really nervous as I opened my door and got out of the car. I intended to apologize to him for hitting his car. The guy was about a foot away from my face and he was yelling at me that I had hit his car. I was about to tell him I was really sorry, but he didn't give me the chance. He said, "You've been drinking!" and he immediately swung at me, hard, hitting me with a sucker punch right in the face. *Wham!* I couldn't believe that I had allowed myself to get suckered again! Hadn't I learned anything when I was a kid? With the initial impact of his punch, I actually blacked out and started instinctively swinging with both rights and lefts, as hard and as fast as I could. It happened without any conscious decision on my part, as if something took over my body. I was in survival mode. Over and over again I could feel the heavy pounding of my fists against his face until all at once I was swinging at thin air. When I came back to my senses, and my vision returned, he wasn't in front of me anymore. I glanced down and there he was, peacefully sleeping, knocked out cold on the sidewalk at my feet. By this time, my date was cowering in the passenger seat of my car. My assailant's wife was standing outside the passenger door of her car in the middle of the street. I could see the silhouette of her in the dark, holding a baby in her arms. I looked down at him and then over at her and said, "Should I boot his face in like he would do to me if I was down there?" His wife answered, "No! Please! He's had enough!" I got down on top of the guy and held him down on the ground as he was coming to.

He looked up at me not knowing where he was or what was going on. I had my high school ring and another large ring on that night, and they had done quite a nasty job on his face. Afraid that this guy might return later for revenge and damage my car in some way, I asked him "What's your name? Where do you live?" He said his name was "Kelly", and he told me his address, which was one block away from mine. I told him, "Look! Kelly! I could have booted your face in, like I expect you would have done to me, but I didn't do it. Now I'm warning you. If anything *ever* happens to my car while it's parked here at my house, I am going to assume you did it, and I'll come after you. Do you understand? You can't go around assaulting people because they accidentally tapped your car. You shouldn't have hit me!" He said, "Okay," and I helped him to his feet. He was still unsteady as he made his way back to his car. I remembered back to when I was a little boy, and the kid named "Kelly" from my neighborhood would tease me until I finally outran him and pushed his face into the pavement. I remembered how good it felt to finally stand up for myself. In comparison, it felt *really* good to knock this guy, another "Kelly", out cold. I hadn't assaulted him. He hit me first, with no warning, so I didn't feel bad about what happened at all.

My date and I entered the stairway to go up to my apartment for a nightcap. I didn't hear her following me, so I turned and looked around. She was twenty feet behind me. I asked her what she was doing as she cowered at the bottom of the stairway. She replied, "Are you finished beating people up?" I said "What? Are you afraid of me?" I exclaimed that he had hit me first. She responded by saying she did not see the guy throw the first punch, or any punch for that matter. From her vantage point, I just attacked him out of the blue.

Finally, the only way she believed me was when I showed her the cuts inside my mouth and my swollen lip that resulted from that sucker punch.

The next morning when I woke, I remember that the muscles in both of my forearms were really sore from the strain of throwing those punches. When the adrenaline kicked in that previous night, I had subconsciously put everything I had into throwing those lefts and rights. It would have taken a lot of strain to make my arms hurt in those days because, as a mechanic, I worked my arm muscles constantly. I was turning wrenches, handling heavy truck tires and transmissions, etc., all day. I couldn't help thinking that if my arms hurt this bad, I wonder how that guy's face must feel.

All things considered, it was great living within walking distance of Emerson Auto. On workdays, I would frequent the local South Boston tavern. My regular Southie hangout was Gavin's Tavern, which was later renamed O'Leary's Pub after it changed hands. From the gas station, I could see Gavin's down at the corner of Dorchester and Emerson Streets and monitor whether any of my friends had parked there and gone in.

On weekends I would be off to the Colbert School, a campground in East Bridgewater, or the Nii Hau Restaurant in Braintree. Life was treating me really well.

Chapter XIII

"Forced Busing" And
The Awful Side Effects

The 1970s were very tumultuous years in Southie. Boston was dealing with court-mandated integration of the school system. It was to be accomplished by way of "forced busing," as ordered by Judge Arthur Garrity. Also, because I owned a gas station during those years, I had to deal with the stress and danger caused by the oil embargo and resulting gasoline shortages. It was not a fun time on either of these fronts.

On school days, there would be hundreds of heavily armed officers from the newly formed Tactical Police Force, wearing riot gear and helmets, along with hundreds of angry protesters outside my front door on G Street. At times, there were police sharpshooters stationed on the rooftop of the school. They had to guard and protect the black students as they were escorted to and from the high school each day. There were massive protests. I have to admit that it is easy to get caught up in the mob mentality if you happen to be subjected to it every day. Just starting out as an innocent observer one day, I somehow found myself unintentionally on the front line of a nasty crowd, caught up in the moment. I was almost trampled by the Boston Mounted Police. The horse just pushed me aside as it plowed its way through the crowd.

One of my best friends, Donald (Barney) Bilotas, was a member of the Boston School Police. It was a new branch of the police force, established specifically to patrol inside the schools during the day. After work, Barney would come to the gas station and hang out for a while with me. Just about every day, he would tell me about the numerous weapons he had confiscated on that particular day. He would also describe the many fights he had broken up. It seemed like a lost cause, but he made a difference by doing his best to keep people safe. Barney was a great friend. A year or so after the busing crisis started, when I was back home in Braintree recuperating from major back surgery in a body cast, Barney was the one friend from South Boston that drove out to my folks' house regularly. He spent many hours visiting with me and cheering me up. That meant so much to me. He ended up being best man at my wedding. Sadly, I lost my friend Barney to cancer when he was only in his forties. As sad as the situation was, I was thankful years later that I was able to return the favor of his dedicated friendship by spending time at his bedside during many of his final days.

My friends from the suburbs enjoyed coming to Southie. They liked being at the shop and going to the taverns with me. It was more interesting to them than their quiet town. One summer, while one of my employees was on vacation, my friend Chippa from Braintree offered to pump gas for me while I was shorthanded. This took place when anti-black sentiment was running extremely high in Southie. Forced busing had the opposite of the intended effect on the city. It just fostered stronger resentment and separation of the races at the time.

It was Chippa's first day helping me at the station. We were in the front office, and I was showing him how to operate the cash register. We noticed a car pull up and park in front of the row-houses across the street from the gas pumps. Through the front windows of the office, we could see that the driver was a black man in his late twenties or early thirties. His passenger was a very attractive professionally dressed white girl with long blond hair. The young man got out of his car and walked approximately two hundred feet back up the street to the US post office, which we could also see from the office. He was probably on an innocent mission to pick up mail for the business he worked for. As he entered the building, I remember thinking how strange it was to see a black person anywhere near this area. This was a time when you couldn't even get a black taxi driver to drop you off anywhere in South Boston because they were afraid of being attacked. The same situation existed in some black neighborhoods where white people would not venture. Chippa and I went back about our business. Maybe thirty to forty seconds later, we glanced up and saw a gang of five or six white boys charging in through the front door of the post office. They were all around twelve or thirteen years old, and each boy was wielding a hockey stick over his shoulder as they aggressively sprinted into the building. Chippa and I didn't put two and two together and only realized what was happening when, a few seconds later, the black man came running full speed out of the post office door, desperately trying to get back to his car. The boys were chasing closely behind him, swinging their sticks wildly in the air. At first, Chippa and I were frozen in disbelief at what we were seeing. As the man reached his car, the boys caught up with him on the sidewalk, right outside the window where his passenger was seated. All of the boys started swinging their hockey sticks as fast and as hard as they could at his head and his back! It was as if they were in a competition to chop a tree down as fast as they could. Such rage and hatred I had never seen before in my life. He was blocking as many blows as he could with his arms wrapped around his head, but you could see that he didn't have a chance. He was being beaten severely, and I realized that he might be killed before they would stop. Once the seriousness of the situation hit me, I looked around the office for some sort of weapon, and I spotted the baseball bat that we kept against the wall next to the cash register. I grabbed that bat and headed outside to intervene. As I exited the office, with bat-in-hand, two men happened to be coming out of their front door, just feet from where this was happening. They yelled something at the boys, but did not try to physically intervene. Thankfully, the boys turned and ran. One of them lingered behind the others just long enough to take one last hard swing with his hockey stick. He smashed the windshield of the car, right in front of the blond girl's face, with all his might. This young woman must have been terrified beyond anything she had ever experienced before in her life. A shower of splintered glass must have hit her right in the face. I'm certain that she would have been beaten and possibly killed as well if this attack had not been interrupted. The black man, without hesitation, scrambled to get into his car. He quickly started the engine and drove away while holding his bleeding forehead with one hand and driving with the other. I could see that the girl was crying hysterically. The two men on the sidewalk and I exchanged glances and shook our heads in disgust. I was pretty shaken up just from observing what had taken place. I turned to Chippa and said, "Welcome to Southie!" That was the first and last day I remember Chippa helping me out at the gas station.

All sorts of thoughts linger after observing something like this. I actually felt bad for those boys, wondering what kind of family influence had produced such intense hatred. Can you blame the boys or should their fathers and mothers be blamed for instilling these feelings of hatred in them? I couldn't help but feel sad for humanity as a whole after witnessing such cruelty to a perfect stranger whose only crime was being black in a white neighborhood. I was upset with myself as well, for momentarily freezing and not trying to help that guy sooner than I did. Time seemed to slow to a crawl during that incident. Not comprehending or believing what my eyes were seeing had a paralyzing effect on me.

Forced busing was the cause of a close call for me on another occasion. My friend Pudgy had driven into Southie from Braintree one morning when I was on vacation. We were going to take some guns down to the town of Halifax where we could target practice at the sand pits. We gathered up a couple of rifles and some ammunition and headed down the stairs to the front entranceway of the apartment house. As we were walking out the front doorway into the street, each carrying a rifle, I stopped cold when I saw hundreds of people and Tactical Police officers all over the place. There were several police sharpshooters with rifles up on the rooftop of the school as well. Apparently that morning, shortly after school started, there had been a violent incident in the school between the black kids and the white kids. Tensions were running so high that classes had been suspended for the day. They were in the process of emptying the school and loading the buses. We hadn't made it two feet out the door when I realized that we were in a very bad situation. I grabbed Pudgy by the arm and quickly pulled him back into my building. I closed the door as fast as I could, taking a deep breath in disbelief of the huge mistake we had just made. Pudgy yelled at me, "What the hell are you doing?" I said to him, "Didn't you see all the cops and commotion outside?" He said yes. I told him that this was not a good time for two guys to be walking out into the middle of G Street carrying rifles! If we had tried to cross that street to get to my car carrying those guns, the Tactical Police probably would have shot us down in the street without question. We went back up to my apartment, waited for the school buses to leave and for the police to clear out.

Then we wrapped our rifles in blankets before taking them out to the car. That was a very close call.

Emotions ran extremely high during the "Forced Busing" era in South Boston. Things were definitely out of control, and violence could erupt at a moments notice. The Rabbit Inn was probably the toughest bar on the west side of Southie. It was one of those bars that I felt compelled to go into just once, so I could say I'd had a beer in there. I was driving by the bar one day and my car just pulled up and parked in front, as if it had a mind of its own. It was a bar my friends had warned me to never go into, which made me want to do it all the more. As I approached the front entrance there was a tough looking guy eyeballing me. Next to him was a pile of broken bricks on the sidewalk. To make conversation, I smiled and asked him, "What are the bricks for?" I guess that was becoming a common question in Southie back then. People would ask me the same question at the gas station when they saw the half-bricks on top of my gas pumps. Mine were there to deter drive-offs. The answer he gave me about his pile of bricks was, "They're here in case we see a car or bus go by with a nigger in it." I just continued into the bar and sat down. The usual silence and threatening stares took hold, but this was by far the coldest reception I had ever encountered in a strange bar. I have to admit that I was pretty scared, thinking I should have heeded my friends advice and not ventured into this forbidden territory. Thankfully, as had happened on other occasions, somebody at the bar recognized me from coming into Emerson Auto. I noticed him give a nod at the bar indicating that I was "okay." Once it was affirmed that somebody knew me and that I was not a cop or a threat from another group, the conversations resumed. I left the bar after my one beer, and earned the right to boast to the guys at the garage the next day that I had stopped for a drink at The Rabbit Inn.

There was a very serious incident that took place in that bar. Apparently, a score had to be settled between some members of the Tactical Police Force and the patrons of the Rabbit Inn after a senior officer was injured during a confrontation outside the bar. One day, a large group of "TPF" officers dressed in full riot gear stormed the bar, and they were swinging their clubs with a vengeance. I heard on the street that none of them were wearing their badges or any other visible identification. They were in and out of that establishment very quickly. The inside of the building was nearly destroyed and numerous bar patrons were badly beaten and left bloodied on the floor. Twelve people needed to be hospitalized. The TPF's actions led to a reputation of them being a lawless group of thugs. They became hated by certain factions in Southie and received plenty of very negative media coverage. There were calls from the public for the Tactical Police Force to be disbanded, and eventually they were.

Sometimes an experience is so surreal and disturbing that I think a person has a hard time accepting that it really happened. It is an incident so terrible and horrifying that we want to believe it never took place. I am about to describe an example of just such an experience. It took place after a long night at Gavin's Tavern during which I had an exceptionally good time. I was now living on G Street, which meant I could party up a storm and not have to worry about driving home on the expressway. I had switched from drinking my usual beer to drinking vodka and grapefruit juice. Often when I made that switch, things happened that I wish I could change or forget, but I was a slow learner, and this was one of those nights. I had left my car at the gas station after work and walked down to Gavin's. It was probably closing time when I left. I was drunker than I had been in a long time, and I recall staggering out the front door of the bar, down the couple of steps, and out into the street. I remember that the roads were wet as I slowly tried to make my way across Dorchester Street. It was totally silent at that time of morning, but I could hear a car off in the distance, and it was approaching. The headlights reflected off the wet pavement as it came toward me at a fast rate of speed. There was the sound of laughing and yelling from a few young men as the car got closer. I tried to make it to the other side of the road, but my unsteadiness made it impossible to move fast enough. They certainly had deduced that the guy trying to cross the road was really intoxicated. Almost hitting me, the car drove up and came to an abrupt stop directly next to where I stood. I remember walking right into the side of the car, at the open back window, and holding onto the roof of the car as I stood there. Three or four young white guys were sitting inside. One that was sitting in the backseat looked up at me with a big grin and loudly said, "Hey! Wanna see a dead nigger?" With that, he propped up what appeared to be the body of a young black man for me to see, using the hair on the boy's head to hold it up. After a second, he let go of the hair and the head of the boy fell limply back onto the body's shoulder. It looked to be a black boy in his late teens or early twenties, but there were no signs of trauma or blood that I could see. His body appeared so limp that he was either dead or he was an Oscar-winning actor. Then, as quickly as they had pulled up to me, they sped off and disappeared into the darkness. All of this happened in a matter of just a few seconds. The dead silence of the night returned as I stood in the middle of that dark wet road. I remember just standing there, in stunned disbelief, trying to decipher what had just happened. I glanced back at the entrance to Gavin's to see if anyone else had observed this. Nobody was there. As I made my way up the street, got into my car, and drove the two blocks to get home, I kept thinking to myself, did this really just happen? Did I really just see this? I tried to convince myself that it was just a hoax or it didn't really happen at all, and the alcohol had me hallucinating. I got to my apartment and collapsed into bed for the night. When I awoke the next morning, that incident was the first thing I thought of. I was close to calling the police when I tried to remember what kind of car I had seen or what the occupants had looked like. I drew a blank on all of those details. All I could remember in any detail was seeing the black boy being held up in the darkness right at the window where I was standing. I would be useless to any police investigation. I asked myself again. Did this really happen? I checked the newspapers for the next few days to see if there were any stories about a young black man either missing or murdered, but I saw nothing in the papers or on the news. Of course there were many murders, shootings, and the like that never made it to the papers. Poor people disappear all the time, and they unfortunately get no media attention.

Years have passed, but I never forgot that night. Could it all have been a manifestation of my mind caused by the hostility I observed between the whites and the blacks due to "forced busing?" Was it really just a bad dream? I try to keep the possibility alive that it really didn't happen, but down deep, I cannot convince myself of that.

My Southie apartment at the top of G Street hill had a great view of the harbor from the glassed-in "widow's watch" on the roof. It was located directly across the street from South Boston High as shown below. During "forced busing," many conflicts and near riots took place between protestors and the Tactical Police Force right at my doorstep.

Evidence of the times:
These stamped dollars circulated throughout
Boston as a protest to court-ordered "forced busing."

During the violent times of "forced busing," Don (Barney) Bilotas
patrolled the halls of Southie High as a member of the Boston School
Police. He would break up fights and confiscate weapons daily. He
was the best of friends and a devoted husband and father. He was best
man at my wedding and loved cruising Boston Harbor with me in the
evenings as a way to unwind from the stress of the day.
Tragically, we lost him to illness at much too young an age.

Barney is ready for another day of keeping the peace
in the halls of Southie High.

Chapter XIV

They Said I Wouldn't Come Back

As time went on, my back pain became unbearable. Wearing the brace to stop the scoliosis from progressing had not worked as hoped. The curvature had worsened to over forty-five degrees, and my ribcage was now distorted. There was a pronounced hump on one side of my back, and I was concave on the other side. My right leg was going numb and sometimes would collapse right out from under me. When breathing became very painful and my heart enlarged from rubbing against my spine, our family physician, Dr. Krisiukenas, referred me to an orthopedic surgeon named Dr. DeLorme. I was told he had operated on Bobby Orr's knees. Orr was a Boston Bruins hockey star, so I had confidence in the doctor.

Shortly after the Blizzard of '78, when I was twenty-five years old, Dr. DeLorme operated, installing a Harrington rod in my back. He also fused the majority of the vertebra in my spine using bone he removed from my hip. My spine would now be straighter and hopefully solid, from vertebra T6 to L3.

This was quite a complicated and fairly dangerous operation. Halfway through the surgery, they brought me out of anesthesia just enough to communicate with me. They needed to check to see if I could still move my arms and legs. Because I surprised them and turned out to be a major bleeder, they almost lost me. After receiving eleven pints of blood, and enduring three days in the intensive care unit, there would be a long painful recovery ahead.

While waiting for the incisions to heal so they could remove the 110 stitches, I spent several long and extremely painful days in a Stryker frame. That is a sort of rotisserie for humans that allowed the medical staff to sandwich me between two platforms and flip me over every so many hours without disturbing the alignment of the newly fused spine. There were four long hours between morphine shots. As the clock crawled toward medication time, I would be crying in pain, begging for that shot. The relief from the morphine was instantaneous, only to have the pain rear its ugly head once again a short time later. I remember that my friend Steve Natali came to visit me soon after I was moved out of intensive care. I felt bad having to do it, but I immediately asked him to leave. I was in tears and in way too much pain for company.

Eventually, the stitches were removed and it was time to apply the plaster cast. I was put on a special table and had a harness attached to my head and another to my feet. The doctors cranked and cranked the apparatus, slowly stretching my body out to the point I was truly terrified that my head was going to pop out of its socket, paralyzing me forever. I could only moan with pain, unable to protest because my mouth was forced shut so tight. I would have thought you would find a device like this in a medieval prison, being used for torture, not in an American hospital. Once I was fully extended, the plaster cast was applied. Unfortunately, my cast was very heavy; nothing like the lightweight casts of today. The modern version is made of fiberglass sections that, after a few weeks, are removable, enabling the patient to shower and sleep without the cast. I would have loved one of those.

I wouldn't be allowed those luxuries until after my cast was removed, six months later.

Prior to entering the hospital for the operation, I had given my landlady in South Boston three months rent in advance. I was optimistic, thinking that I would be able to return to my apartment within a month or so after the surgery. I was *so wrong*. I soon realized that it would be impossible to live alone during my six months in that cast. I had to give up the apartment and the independence that I had grown to love. My mom, my dad, my Aunt Marion and Uncle Dick took their cars into South Boston to empty out my apartment. They brought all my belongings back to our house in Braintree.

Two or three months after moving back in with my folks, I was in for a real surprise. Mom had just driven me home from the hospital after my monthly x-rays. When we arrived back in Braintree, she stopped to let me out directly in front of the house, near the front door. I had ridden in the front seat of her car, with the backrest completely reclined as she drove. After I managed to get out of the car, I glanced at Mom's garden along the front of the house. About twenty feet from the edge of the street, I noticed a line of tall plants, about three feet high, which had no flowers on them. To me, those plants looked out of place because all of her other plants had brilliant color. I asked her, "Mom, what are those tall plants along the front of the house?" She replied, "Oh! Those are the plants that were hanging in pots in the front windows of your apartment. Marion and I brought them home. Your landlady said she had been watering your plants every day while you were in the hospital. They got too big for the pots, so I transplanted them outside into the garden. They've done very well! What are they?" At first I was puzzled, not being able to figure out what plants I could have possibly had that would get that big. Then I gasped when I realized what had happened. I had totally forgotten about something I had done shortly before ending up in the hospital. In order to explain, I have to make a confession. While living in my apartment during the 1970s, occasionally, a friend would want to share a joint while we visited. Unlike Bill Clinton, I actually inhaled. Marijuana seeds were usually just thrown away, but after my friends left one night, I decided to do an experiment. There was nothing growing in the hanging flowerpots in the front windows of my apartment. I scattered the leftover marijuana seeds into those pots, just to see if anything would actually sprout. After planting them, I forgot all about it, and then I ended up in the hospital. Time went by, and my unsuspecting landlady nurtured and watered all the plants I had, including the hanging pots. Apparently, those seeds did sprout and the seedlings prospered under her care. When my loving family struggled down those flights of stairs, moving all my belongings out of the apartment, they were inadvertently transporting marijuana plants. Now those plants were proudly displayed right in front of my parent's home on a public street. Even more bizarre was the fact a Boston Police detective lived directly across the street from our house at the time! He came and went from his home, just fifty feet away. He had even stood in front of our house having conversations with my folks, but he never noticed the three-foot high illegal weeds that were hidden right there in plain sight.

When I realized what those plants were, I was totally shocked! I said to myself, "Oh my god!" I hobbled over to them in my body cast and started pulling them out of the ground one by one, as fast as I could. Mom went and parked the car in the garage and then yelled at me saying, "What are you doing? You're gonna hurt your back!" I said, "Ma, you don't want these plants out here. These are just weeds! Take them and toss them in the woods behind the house."

She said, "Oh! They were such nice-looking plants. I thought they were something you wanted." I never did tell my mom what those plants were. She is going to be quite surprised at these details if she reads this book.

Both before and after my surgery, I was told I probably would not be able go back to being an auto mechanic because of all the bending and lifting required. There were many days when I felt hopeless, lying at home, sometimes in tears, worrying about the future. The things that saved my sanity when I was in that cast were my wonderful family and my loyal friends. Mom took great care of me. She even devised a tool to ease the itching I developed under the cast. She got a long flexible spatula and sewed a sock around the end of it. We would wet the cotton sock with alcohol and then slide the spatula under my cast to relieve itches and to keep me clean and fresh. That was such a tremendous relief! Because it was virtually impossible to sit down with the cast, my mother set up all my meals on the half wall at the top of the stairs from the entrance of the house. I ate comfortably while standing on those stairs for the entire six months.

My friends were great to me as well, often coming to visit at the house. As the months went by, and I got stronger, I would walk the mile or so to the Nii Hau just about every day. I could visit with friends, have a drink or two and then walk back home. I must have been quite a sight to see, walking down Granite Street, but I didn't care. I was just happy to be out of the house. One day while at the Nii Hau, I was standing at the bar sipping a Black-Russian. Not being able to sit, I would rest the bottom edge of my body-cast on the barstool and stand there, leaning back slightly to take the weight off my feet. The balancing act I was learning was the next best thing to sitting. I couldn't tip my head back because of the cast, so I had to lean back more and more as I drank my drink. About halfway through my Black-Russian, I leaned backward to take a sip, and I leaned a little too far. I felt the top-heavy cast pulling me over backward. There was absolutely nothing I could do to stop it once I started to go. Just like a falling tree, I slowly tipped farther and farther backward until the cast was against the backrest of the barstool and my feet came off the ground. Stool and all, I fell over backwards to the floor with a crash. I was really glad that there was nothing directly behind me to hit my head on, such as the edge of a nearby table. That would have finished me off for sure. The entire bar went silent as everyone turned and stared at me lying there. I'm sure they were thinking I must have broken my back all over again from the fall. I lay there holding my drink in an outstretched hand. Remarkably, I hadn't spilled a drop. Several of the guys I knew came over to see if I was hurt, and I asked them to stand me back up. It was all very funny once everyone realized that I wasn't hurt at all.

Toward the end of my recovery, the cast became the subject of lots of fun. The Braintree cop named Bubba, that seemed to dog me for years, had spotted me drinking again at the Colbert School one night. He couldn't fit me into his cruiser with that cast on, so he actually marched me home from the school yard. It must have been quite a scene to see. As I walked in the middle of the street, I had Bubba in his cruiser following twenty feet behind me with the blue lights illuminating the night. With me waddling in front with a spotlight trained on my ass, we turned the corner of my street and continued right to my front door where he delivered me once again. My neighbors must have been enjoying the show.

That summer, I drilled holes in the cast and used myself as a rocket launcher at my friend Bob's annual Fourth of July party. I believe I was the only non-family member to be invited to this great event each year.

The party was held at his mother's house, and they served unlimited lobsters and corn-on-the-cob. They were great hosts. Every year we were assured of a visit from the Braintree Police as the fireworks got bigger and louder. After all of us had indulged in a few beers, Bob and his brothers, Tommy and Al, jokingly threatened to hang me by the neck of my cast, saying it probably wouldn't bother me at all. I said, "Go ahead!" They tied a rope around the neck of my cast, threw the rope over a beam in the cellar, and before you knew it, they were swinging me back and forth through the air, hanging by the neck, with my feet dangling in the breeze. It wasn't hurting me in the least. Looking back, I'm really glad that plaster cast didn't break! Everyone was laughing their asses off so hard at the sight that Bob's mother came down the cellar stairs to see what all the noise was. Her sons had a history of getting into mischief. Just because they were adults didn't mean she no longer had to check on them. She let out a scream when she saw me hanging there, swinging, and she started yelling, "Cut him down! Cut him down!" It was so funny watching her panic. She had no idea that everything was just fine. She had a few choice words for us all after they cut me down.

When that cast was finally removed, it was like a rebirth to me. I felt as light as a feather, yet I was still in great pain with every movement. As soon as I felt up to it, I took the cast to the Halifax sandpits and used it for target practice. I fired a 12-gauge semiautomatic shotgun into it at least twenty times. To my dismay, not even that heavy artillery could destroy that instrument of misery. Just a small puff of white powder would be visible when the bullets hit, and the cast was still sitting there in one piece. I finally just left it there for the next group of shooters to work on.

Determined to get back to a normal life as soon as I possibly could, I began to concentrate on building up strength in my back muscles. They had all been cut through during the surgery and had since lain dormant for months. Remarkably, I don't recall that any physical therapy was offered to me after the cast came off. I was left on my own to figure out how to regain my strength. Little by little, there was slight improvement, and I tried to resume some duties at the garage with my dad. Just pumping gas and doing the paperwork was a drag to me. I missed being on the road with the tow truck and working in the shop as a mechanic.

I found out quickly that leaning over fenders while working on an engine was impossible because of the intense pain and muscle weakness. Then I made a wonderful discovery. The solution was so simple! If I just *laid* my chest across the fender of a car instead of leaning over as I worked, I didn't have to strain my back muscles at all. I would use the strength in my arms to raise and lower myself off the fender. I was able to work this way without much trouble at all. As the months and years went by, I slowly gained more and more strength. Finally, Dad could begin enjoying retirement as I took over the business. I continued paying him handsomely every week until he said the shop was mine. He enjoyed visiting the shop a couple of times per week until his unexpected death in 1985, at the age of sixty-nine.

While recovering from back surgery, the mile or so walk each way
to the Nii Hau every day served as good therapy.
There were always good friends to be found there.

Friends and neighbors from Southie sent me this get-well poster.
It was signed by so many that it meant the world to me.

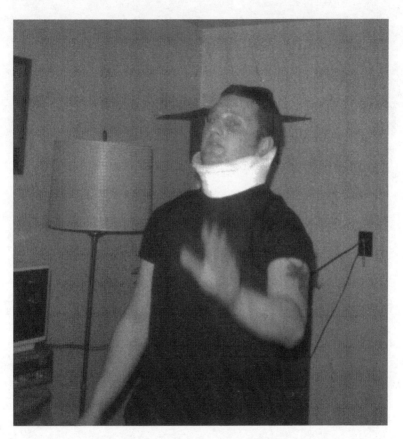

A day I was not in the mood for photos

After six months in the body cast, it was good to finally be back at the shop.
Mom would stop in for a fill-up once in a while to check on me.

This statue of Admiral Farragut is located at the end of East Broadway.
During the long recuperation, I missed my pre-work ritual of having coffee
each morning while watching the sunrise silhouette him by the bay.
(The cover photo is an example of a sunrise, which I photographed.)

Chapter XV

Whitey Bulger Pays Me A Visit

The gasoline shortage of the 1970s was a very difficult time to own a gas station. We were normally selling between 1,000 and 1,200 gallons of gas per day. Most of that fuel went to our commercial account customers. When the oil embargo hit, we were put on a ration that averaged six hundred gallons per day. Like other stations, we tried many methods of working with the supply we had available to us. The main concern was to save enough gasoline in our tanks to keep our regular and loyal customers supplied. With no gas for their trucks, our account customers would be out of business. We had to take care of them during this crisis, or they would certainly not remain loyal to us when the gas shortage was over. Trying to deter the masses from lining up at the pumps, we put up signs that read "Commercial Accounts Only," "Regular Customers Only," and at times we posted signs stating "$2 Limit." At the time, $2 would buy you three or four gallons on gas. None of those efforts seemed to work. Cars would still line up from the gas pumps all the way down the street past the post office. People played ignorant, just disregarding all the signs. Sometimes a person waiting in the "$2 Limit" line would observe me putting ten or fifteen gallons of gas in the truck or car belonging to one of our commercial account customers.

An argument would immediately ensue at the pumps as people couldn't understand why that guy was able to fill up, and all they could get was two dollars' worth of fuel after waiting in line for an hour. People were increasingly short tempered, and situations often turned ugly. At the end of the day, when we wanted to close up for the night, I would have somebody stand at the end of the line, holding up a sign saying "Last Car", and people would still pull in and form a line behind the guy holding the sign. We heard all kinds of stories from people we had never seen before. They would explain how their uncle owned this company or that company that was a good customer of ours and so on. It got so bad that when I needed gas in my own car, I would park it inside the shop late at night and run out to fill a gas can in the dark when no cars were going by. Then I would bring the can into the shop and dump the gas in my car. If we opened our pumps for just one instant in view of drivers, they would flock to the pumps like bees to honey.

It got really stressful and dangerous pumping gas. Understandably, people were extremely mad and very frustrated by this whole gas-shortage situation. There were stories floating around town that the shortage was not real, and that the major oil companies had fabricated the shortage so they could boost the price of gas. (Gee, that couldn't be true, could it?) People would say they heard there were "three tankers anchored way out in Boston Harbor, full of gasoline, and the oil companies were refusing to let them unload." The executives at Mobil and Citgo were certainly not feeling the sting of all this while sitting in their cushy offices. Heck, they were moving half the usual amount of product while taking in two or three times as much money as before!

It was the gas jockeys and small dealers like me that had to deal with the nastiness and danger of the front lines. Some customers would explode into an out-of-control rage when I had to say no to them. They chose to ignore our signs, which initiated the confrontations, but that didn't make any difference to them. I almost came to blows several times every day during this horrible period. I would be threatened, cursed like you wouldn't believe, and even spit at.

A customer drove in one day, during the height of all of this chaos and said, "Tom! Did you hear what happened up at so and so's gas station? Somebody just shot the guy that was pumping gas. He's dead." When I heard that, I got boiling mad, and I remember immediately saying that the oil companies should be charged with murder because they concocted this shortage in my opinion. It was all about greed and price gouging! There were already lots of stories in the news about fights at gasoline stations around the country, but now it was getting serious. It had come to the point that you actually needed protection from the public while pumping gas.

My very good friend, Lyle, worked in the area. He was a decorated World War II veteran who had been wounded badly several times during the war. Lyle was never afraid of a confrontation. When he heard about the shooting at the gas station on the other side of town, he offered to stand guard in my office with his .380 automatic at-the-ready, for as long as he could each day. He knew I had already experienced some nasty confrontations at the pumps. I also felt the need to start carrying my .32 Beretta in my pocket. I had previously kept that gun in the office safe during workdays and at home on weekends. The sad fact is that my gun wouldn't really do me much good if somebody pulled a pistol on me unexpectedly. By the time I was able to react and pull my own gun, it would be all over. It would be far better to have Lyle make a move from inside the office. I truly hoped it would never actually come to that.

One day, the line of people waiting for gas had dwindled down for some reason. We had our "$2 Limit" sign up when a large Caddy, Buick, or Oldsmobile pulled up to the pumps. The driver, whom I had never seen before, was wearing a hat and no glasses. Even though the guy appeared to be around forty to forty-five years old he was very well built, somebody who definitely worked out. He pulled in next to the pumps and looked toward me, but he didn't look me in the eyes. He barked out, "Fill it up." In a fairly loud voice, I said to the guy, "The sign says $2 LIMIT! Can't you read?" I could be a little short tempered with people after dealing with this crap over and over again, all day long. Plus I couldn't help the fact that I had acquired a certain amount of my dad's people skills after observing him for so many years. Well, my assertiveness didn't go over well with this particular guy. Before I knew it, I had a chrome-plated semiautomatic pistol pointed right at me! He leaned his head partially out the window but kept the pistol close to his chest. I heard the following five words very clearly. "I said, fill it up!" I replied, "Okay! Okay!" As I turned and walked toward the gas pump, I made a facial signal toward the office, hoping that Lyle would see my alarmed expression. Lyle was better than that. He had already seen the guy pull the gun and was waiting for me to get out of the way. As soon as I was clear, the front door of the office swung open in a flash, and there was Lyle, arms extended, pointing his gun directly at the guy's head, which was only ten feet from the office door. The driver reacted amazingly fast! He closed the car window so fast that he almost didn't get his head back inside in time. The brim of his hat caught in the window as it closed. He must have kept the car in drive this entire time because he pulled away very quickly, with his hat stuck in the window.

It was really funny to see how this guy took off. When I walked into the office, Lyle's eyes were gleaming. He chuckled with his usual raspy voice and said, "Did you see that asshole take off when he saw my gun? Huh? Huh?" Except for the cigar that was clamped in the corner of Lyle's mouth, he looked like a teenager sporting a huge smile. We laughed really hard about what had taken place, and I sent one of the guys to get some beer so we could celebrate the latest excitement.

Even though he refused to look directly at me, that man's face and his blue eyes were imprinted in my memory. When somebody points a gun in your face from only a foot or two away, you are not likely to forget that face. At the time, he was just a stranger that I had a run-in with. We didn't even bother calling the police. I figured that was the last time I would ever see that guy.

I had heard of Whitey Bulger many times, but had never met him, that I knew of. I had not even seen a photo of him. All I knew was that he was the ruthless leader of the Mob on the west side of Southie. It wasn't until years later, when some photos of Whitey started to surface that I realized that he had paid me a visit. He was the one who had pointed a gun in my face that day at the gas pumps. I have no doubt about that. When I saw his mug shot on the FBI's ten-most-wanted poster, offering a $1,000,000 reward, I instantly realized how close I had come to an untimely end that day. Lives meant nothing to him. He had killed numerous times over issues both large and small. I'm probably one of just a few people that have had Whitey aim a gun at them and lived to tell about it. The very nature of my business almost guaranteed that I would eventually come in contact with virtually every individual in my section of the city. Whitey probably passed by my station a thousand times.

He hung out with his friends in a house on the same street as the gas station, East Third Street. He and his friends were killing people in that house and burying them in the cellar, right down the street from me.

A short time after that incident with Whitey at the gasoline pumps, I would be in for a shock upon arriving at work. While picking up my morning coffee down at the corner store, I glanced down the road toward the gas station and noticed that something didn't look quite right at the front of the building. As I started driving in that direction, my fears were confirmed. I realized that both gas pumps had been smashed into and destroyed. All I could think of was how thankful I was that they had not burst into flames. As I was assessing the damage and trying to figure out how this could have happened, a neighbor named John walked over from his house. I said to him, "Somebody must have been drunk and crashed into the pumps last night!" John gave me the news that it was no accident. He lived directly across the street, on the third floor, and had a bird's-eye view of the pumps. He said he was sitting at his front window about one in the morning having a smoke when this "big black Oldsmobile" drove up to the pumps and then drove backward into one of them, smashing it and knocking it over. He said his first thought was that the guy just didn't see that there was a pump there, but when the car left, went around the block and then returned, he knew differently. As John watched from his perch, the car did the same thing to the other pump, smashing it to the ground! He said he was really afraid that there was going to be an explosion. That would have been a disaster in this neighborhood of ancient wooden two- and three-deckers, filled with sleeping people.

As it turned out, whoever had done this to my pumps did me a huge favor. When the gas shortage started, gas was cheap.

By the time the oil companies had achieved their goal, gas was so expensive that gasoline stations had to replace their old pumps because the meters didn't display dollar figures high enough. The days of $7.95 fill-ups were over. The old three-digit pumps needed to be replaced with pumps having four-digit meters. For small independent dealers like me, this was a huge expense. I had been holding off on replacing my pumps for as long as I could, but now was my golden opportunity. I called my insurance agent and told him of the loss and I took several photos of the old smashed pumps. I anticipated that the insurance company might try to pay me a lesser amount, claiming that the old three-digit pumps were obsolete and needed replacing anyway. I was happy when the issue never came up. With commercial account customers lining up and needing fuel, I couldn't wait for an insurance adjuster to show up. I called a service station equipment company in Braintree that was owned by an Italian family that I knew. Their son hung out at the Colbert School. Within just a couple of hours, they had delivered and installed two new four-digit pumps. The new pumps were up and running before the insurance adjuster had even called to schedule his inspection. The old pumps were already gone to the gas-pump graveyard, and were nowhere to be seen. I explained to the adjuster that I couldn't wait for him to come and look at the damage because I had companies that depended on me to fuel their business vehicles. When he finally arrived, I handed the adjuster the photos of the damage, and showed him the bill for the new pumps. We had a great insurance representative, and he took care of us right away. The new pumps were paid in full. If it was Whitey Bulger who paid my pumps a visit and destroyed them, I would like to send him a thank-you note. Does anyone have his forwarding address?

Mom's front garden, where she unknowingly
nurtured my illegal Hawaiian Gold plants.

Ken Saunders, Vito, and Lyle

(Left to right) Ken Saunders, myself, and friend, Lyle Lindberg
Lyle was a Navy veteran and survivor of the attack on Pearl Harbor.

The gasoline pumps after being methodically smashed by a black Oldsmobile in the middle of the night. John Foley, my friend and part-time gas jockey, observed the entire episode from his third floor window across the street.

The MOBIL sign would soon be gone.

From the gas pumps at the shop, I could see Gavin's Tavern/O'Leary's
Pub on the first floor of the three-decker down the street. It was the
scene of fun, fights, IRA posters, and a machine-gun attack.

One of my cable TV friends installed a new sign for me after
I decided to become independent from the major oil companies.

Chapter XVI

An Offer I Better Refuse

One thing you could always count on in Southie was that a good deal on *something* would come along every so often. Occasionally, there would be a trunk full of watches or cases of whiskey that I would be shown while I gassed up a car. Then there was the ice cream-truck guy that went through the neighborhood every day during one particular summer. He always had something other than ice cream to sell in the back of his truck. I was young, and it was such a common and accepted practice in Southie that I never gave a thought to where these items must have come from. The guy in the ice cream truck was named "Robert Newitt." I got to know him very well. At least I thought I did.

After getting some really good deals from him, ranging from watches to amplifiers, he came in one day with the best proposition yet. He said he had a line on some twenty-five-inch color TVs. He asked me if I wanted one for $80. I jumped at the chance! I asked him how many he had access to, and he answered, "Ten." Wanting to share this great opportunity with my friends, I went around Southie and collected $80 from seven people that I knew very well. Some of the folks that gave me money were variety store owners etc. When I told Robert that I wanted eight TVs, he asked me if I wanted them delivered all at once or one at a time. He said he had access to a big van. I trusted him at this point because he had always come through in the past without a problem. I told him, "Why make eight trips? Bring them all at once." He told me he had to pay the guy for the TVs when he picked them up, so I handed him all the money I had gathered, $640 in cash. Delivery was to be the next day.

About an hour past the scheduled two o'clock delivery time, the phone rang at the shop. There was a stranger on the other end of the line. Almost in a whisper, the caller said, "Robert got arrested. The cops got him, the TVs, and all the money." Then the caller just hung up. There would be no TVs delivered.

Something didn't feel right about this situation. After a couple of days of not seeing Robert's ice cream truck come by, I asked "Paul," a big Irish cop who was a good friend of mine, if he could check and see if there had been any arrests in Boston that might have involved a "Robert Newitt" or some hot TVs. Later that day, Paul came back to the shop and told me that no arrest like that had taken place. He also told me he had checked out the guy whose name I had given to him. He said, "This Newitt is a bad guy, and you would be smart to not get involved with him." My policeman friend never asked me why I was inquiring about Robert and hot TVs. He just gave me that friendly warning.

With the knowledge that I had definitely been screwed and there would be no TVs, I went around to all those folks who had given me their money. I explained the situation and gave them their money back, out of my own pocket. Now that I think back, giving those refunds so quickly was probably a mistake and a dumb thing to do. Some of those friends were pretty tough and might have helped me find this guy if they had money to get back, but I felt it was my responsibility to give them a refund.

Later that same day, my good buddy Lyle came into the station, and I mentioned what had taken place. Lyle was just as pissed off as I was. I think Lyle thought of me as a son. He told me he knew a guy that would help me recover the money and teach Newitt a lesson. He said if I wanted to talk to the guy, he would take me to him. I agreed right away, and within a few hours, we were off to meet "Big Mike." We met him at a warehouse somewhere down off East First Street. Mike was the big serious type and a guy you wouldn't want to see waiting for you on your doorstep. He seemed like the right guy for the job. I gave him all the information that I had about Robert, which was virtually nothing. Big Mike said if he didn't recover the money, I owed him nothing. I guess he was very confident in his ability to be successful. If he recovered the money, he would take $475 of it. I told him I didn't care about the money. I just wanted this guy to pay for what he did to me. I started to get concerned as to how far Big Mike would go in trying to accomplish his mission, so I asked him straight out. Big Mike said he would find this guy, and the worst he would do was "break the guy's legs if I have to." Acting on the rage that was still fresh in my mind, I said "Fine. Go for it."

I couldn't believe it when it took Big Mike just a couple of days to find out where Newitt lived and where he hung out! Mike called to tell me that he "found the guy in Cambridge." He had staked out his house, saw him come and go, and would "move in when the time is right." He told me he also found out that Robert was "a homo" (Gay wasn't the common word to use yet). Big Mike named two bars that Robert frequented. One was The Other Side and the other was Jacques. Both clubs were in a rough section of Boston. I was glad he found the guy, but at the same time very nervous because I didn't like the thought of hurting somebody. Big Mike should have worked for the CIA. I have no clue how he was able to find out all this information about Newitt, even his sexual orientation! All I had told him was the guy's name and that he drove an ice cream truck. For all I knew, the name was possibly an alias. I was quite impressed with the fast results.

The next day, the situation took an interesting and very scary turn. A well-established and well-connected bookie / loan shark pulled in for gas, driving his brand new Lincoln Continental. I had known him since I was a kid. He had been a regular and faithful customer for many years and had always gotten a full tank of gas from me, even during the height of the fuel shortage. I always took good care of him. Normally, he would just sit in his car, counting money in his lap as I pumped his gas. Over the years, he was never one to make a lot of small talk. That's why I was surprised when on this particular day he got out of his car and stood right next to me as I pumped his gas. He looked at me with ice-cold eyes and said something that shocked me. "Tom, I heard you hired a guy to go after Robert Newitt." My heart seized up for a second or two. My first thought was that Newitt must be somehow connected to the Mob, *one of them*, and they weren't happy with me for sending a leg breaker after him. Not being one to stop and think before speaking, I immediately replied, "Yes I did. He screwed me!" The bookie simply stated, "Call your guy off." I wanted to know what his interest in the situation was, so I asked, "Why do you want me to call my guy off?" He held out his hand and repeated, "Call your guy off and give me 67¢." I said, "Why do you want 67¢?" He replied, "You buy the bullet, and Newitt is history." I couldn't believe my ears. He was offering to *kill* this guy for me! I could have the scumbag wiped off the face of the earth for just 67¢. (Today it would probably be $2.99 with inflation) That was all I needed to hear. I told him "Thanks. I appreciate the offer, but I don't think a few hundred bucks are worth a guy's life." He said, "If you change your mind just let me know." I think that was the extent of the conversation with him. Mainly, I was shocked that my situation involving Bob Newitt and the hiring of Big Mike was information that was somehow out on the street. I would love to know how they got the information. Maybe Big Mike also did work for them.

I realized what motivated the Mob to make such a generous offer to me. They really would love to have a friendly garage the size of mine at their disposal. Just watch any gangster movie to see my point. Shops like mine are versatile places with so many possible illicit uses. I had been approached with propositions to use the garage several times before, and I was able to politely say "no" every time. I imagine that once the Mob kills someone for you for a fee, albeit a small one, you would be indebted to them for life. Saying no would never be an option again. I would never have considered letting them carry out that deadly deed regardless of their motives. (Did I previously say *never say never?*).

After the Mob's generous offer of a virtually free contract on Newitt's life, I was actually scared. I realized that this situation was getting out of control. I called Lyle and told him to come to the shop right away. When he arrived, I explained what happened, and he arranged for us to go see Big Mike. When I met with Big Mike, I told him I had reconsidered, and that I didn't want this *thing* to go any further. Mike was disappointed, saying that he was planning to make his move on Robert that night. I told him firmly, "Drop it. Just tell me what I owe you." He said "Nothing, forget about it. Lyle says you're *okay.*" I couldn't believe that Big Mike had done all that work and wouldn't take any money. Now that the killer and the leg-breaker were out of the picture, I felt better. Nobody was going to die or get badly hurt over this.

On the other hand, as the days passed, I was still very pissed off. I was having a hard time letting this thing go, so I decided I would hunt down and confront Newitt myself. I couldn't just let him off scot-free. I soon would realize that going after him myself was not a smart choice.

It was a Friday or Saturday night, and I asked a few people to go with me to check out the clubs that Big Mike said Newitt frequented. The first club we found was The Other Side. Today you would refer to it as a gay bar. Based on Big Mike's information, there was a chance we might find Robert there. When we arrived, we got a table directly below the raised dance floor. The place was packed. As expected, it was packed with guys. I looked around, scanning all the tables in the place, but I didn't see Newitt. I was thinking that we had struck out and wasted a trip. Then I happened to look up at the dance floor right above where we were sitting, and there he was! He was only ten feet away from us, dancing with another guy. He was easy to spot due to the bright white medical tape he used to hold his broken eyeglasses together over the bridge of his nose. Even if he did glance down, I was pretty sure he wouldn't recognize me nicely dressed and in a leather jacket. I told my crew that I had spotted him. The song ended, and we watched as Newitt walked away from the dance floor. He sat down at a table a good distance from where my friends and I were seated. Lacking any real plan of action, I told my guys to sit tight as I got up to go and pay Robert a surprise visit. Newitt's table was almost in the corner, near the entrance of the club. It was quite dark in the entire establishment, but especially dark at the location of his table. He probably liked it that way. I walked up to within two feet of him and just stared down, waiting for him to notice me. Sure enough, he looked up at me and smiled. It was obvious that he didn't know who I was—all cleaned up and without my greasy gas station uniform.

Up to this point I failed to mention that Robert Newitt was quite a big guy with totally masculine mannerisms. Nobody would ever peg him as gay. He was big enough to kick my ass for sure. I looked down at him and said "Hi Robert! You owe me some f—n money!" As soon as I said those words, you could see the smile leave his face as he realized I wasn't there to ask him to dance. He slowly opened his jacket to the side so I could see what appeared to be a .38 caliber revolver stuck in his belt. He had no idea that in the pocket of my leather jacket, my finger was already on the trigger of my Beretta, aimed right at his chest. I had pulled the hammer back and it was ready to fire, just in case he tried to stab me. For some reason, I didn't picture him as someone who carried a gun, so that was a surprise. Before any further words could be exchanged, I felt something press against my lower spine. I turned my head and saw a very tall man standing directly behind me, right up against me actually, and he had a gun barrel stuck squarely in the small of my back.

I doubted they would just shoot me in front of all those people, so I calmly said, "Okay, Robert. You got me this time, but now I know where you are, and I'll be back." Newitt never said one word to me throughout the entire confrontation. I told him and his friend with the gun, "I'm going to turn away and walk back to my table." And that's exactly what I did.

Amazingly, before I could fill my companions in on what had just taken place, I encountered a major distraction. Standing right next to my chair when I returned was an absolute-knockout, gorgeous platinum blond. I had to squeeze by her in order to sit down. All 110 pounds of her beauty were perched on six-inch heels, and squished into a tiny, white-sequined dress that was overflowing in all the right places. She was holding a white toy poodle in one hand and a banana in the other. Occasionally she was stroking and licking the banana as she stared up at the dance floor. I sat back down, only a foot away from her and couldn't stop staring at her performance. I was in a trance, totally forgetting why we were even in this place. A guy at the next table reached over and tapped me on the shoulder. He smiled and said, "You like that, huh?" I turned and said, "Yeah!" He paused for a second and said, "It's a guy." I was shocked! I could not believe it. I thought to myself, "Get me out of this place!"

I regained my focus and informed my group about the interesting encounter with Robert and the guns, suggesting that we should probably leave after we finish our drinks. Before we could make our exit, a heavyset guy, well over six feet tall, approached our table from the opposite corner of the club from where Robert was. He was wearing a long green trench coat. I had no idea who he was, but as he came closer he made me nervous. The man leaned over to say something in my ear. After I heard his voice, I was relieved. I recognized him as Jimmy, a truck driver from Southie who often got gas and repairs from me. He told me, "Word is going around the club that at the end of the next song, everybody in here is going to pounce on your table." There were probably seventy-five weird people in this place, and that was a very scary thought. Then he said to me, "Don't worry Tom. They came to the wrong table when they came to us. Look over in the corner," he said. "There are ten of us Southie guys over there. We're with you." I asked him what the hell they were doing in a place like this. He said "We come here every once in a while just to laugh at these fags." He walked back to his corner where all the Southie guys were sitting. They were about thirty feet from our table, and they all had trench coats on. They were glancing our way, and smiling. The song ended, and we waited for all hell to break loose. We looked around at the other tables but nothing happened. They must have noticed my reinforcements in the corner and decided against the attack. Trench coats were never a good sign if you were looking for trouble. You never knew what might be under those coats. I bet everybody in that place was packing, but probably not as heavily as my Southie friends were. It pays to be "*in*" with these Southie guys.

I turned and saw that Robert's table was empty. Newitt and his friends had left the club. We left as soon as we finished our drinks and I never went looking for Newitt again. I'm sure that someone down the line probably gave him what he deserved. The old saying, "What goes around, comes around," seems to be true. Within a year of that night at The Other Side, I found out that Jimmy, the guy who had bailed me out of that terrible situation, had been murdered. I never asked any of the details surrounding his murder. I just remember feeling very sad when I heard he'd been killed. I really liked him. Every time I had dealt with him at the garage, he was very friendly and polite. He seemed to be a hardworking, honest guy. But I learned that you never could tell what people might be involved with by just talking with them.

There was one other night that Southie guys saved me from getting seriously hurt. My friend Bobby and I had gone to a strip club called the Pic-a-Dilly Lounge. It was located in an area of Boston called the "Combat Zone." We left the club quite late and were headed back to my car. Suddenly, from silence, the deserted early morning street instantly transformed to chaos as a fierce battle broke out on the sidewalk, twenty feet behind us. Bob and I turned around and saw a gang fight going on between eight or ten guys, and it was a really vicious one! Fists and boots were flying and connecting over and over again. One group quickly got the better of the other, using sheer speed and brutality. They were obviously skilled street fighters, virtually beating the other group to a pulp. The littlest guy from the winning side picked up a Heineken bottle from the gutter. I watched in disbelief as he wound up and pitched it like a fastball with all his might. It smashed directly in the face of his opponent, from just six feet away! I remember thinking to myself, "Oh my god! If that bottle hadn't broken, it probably would have killed that guy." Somehow, the defeated group managed to run off and get away. Bob and I didn't have a clue at this point as to what in the hell was going on. None of the combatants had bothered to come after us. Then I recognized the victorious group as being guys from South Boston. I didn't personally know them, but I had seen them hanging around up on Broadway a few times. As they approached Bob and me, we had no idea what to expect. We were really relieved once they explained the reason for the fight we had just witnessed. They said they had overheard those guys making plans to attack and rob Bob and me! We had no idea that as we were walking along, we were being followed by that gang. When the South Boston guys heard the plan to mug us, they followed to intervene because they knew I was from Southie. Just as they were telling us this, a police car pulled up with its lights flashing. The Southie guys took off running, leaving us there to explain to the cops what had just taken place. The police were not thrilled with us. They loaded Bob and me into the back seat of the cruiser and transported us right to my car in a nearby underground parking garage. They instructed us to "stay out of the zone" and not be seen around there for a while.

Bob was really glad those cops had not taken notice of the jacket he was wearing. It was a stolen Boston Police motorcycle jacket that he had grabbed off the back of a police bike in "the zone" earlier that night, because he was cold. He had removed the badge but you could plainly see the worn impression in the leather where the badge used to be.

Chapter XVII

People, Characters, and Strange Events

There were so many wonderful people that were part of my life in South Boston. Many of them were quite unique as well.

One of the most wonderful people I ever met in my life was Anthony (Tony) Banna. He was born in Greece on May 25, 1888, and came to Boston in 1942. Tony had graced the gas station with his presence since before I had ever set foot in it. He was now in his nineties and lived by himself, across the street from the pumps. With the assistance of his cane, he would walk over to the office each morning, usually wearing a hat and tie, and keep me company as I opened up before 7:00 AM. He was a retired baker, having worked at the Waldorf Hotel in Boston for decades. Tony would watch the front office and yell to me if a gas customer drove in while I was out back working. Two or three times a week, he would walk up to the Shawmut Bank on Broadway with the gas station deposits. He did this for us for many years. It would take him quite a while just to make it down to the corner of the street because of his age. Finally, he would be out of sight. During most of those trips up to Broadway, Tony would be carrying around two thousand dollars in cash as he walked slowly to the bank. Everybody in the neighborhood new he made these bank runs for me, and nobody ever bothered him.

Regardless of his age, he was a lot of fun to be around. Many afternoons, as the garage work would wind down, Tony would share a beer with me and the guys at the shop. Each year, on May 25, I would throw a birthday party for him either at the station or at my house. His grandchildren and great-grandchildren lived pretty far away, and he usually just saw them around Thanksgiving and Christmas.

Over the years, Tony offered me some wonderful advice. He said the keys to a long and healthy life were as follows. "Don't drink anything too hot or too cold. Don't take really hot showers." And when drinking alcohol, "Take two, no more." The "take two, no more" was probably the best advice of all.

Sometimes after a long day of walking in the city, Tony would still not be home when it was time to close up the shop. I wouldn't worry, because that happened every so often. The next morning he would come into the office bright and early with a big wide grin and eyes squinting mischievously. He would tap his cane on the floor in front of him, and when nobody else was around, he would say to me, *"Catchum lobsta last night."* That meant he had run into a willing female during his outing the previous day, and to put it nicely, hooked up. I was so happy for him that he was still literally having a ball even though he would soon be pushing 100. Tony was a very religious man. He walked all the way from Southie to Saint Anthony's Shrine on Arch Street in downtown Boston several times per week. Anytime somebody had lost something, he would tell him or her to say a prayer to Saint Anthony. Whatever had been missing always showed up. He never hesitated to give good wholesome advice to me. I loved and respected him, and he was the closest thing to a grandfather I ever had. All of my grandparents died when I was too young to really remember them. Plus, even if they had lived longer, they spoke only Italian, which I never was taught.

In spite of the surgery I had undergone to correct my scoliosis, the back pain once again started to rear its ugly head as the years passed by at the shop. Eventually, the constant pain wore me down to the point that I couldn't handle the mechanical work and frigid working conditions any longer. I set an appointment with the most reputable scoliosis specialist at a top notch Boston hospital. My x-rays showed that I had developed severe osteoarthritis of the spine, and soft tissue buildup surrounding the metal rod in my back. The doctor said he would have sworn he was looking at the x-rays of a much older man. He highly recommended a warm climate and less strenuous work. Wanting to hear a better solution, I asked him what else I could look forward to in the way of surgery, or anything that would lessen my pain. These were his exact words. "Well, one thing you can look forward to is that someday you're gonna die." He said it with a smile, but I still think he needed a brush-up class on bedside manor.

I knew it was time to sell the garage. Tony was ninety-eight years old when I told him I was going to sell the business. As soon as he heard those words, he matter-of-factly said to me, "When you sell gas station, I die." I said, "Tony! Please don't say that! I'm sure whoever buys this place will be nice, and you will fit right in. You will still have this place to hang out at. I'll make sure of it." Tony wasn't acting mad. It was as if he was just telling me his plan. I felt terrible at hearing him say those words, but I had to do what I needed to do at the time. The cold weather and outdoor work was taking a terrible toll on my back. It was impossible for me to keep doing that type of work for much longer. Luckily, I sold the business to Gary Grossberg. He had known Tony for years and was very fond of him. Gary and his family already owned Ross Motors, which was my main auto parts supplier, so he was a good fit for the business.

I was happy knowing that Tony would feel comfortable with the new owner. The date of sale was December 15, 1986. I stayed on at the shop for a week or so after the sale closed until Gary was familiar with the customers and routines. I also used that time to say a sad farewell to the many wonderful customers and neighbors that I grew to love over the years. In June of 1987, after selling the house in Weymouth, my wife Diane and I relocated to Fort Myers, Florida.

Just one month after settling into our new home, I received a phone call from South Boston. Gary sadly informed me that Tony had passed away after suffering a massive stroke. He had been at home, and it happened very quickly. That was a very sad day. He was ninety-nine years old.

The following May 25, while sitting out on the screened lanai at our house in Florida, something just didn't feel right. I suddenly realized what was missing that day. I called to Diane who was standing in the kitchen. She could see me through the open window to the lanai. I said, "Di! Guess what day this is?" She asked, "What day?" I said, "This would have been Tony's one hundredth birthday!" Upon saying that, I reached for my drink, which was on the table next to my lounge chair. I raised my glass and declared out loud, "HAPPY BIRTHDAY, Tony!" The very instant those words left my lips, the dartboard that I had mounted on the wall right behind where I was sitting came crashing to the floor. The screw, which was tightly installed into a drilled hole in the concrete wall, had popped out. I had drilled the hole and mounted that dartboard myself, when we moved in. You could have safely hung a one-hundred-pound weight from that mounting, yet it had dislodged itself the very second after I toasted Tony's special day. I was convinced that this was his way of letting me know he was there with me that day.

I repeated once again, "Happy birthday, Tony!" I have continued to wish him a happy birthday every May 25 since. Thankfully, he has decided not to break anything else as long as I continue to do so.

Although Tony comprises some of my fondest memories, Southie had some very strange characters that were quite unforgettable as well. When I was very young, I can recall a man who would walk by the gas station just about every day, thankfully, on the opposite side of the street. He was a tall dark-haired man who would be talking to himself. After walking ten or twenty steps, he would abruptly stop and loudly speak, blurting out just a few words. He was very animated and would be wide-eyed while waving his arms as he turned to address his invisible friend. It always seemed to be an amiable conversation. He would then proceed a ways down the street until he repeated the ritual. People would just walk on by him as if he was a normal part of the landscape. As a youngster, I found him to be quite scary. There was another gentleman that would stop in his tracks every so many feet and break into an elaborate dance. His feet would be shuffling and his arms swaying to the silent rhythm in his mind. He also seemed to be a very happy individual.

Then there was the not so happy old lady who would often walk directly past the gas pumps with fire coming out of her eyes. She would be cursing like the devil at nobody at all, or at anybody that happened to be close by. If I happened to be outside pumping gas as she passed, I sometimes made the mistake of quickly glancing at her as she made her way by. She would loudly exclaim to me, "Go f—yourself, c—k s—r!" Customers would ask, "What was that all about?" I would say, "I don't know. She does that every day." Once, she decided to come in and make herself comfortable in my office. I had a hell of a time getting her to leave. Over time, I learned how to deal with all types of unique personalities, sometimes being compassionate and at other times forceful, depending on the situation.

Gas stations are a great place for guys to hang out. We always had a few regulars who would stop in for coffee or a beer. Some of my favorites were well known in Southie for their individual skills or interests as was reflected in their street names. Sometimes there was no obvious reason for the names. I never questioned the origins. There was Flash Gordon, Mike the Plumber, Mary Roadrunner, Tubby, Chunky, and Dumbo, etc. One of the more interesting was "Tom the Bomb." I liked Tom, but you never knew which Tom was going to be coming through the door into the gas station office. Sometimes it was the calm and friendly Tom, and other times it was the hyper, nervous wreck, the "Quick! Find me a straight jacket," Tom. He was a longshoreman who worked the docks in Boston, unloading foreign freighters, and he was built accordingly. I somehow felt that if I ever needed backup, Tom would be there for me. Tom knew that I had a boat, and that I frequently went out in Boston Harbor. One day he came into the station and said, "Tom, do me a favor." He asked if I would be going out on my boat over the weekend, and I said yes. He handed me a metal coffee can that was very heavy, as if it was full of small pieces of iron. It was taped up securely with duct tape. He asked me to take it way out in the harbor and throw it overboard without asking any questions. I reluctantly agreed to do it for him. Honestly, I was a little apprehensive as to what his reaction might have been had I said no. That weekend I happened to be taking my close friend Barney out on the boat. We were fishing and having a few beers. As the sun was setting, I spotted the coffee can that Tom the Bomb had given me. It was on the floor next to my feet. I yelled over the engine noise. "Barn, do you think this will sink?" I tossed him the can. He answered, "I'm not sure.

There's quite a bit of air in there." I said, "Do me a favor! Rip it open and dump it overboard." Barn yelled back, "What is it?" Then, quickly thinking twice, he said, "Never mind! I don't want to know." He tore the cover off, tape and all, and dumped the contents overboard, and then he tossed the can. Whatever Tom the Bomb wanted to get rid of, he had spent a lot of time preparing it for disposal. He must have been up all night with a hacksaw. The coffee can was never brought up in conversation again.

Despite Tom the Bomb's tough demeanor, he still found a way to get beaten up pretty badly on one occasion. He came in the shop one day, badly bruised and swollen around his head and face. He also had several obvious human bite wounds on his arms. When I asked him what the hell happened, he said he had gotten beaten up by a local drug pusher the night before, for no reason. He said he was sitting in his car in front of the Italian American Restaurant (known by the locals as the I & A), minding his own business when this guy just picked a fight with him and attacked him through his open driver's window. Who knows what really happened. I knew the dealer that he had fought with, and he wasn't the type to attack for no reason. All I know is that I personally tried to get along with everybody I could, and there were just a few exceptions over the years. It was impossible to avoid all conflict. Some people just wouldn't allow that to happen.

Many of the families that I became close to were truly wonderful and hardworking. They were honest and extremely supportive of each family member. March 17th was a very special day for Southie families and friends to gather. They put all their troubles on the back burner for that day. Saint Patrick's Day was something everybody really looked forward to. Once accepted as part of the Southie community, I would be invited into several house parties in the neighborhood on St. Paddy's Day. I was Irish for the day and would share in drinks at each apartment I visited before heading off to see the parade. Everyone there was made to feel like part of the family. It was a wonderful feeling that I think you'd be hard-pressed to replicate in any other neighborhood of this city.

It was surprising to me that many of these fine and loving families would have the one proverbial *bad apple*. Sometimes that apple was a *very* bad apple. I had been the mechanic for this one particular family for several years and worked on the cars of the father and all the other family members. They trusted me, and I enjoyed taking care of each of them. One of the sons was in a rock band and had actually dated disco queen Donna Summer for a while when she sang with his band. That's what he told me, and I believed him. This was a short time before she became a national celebrity. I felt that my relationship with this family was a mixture of business as well as friendship. Suddenly, a brother that I never knew existed showed up at the garage. I just assumed that he was going to be as pleasant and nice as the rest of his family had been to deal with. I couldn't have been more wrong. Although he seemed quite normal during my first contact with him, after just one small job on his car, he accused me of screwing him and screwing his whole family. Just inches from my face, he swore he was going to "get" me! He went on and on like a madman! At first I thought he was just kidding around, but then I realized differently. He refused to pay me for the work I had done. He just grabbed his keys off the peg-board, took his car, and left. When his father and one of his brothers came in for gas, I told them what had happened, and I asked, "What is going on with this brother of yours? He wants to kill me!" I told them that I had treated him extremely well, and I had no idea what he was upset about. I could see the seriousness enter their faces.

They told me that the brother was heavily into drugs, and he had been in all kinds of trouble with the law. The family had nothing to do with him at all anymore. They felt bad that he had found out where they had their automotive work done and advised me to not get involved with him. As the days went by, that scary maniac drove by the gas station several times. He would go by very slowly and stare at me if I was outside. This creepy behavior was making me very nervous. After a few days of this, I happened to be at the side of the building using a paint scraper to prepare the bricks for a fresh coat of paint. As he was driving by, he spotted me outside and alone, and he pulled over. He got out of his car and got right up in my face. I didn't respond to him, or move at all, as he leaned into me repeating his threats with a wild look in his eyes. I remember just grasping the long heavy paint scraper as tightly as I could, and at the first real physical move he made, I was going to smash him in the head with this thing as hard as I could. It was all metal and was a formidable weapon. If he had just poked me in the chest, I was going to move quickly against him. I had no idea what this jerk was capable of and I was going to end this craziness right there and then if I could. After what seemed like forever, he just walked away, got in his car, and drove off. He didn't know how close he came to leaving the gas station in an ambulance.

Apparently, I wasn't the only person that was having trouble with this jerk. His brother came in for gas the next day and said to me, "Well, you won't have to worry about my brother bringing his car in here anymore." I asked what he was talking about. He said, "I just saw his car up on East Fourth Street. Somebody pulled a street sign, post and all, right out of the ground and smashed his car all over with it. They smashed all the windows too and then rammed the signpost through the dashboard. It's still up there with the post sticking out of it. It's totaled!" This was a common practice in Southie. If somebody pissed somebody off, but that somebody didn't want to "get them" bodily, they would "get" their car or some other property that the person owned. I would hear about this happening quite often. Several of my friends in Southie knew about the trouble I was having with this guy, and how upset I was about it. I suppose it is possible that one of them took it upon himself to send a message and take care of the situation for me, without my knowledge. I wouldn't put it past them. Thankfully, I never saw or heard from that particular jerk again.

Conflict was always just a moment away in Southie. Being one of just a few automotive inspection stations in town left me open to arguments with irate customers all the time. My shop abided strictly by the rules that the Registry of Motor Vehicles dictated. Otherwise, I could have lost my sticker license. People with old junkers had a knack for coming in for a sticker just as I was closing up to go home. Inevitably, those last minute people would have problems with their vehicles, which mandated that I reject them. Terrible arguments would result. These were not our regular customers. They had probably been turned down for a sticker at a few other places before coming to me, and tempers would flare when I would have to turn them down. One scary guy really made an impression on me. He drove up five minutes before closing with a car that looked pretty good. Expecting it to pass, I directed him into the inspection bay. Upon checking the car, I found that the windshield wipers didn't work. I couldn't give him a sticker, and there was no time left for repairs that day. At the time, there was a "sticker season," and this was the last day for inspections. You would be subject to a ticket and a fine if you didn't have a current sticker by midnight that day. It wasn't my fault that this guy let forty-five days go by and waited until the last minute. When I told him he would have to have his wipers fixed before he could get a sticker, the guy jumped out of his car and started ranting and raving in my face like a madman. He was yelling at me saying, "You don't know who the f—you're dealing with! I'm a f—in' parole officer! I deal with scum all day that are a lot tougher than you, and you tell me I can't get a f—in' sticker! I'll kick your f—in' ass!" I picked up the crow bar, which was leaning up against the post right next to me, in case he attacked. He went on and on as I tried to keep things from getting out of hand. My dad was in the office, thirty feet away, observing the problem I was having. I glanced toward the office because I was genuinely scared that this guy was going to attack me. There was Vito, ready for action. He was standing in the doorway to the shop. His arms were fully extended with the Beretta from the safe in his hand. He was in a firing stance with the gun pointed right at this guy. The customer was not even aware that my father was standing there. I finally told the guy to get out of my shop, and I yelled toward the office, "Dad! Call the cops!" This guy may have been lying to me about being a parole officer because when he heard the word cops, he decided it was time to leave. I went into the office after he drove away and my dad said to me, "I was ready to pull the trigger if that guy made one move toward you!" I believe he would have shot that guy without hesitation. I'm thankful that he didn't have to do it.

Because we were located in a blue-collar section of the city, there were a lot of older cars around. Many of them were not in great shape. Even when people *knew* their cars had obvious problems which warranted rejection, such as loud exhaust system leaks, they would still come in, hoping to slip through and pass inspection. People would use all kinds of tactics to try to get a sticker. Some occasionally would offer me money. In fact, when my friend "Chad" would come in for a sticker with one of the many cars from his antique car collection, he would always hand me a folded up registration certificate. The first time he did this, he forgot to mention that there was a $100 bill folded up along with the registration. I took his registration and walked through the small doorway into the rear bay of the shop to write out the sticker. I was surprised to find the large bill when I unfolded his registration. I wrote out his sticker and went back over to his car. I handed the money back to him, jokingly saying that his car passed inspection so there was no need for a bribe. He laughed and then explained that he kept a "C-note" folded up inside all of his car registrations, so that if he got pulled over by the police, there would always be an incentive there for the cop to give him a friendly warning, instead of something worse. From that day on, I just refolded the $100 bill back in with his registrations every time he got a sticker, without mentioning it.

Young women would sometimes drive into the sticker bay scantily clad and flirt with me as I was inspecting their vehicles. They would be smiling at me through the windshield and using all their charms. A blouse might be partially unbuttoned, or a skirt would be noticeably sliding up in their lap. Some were absolutely HOT and extremely hard to say no to. But I was a hard ass and stuck to the rules, even with friends. It was the way I was taught. Giving in to bribes or female charms would have been the easy route to take.

Many times, customers would leave their cars with me for work and to get their stickers at the same time. They would tell me, "The registration's in the glove compartment." Over the years, I saw some very interesting items in various glove compartments. I opened one "glovy" to find a huge roll of large bills held together by a couple of fat elastic bands. I couldn't resist checking to see if they were all $50's and $100's, which they were. There were several thousand dollars just sitting there along with a loaded .44 magnum keeping the money company. That customer was a bartender at an establishment on the west side of Southie.

With the price of gasoline no longer being a bargain after the so-called gas shortages, people driving off without paying became a major problem for gas station owners. After several such incidents, I had to think of a deterrent, something to force people to think twice before just driving off. I decided to break a brick in half and place one half-brick on top of each gas pump. When a stranger would come in for gas, I would pick up that half-brick and toss it up in the air from hand to hand, juggling it in plain sight of the driver as the gas pumped. Some drivers would even ask me, "What's the brick for?" I would say, "Try driving off without paying, and I'll show you." Of course, I would say that with a smile, as if I *might* be joking. Drive-offs almost came to a complete halt after we began exhibiting the bricks, but occasionally there was the *really* stupid person who hadn't figured it out.

A driver in his late teens or early twenties pulled in with a big old Buick one afternoon. How I knew he was going to make a run for it, I don't know, but I just *knew*. I made sure he couldn't miss my brick-juggling exhibition as I was filling up his tank. Sure enough, my gut feelings once again proved correct. As I was putting the gas cap back on, he started the engine and took off! I had placed the brick down on the ground right at me feet so I quickly grabbed it. With all the power that the instant adrenaline could muster, I wound up and whipped the brick as hard as I could at the car! He had only made it twenty feet away when the brick hit the top edge of the trunk lid with a tremendous *bang*! It sounded as loud as a gunshot. The extensive damage to the left side of the trunk was very evident as the car continued to peel off into the distance. I had lost a few gallons of gas but gained the satisfaction of knowing that the driver of that car would be reminded of his stupidity each and every time he saw the back end of his car. Better yet, maybe it was his dad's car!

Later that day, the reality of what could have happened hit me. What if that brick had struck the car five inches higher? The dent in the trunk was perfectly lined up with the driver. If the brick had gone through the rear window with the force I had used, it would have hit that driver right in the head. I could have killed another human being that day, over a tank of gas. How many people in this world wish they could go back and change one turn of events or one dumb decision from their past?

Most people learn from their mistakes. Some, I'm sorry to admit, tend to repeat them. I walked from the shop to the front office one afternoon while an always-helpful neighbor was pumping gas for me. John was standing by the pumps, facing away from the office. With one hand on his hip, and a gas cap in the other, he was yelling loudly, "Hey! Hey!" I walked out, wiping the grease off my hands, and asked, "John! What's going on?" He said, "That truck didn't pay!" There was a large white panel truck off in the distance. It was taking the right-hand turn to head up toward Broadway. Knowing that escape routes from the area were limited, I ran to my Eldorado and jumped in. I figured I had a great chance of catching those guys because they didn't know anybody was after them, and they didn't know my car. When I got to the top of the hill at Broadway, I looked both ways. There was no panel truck in sight in either direction. They had to have taken a quick turn to get off Broadway. I knew they were most likely heading toward the boulevard to leave Southie. All of the streets that headed down toward the beach were "one way" in this area. I took a right onto Broadway and then a quick left onto the closest one-way street they could have taken to head out of town.

That was G Street. When I made that turn, I looked all the way down the long, steep hill to the waterfront at Day Boulevard. No truck was on the road, and they couldn't possibly have had time to make it to the end. I surmised that they had to have turned off before reaching the bottom of the hill, so I took a quick right. I was heading around the big circle, which leads around South Boston High School and Thomas Park at Dorchester Heights. I had almost made the entire loop back to G Street when, *there they were*! This was perfect! The truck was parked along the curb on this narrow one-way street. They didn't know I was after them, so the sight of my car did not alarm them at all. I slowly drove by the wide-open sliding driver's door of the truck, and I could see two guys with beards sitting in front. It looked like the passenger was leaning forward, rolling a joint in his lap. After driving about fifty feet past the truck, I pulled the Eldorado crosswise the narrow one-way street, blocking their exit completely. Reaching under the seat, I grabbed the solid oak axe handle that I kept there for protection and jumped out of the car, leaving the engine running and the door wide open. They were just sitting there, preparing to get high, reveling in the glory of the caper they had just pulled off. I saw that they were totally oblivious to the fact that I had blocked the road, and I was approaching their truck with the club in my hand. I was only eight feet from their door when the passenger glanced up and spotted me. He yelled to his partner in crime, "Watch out!"

The startled driver quickly slid shut and locked the door just as I reached it and instantly started the truck. I was thinking, where does he think he can go? He jammed the truck into reverse and started backing up as quickly as he could down the narrow one-way street in the wrong direction! He was barely missing the parked cars. I have to admit, that was some fantastic driving. I was running as fast as I could and he was backing up using only his mirrors, swerving from side to side around this narrow curvy road! It was lucky for him that no traffic had entered the road behind him during this incident. He was gaining ground, so I stopped quickly in the middle of the street, wound up, and launched that axe handle as hard as I could, aiming for the massive front window of the truck. The heavy club hit hard just below the glass, directly in front of the driver. I resumed the chase, picking up the wooden weapon again as I passed it on the road. The thieves continued backing up with me running along after them with club in hand. Remarkably, those lucky bastards made it all the way back out onto G Street where they had to stop and put the truck in forward gear. I continued running toward them until they were ready to pull away. Amazingly, we were now in the street directly in front of the house in which I would eventually end up living. Facing the driver's side window from about fifty feet away, I stopped and whipped the axe handle one more time, and with all my might! I aimed a little low because I was afraid that if I missed the truck, the club would go through a window, into a house. It's a good thing I aimed a little low. The blunt end of the axe handle hit the door of the truck with tremendous force, just two inches below the driver's side window. Just inches higher and I would have hurt that guy really badly or possibly even killed him. I was glad I missed the driver, but angry that they had gotten away. I walked over and picked up the club while catching my breath and getting ready to walk the long distance back to my car. A minute or two after the truck had pulled away, a good friend of mine, named Grafton, came zooming up G Street in his Ford LTD. John, at the gas station, had told him what had happened and Grafton, wanting to help, somehow found me. I yelled to him that the truck just left. Pointing him in the right direction, I said, "See if you can catch up with them and get a plate number."

He took off like a bullet, but was unable to locate the truck. Anybody who happened to be looking out of their front window that day would have had a great show to watch.

When I arrived back at the shop, I was really happy to hear that John had written down the truck's license plate number after it drove away. I called down to Station Six at D Street, and they sent an officer who took a report. Within a day or so, I got a call that the police had tracked down the truck and the owner. The driver offered to come back and pay for the gas, and the cops asked if I wanted to press charges. I didn't want to go to court, so I agreed that if they came back, paid, and apologized, I would let it end at that. He showed up as planned and paid what he owed. I *had* to say something to this driver whose dumb stunt had led me into a situation where I had almost hurt and possibly could have killed somebody. I asked him if he knew what a stupid thing he had done, and I told him he was very lucky that he hadn't ended up getting hurt. I couldn't believe my ears when his reply was "Look at the damage you did to my truck," and then he had the nerve to ask for his gas cap back! At that point, I almost wished I had hit him in the head with that club. Being caught off guard by the request, I reached behind me and retrieved the gas cap from the oil display shelf and handed it to him. I should have said we didn't have it so he would have had to buy a new one. Oh well, a jerk like him probably would have just stolen one from another truck. Who would believe that selling gasoline could be so exciting!

Think back to the events that shaped the
unique individual that you are today.
What person or experience can you just
not get out of your mind?
If you don't hold back, the results may surprise you.

Reader's Notes

Reader's Notes

Reader's Notes

Reader's Notes

Chapter XVIII

When is a Game Just a Game?

There were plenty of interesting regulars down at Gavin's Tavern. A few of them had names such as Fast Eddy, who was good at pool; TV Eddy, who was good at TV repair; and so on. All told, there were dozens of guys and a few girls that always made me feel welcome down at the tavern. Some liked to play pool, some liked to challenge me on the pinball machine, and others would just like to shoot the breeze. Because I now drank with the best of them, I felt truly accepted, which was an experience that had been rare in my life. It was a very good feeling. I can truly understand how some kids, and adults as well, end up in gangs just so they can experience this feeling of belonging.

On occasion, I could be found tussling with guys out on the street after a few too many vodka and grapefruits. Those exhibitions were usually just good clean fun, to see who could get the better of the other guy. Mom would have been so proud. I have several chipped teeth as a result of those fun times.

There were certain things at Gavin's/O'Leary's that I didn't really understand and didn't dare to question for fear of looking ignorant. I only recently found some answers to one of those mysteries as I read the books titled *Brutal* by Kevin Weeks and *A Criminal and an*

Irishman by Patrick Nee. Both books focused on South Boston and the activities of mobster Whitey Bulger. The books also mentioned the IRA, which stands for the Irish Republican Army. There was a very large poster high up on the wall at the tavern during the 1980s. I remember the name of the man on that poster was Bobby Sands. He was a good-looking young Irishman, with a pleasant smile. I believe the word "Martyr" was incorporated into the poster. I had no idea who Bobby Sands was or what his significance might be. But I recently read that Bobby Sands was an Irish Republican Army activist. He had actually been elected to the Irish Parliament in 1981 while he was imprisoned. Mr. Sands was in the fortieth day of a hunger strike at the time of his election. He died on the sixty-sixth day of that hunger strike and was revered by those who wanted the English out of Northern Ireland. At the time, I didn't know how closely connected South Boston actually was to the IRA. Much of the funding and weaponry being supplied to the IRA was coming from Southie. Whitey Bulger allegedly helped fund and arrange a huge shipment of weapons and ammunition using a Gloucester fishing boat named the Valhalla. Besides the huge stash of illegal weapons already secured, many of the weapons that were eventually loaded onto that ship were being purchased legally via mail-order and delivered to a yacht club in South Boston where they were stored. Lockers at the club were secretly being used as weapons caches, awaiting shipment. Lockers are small rooms, which are normally used by club members as sleeping quarters and for the storage of boating equipment. A good friend of mine, who was a Boston police officer, had a locker at a yacht club right next door to the yacht club being used as a weapons storage point. As a guest to the club, I had visited my friend's locker, which was set up with a bunk and it was nicely decorated with numerous nautical items and artifacts.

I would imagine that many of Boston's most prominent citizens must have had lockers at South Boston yacht clubs at the time. It was quite prestigious to have possession of such a locker, and there was always a long waiting list to get one. It could take many years for those on the list to finally be granted a locker. Little did they know that these weapons were sitting there right under their noses at one such club. The Valhalla arms shipment made it all the way across the Atlantic only to be seized a short distance off the coast of Ireland near the planned rendezvous site. History shows that IRA sympathizers could be found all over South Boston.

As it was with most of the bars in town, Gavin's/O'Leary's had the usual pinball machine and coin-operated pool table, but there were also a couple of other machines which were games of chance. I never fell into the habit of playing the gambling machines, but I observed them taking in a lot of money from people over the years. The player could bet various amounts of money on the numbers he wanted to come up as the balls dropped into holes on the playing field of the pinball-like machine. If the player won, the bartender would pay out cash. I guess these machines were quite profitable for the bar and also for the owner of the machines.

On one particular Saturday afternoon, I headed down to the corner tavern and had a drink or two before heading home. As I usually did, I called Diane from the payphone at the tavern to let her know I was on my way home. I had no sooner walked in the front door of our recently purchased home in Weymouth when regular TV programming was interrupted with a news bulletin. Diane and I watched as the reporter announced that a South Boston bar had just been machine-gunned. They had live news cameras there, showing policemen carrying pinball-like gambling machines out the front door of a bar and down the two or three stairs. They were loading the machines into a truck as several other police officers looked on. Suddenly I recognized the bar and I was stunned! I announced to Diane, "Oh my god! I just left there! That's Gavin's/O'Leary's!"

Apparently, just minutes after I had left the tavern, a white Corvette pulled up in front of the bar and stopped in the middle of Dorchester Street. In broad daylight, the driver got out of the car and emptied a fully automatic M16 rifle into the wooden front wall of the bar! The shooter then got back in his car and drove off. It was a real miracle that not one person had been hit by the bullets! When I left the tavern, there were only four or five guys there, and they were sitting at the bar. Thankfully, the bar sat at the far end of the establishment, away from the front entrance and the street. The angle of the bullets coming from the street, which was slightly lower than the bar, worked out really well for those guys. After the bullets entered the front wall, they traveled higher and higher as they went farther into the barroom. By the time the projectiles reached the bar area where the few patrons were sitting, the bullets were hitting the ceiling. I'm sure that the fact nobody was injured or killed was pure luck. The intent of the shooter was far more sinister than to just destroy property or they would have done this in the middle of the night, after closing time. Either way, the point was made. Whoever did it, meant business.

Monday, when I went down to the bar after work, it was open for business as usual as if nothing had happened there. I was told that the reason for the shooting was because one gang wanted to take over the gambling operation from the existing gang. It was a dispute over whose wagering machines would be allowed to operate in the tavern.

Inside the bar, evidence of the shooting was everywhere. The phone booth to the right of the entry door was riddled with bullet holes.

If I had been on that pay-phone just five minutes later, calling Diane to say I'd be home soon, there would have been no escaping those bullets. The thick wood paneling of the exterior wall of the tavern was splintered. You could see daylight through the holes to the outside. To the left of the entrance, the wall by the regular pinball machine was peppered with bullet holes as well. The iron frame around the grate that covered the exterior window looked like somebody had taken a paper puncher to it. The perfectly round holes were directly in front of where I would normally be standing while watching my pinball opponent play his ball. There were chairs and tables with bullet holes, and holes in the ceiling tiles as well. I have to admit that it felt pretty cool to be standing in the open doorway to O'Leary's drinking a beer as curiosity seekers slowly drove by, staring at the bar that had just been in the news a couple of days prior. For now at least, it had a reputation as a tough bar and a dangerous place to be. This was the Southie of the 1980's

On any given night, quarters would be lined up on the edge of the pool table at the tavern. Players waited their turn to challenge the winner of the previous game. Usually we played for a buck or two per game, but those stakes would escalate as the evening progressed. There were some guys that you knew better than to play against for money.

If you play pool three or four nights a week, you do tend to get better at it. I was never really a good pool player, but I could hold my own against most of my friends at the tavern. Remarkably, I was the type of player that became better at pool as I drank more—up to a certain point. I believe I tended to overanalyze my shots when I was stone-cold sober. Once I had a few drinks in me, I would be relaxed. My shooting became more fluid and accurate. One particular evening, it was getting quite late as I was experiencing an unusually long lucky streak while playing my opponents. Two guys that I had never seen before had walked into Gavin's/O'Leary's Tavern earlier that evening. Both were in their twenties and were well dressed. Strangers would not have been welcome in the bar, but apparently some people knew who those guys were.

It wasn't long before they started placing their quarters on the pool table and challenging me. They also wanted to raise the stakes of the games. First I agreed to $5, then $10 per game. For some strange reason I just *could not* lose a game that night. Everyone else had dropped off the table and it was just the two strangers and me playing over and over again. The games didn't last long, and the money was piling up in my pocket. After a while, instead of handing their losses to me after each game, I noticed they were now just throwing the money onto the table, arrogantly and in disgust. I just kept sucking down the vodka and grapefruit juice and savoring the moment. Everyone in the bar was watching the games with great interest. I remember telling these guys that we could just play for fun, and they didn't have to keep betting. I think they took that as an insult, which was not my intent. Actually, I knew that I had reached my plateau, and one too many drinks was going to bring my play back on the downward curve before long.

Once again, we began to play. As I popped balls into the pockets one after the other, the two guys happened to be standing very close behind me. The polite thing for them to have done would have been to back away and give the shooter ample room. They stood there, arrogantly not moving, in an attempt to throw my game off. I was bent over my shot when one of the guys made a negative comment of some kind that I could just barely hear. I believe it was something like, "We're being hustled." I chose to just ignore the comment.

As I bent over another shot, I could clearly hear one of them say, "This guy's an asshole!" Without any thought or hesitation whatsoever, I gently placed my pool cue on the table and turned around to face the two of them. I looked the closest one in the eye and said, "What did you say?" He said, "You're an asshole! You're hustling us!" As soon as I heard those words, I took a swing at the guy and punched him right in the jaw. I didn't see it coming, but right after I threw that punch, I felt a hard hit to the side of my head either from a fist or a cue stick. Before I knew it, I blacked out and fists were swinging wildly, mostly mine I guess. I don't remember getting hit more than that one time, but I kept swinging and hitting those guys with a few good shots. I think the bartender and a few others grabbed me. As soon as I was subdued, the two strangers went out the front door and left the bar.

Immediately after they left, somebody said to me, "Tom! What are you? Nuts?" I said, "What do you mean?" He said, "Do you know who those guys are?" I said, "No. Who are they?" My friend replied, "Those are two of Whitey's bookies from the west side! You better get out there and apologize!" I remember saying "Oh shit!" as I rushed out the door. Thankfully, I was in luck. They had not driven away yet. Their white Lincoln Continental was parked along the curb with the motor running. The windows were up because it was raining, so I went to the passenger's door and tapped on the glass. The window opened about three inches and I could not believe what I saw. Here was this big tough bookie, sitting there sobbing, with crocodile tears running down his face. I said, "Hey! I'm sorry I hit you, but you shouldn't have called me an asshole. It's just a game." He looked up at me and his only words were, "You didn't have to hit me!" I repeated that I was sorry as his window went back up and the car pulled away. For the next several weeks, whenever I visited the tavern, I kept a close eye on the front door. I was nervous that some night, somebody might come back to get revenge on me, but it never happened.

There were always incidents that could have been chalked up to acts of revenge, but I considered them to be random and unrelated to the bookies. Occasionally there would be a new bullet hole in one of the gas station windows or doors. More than once, I got a call in the middle of the night from the police, informing me that someone had smashed in the front door of the gas station with a sledgehammer. The neighbors would be awakened by the noise, call the police, and watch as the thieves got in. By the time the police arrived, the thieves were long gone. I would get dressed and go to the garage in the dead of night to secure the building. Each time that happened, I would find that all of the inspection stickers had been stolen. Nothing else would be touched. Stickers were like gold on the streets of Southie and could be unloaded for quick cash in any bar in town. What bothered me most about those thefts was the knowledge that whoever broke into my shop was known to me. They knew exactly where I kept those stickers hidden. They would use the hidden key to the bolted-down lockbox where the stickers were kept. I will never know what really motivated some of those destructive acts. I guess I was always pissing somebody off.

One funny note about inspection stickers: One year, the Registry of Motor Vehicles made a booboo. When they created the new stickers they inadvertently designed them very close in size and resemblance to a pack of Lucky Strikes. People would drive in for gas in old clunkers with no exhaust systems etc. Inside the windshield, where the inspection sticker belonged, there was an imposter. It had the distinctive round red circle surrounded by a square of white color and black printing in all the right places.

But, instead of a legitimate sticker, it was a cut out from a pack of Lucky's, glued in the window. I had many a good laugh at seeing them. It was such a close match to the real thing that you had to look closely to tell it wasn't a real sticker. I imagine many a cop let these people go with just a warning because it didn't seem right to ticket somebody while laughing.

There were all kinds of people that hung out at the tavern. Most were blue-collar workers like me, always in their work uniforms. A few guys worked at the rum-bottling company down off First Street. After work, some of those guys would get so drunk that not one word they said was understandable. Most were happy drunks. Sometimes, the wife of the rum company's owner would drive in for gas with her shiny new Mercedes. Of course, she would charge the gas to their company account. She always looked and smelled great as she sat there, snugly wrapped in a beautiful mink coat. She would be flashing several huge diamonds as she gripped the steering wheel with both hands while chatting with me. She was always very pleasant to talk to. Her husband would also come in for gas. He was a miserable bastard who never looked at me or said anything to the lowly gas jockey that I was. He was so fat that he had to keep a towel on his lap when he drove because the steering wheel unavoidably rubbed his belly. Ironically, sometimes there would be an old clunker waiting in line for gas behind her or her husband, containing a couple of their employees. The guys in the clunker would pull in after their boss had left and hand me a couple of half gallons of 190-proof grain alcohol. I would, in turn, give them a few gallons of gasoline. They had given me instructions on how to make vodka with it, but some of my friends at the Colbert liked to drink it straight.

There were some younger guys that frequented the tavern that had no job at all that I could see. One such young man I'll call "Paulie." He was not your typical street-tough Southie kid. He had experienced a young life much rougher than most. He was the direct result of being left to grow up on his own on the streets of this city. When he was only around nine or ten years old, I noticed that he was in a neighbor's car, removing the stereo system in broad daylight. I knew the person who owned the car, and Paulie knew her as well. The owner of the car had lived in the neighborhood for a long time. She worked nights as a nurse's aid and slept during the day. I couldn't believe that Paulie would steal from a hardworking young lady that he knew was struggling to get by on her own. As I pumped gas, I yelled over to him saying, "Paulie! What are you doing? Get out of that car!" He just looked over at me and then ignored me. He continued systematically removing the speakers. I had to yell at him several times and show him that I really meant business before he stopped. Finally, he walked away from the car, but as he did, he kept turning toward me with daggers coming out of his eyes. Even at this young age, he had acquired the hard look of a desperate soul in his eyes. A few years later, there was a rumor that he was one of the guys who broke into my shop and stole all the inspection stickers. Even though there was a good chance he had caused problems for me, I always felt forgiving toward him because I knew that it was not his fault that he grew up with no respect for anyone or anything. Society had worked really hard to create the person he was. What environment and what choices were even available to him? Finding a way to survive was the only option he had to consider. Years later as a young man, he was hanging out at Gavin's. I was sitting at the bar next to him, and we were having a pretty nice conversation.

I always went out of my way to say a kind word to him whenever I saw him because I knew he hadn't heard too many kind words during his lifetime. As I was sitting there with Paulie, somebody asked me if I wanted to play a game of pinball. I said, "Sure." I was enjoying the game with my opponent when he informed me that Paulie had shot some guy with a shotgun the night before. It was just mentioned as small talk, as if we were talking about the weather or something. It was a casual statement, something like "Oh. Did you hear that Paulie blew some guy away with a shotgun last night?" As I just stood there, pondering what I had just heard, the guy reminded me that it was my turn on the pinball machine. At just about any bar in Southie, you could be sitting next to somebody having a beer and not know that he had shot somebody just hours before or he would be shooting somebody in a few minutes. Shootings became way too common as time crept into the late 1980s.

Chapter XIX

Gentlemen! Show Me Your Weapons!

I don't know why so many people felt compelled to show me their pistols over the years. Adding to the mystery was why they always chose to do so right before they intended to use them.

There was a guy around my age living near the garage that I became friends with. "Rob" was a very likable guy. He was from a family with a history of violence, but he seemed to have turned out okay. He was always fun to be around. My dad had told me about how Rob's mother had come running out of her house years ago after being badly beaten by her now ex-husband. Dad said her eye-ball was hanging out of its socket, bouncing off her cheek as she ran past the gas pumps. Rob had an older brother that I didn't get to meet for many years because he had been away in prison for quite a long time. I got to know most of the family pretty well and grew very close to Rob and two of his three sisters.

It was just an ordinary morning when Rob walked over to see me at the gas station office. But then, the day took an unusual turn. He pulled a chrome-plated revolver out of his pocket and asked me if I had any bullets for it. I said "Yeah." He knew I had a few assorted bullets of different calibers that had somehow collected themselves in the coin tray of the company safe over the years. Many of those bullets were probably there since before I was born. I grabbed three or four rounds that would fit his gun and I was about to hand them over. Something stopped me. I asked him why he wanted bullets. He said he would just like to have some. Actually using good judgment for once, I hesitated and said, "No. I'm not giving you any bullets. I don't want it on my conscience if you go out and get killed or kill someone else." Rob just smiled. I was surprised when he didn't try to persuade me to change my mind. He knew my reasoning was steadfast, so he left to go about his business.

That afternoon, he returned to the garage. Most of the repair bay doors were open. He entered through the shop before coming out to the office where I was doing paperwork. When we greeted each other, I didn't notice anything unusual about his demeanor. He said, "I'm headed over to the house for a few minutes. I left something in the back room, and I'll be back to get it." A red flag went up when he said that, so I asked him what he had left back there. He said, "It's nothing." I told him, "Come with me." We walked out to the last bay of the shop together. That bay was the only one that was closed up. There was a concrete wall separating that area from the rest of the shop. The only opening was a small doorway leading into that section, so it was pretty dark in there. We seldom used that bay except for storage of the old 1942 tow truck and to write inspection stickers. There, sitting on my sticker desk, was a large brown paper bag stuffed to the brim with prescription drugs. I said to Rob, "Get this stuff out of my place!" He said, "Can't I just leave it here for a few minutes?" I repeated, "Get this stuff out of my place!" I didn't ask him where he got it. I just knew I didn't want that bag in my shop. Rob picked it up, gave me a smile, and walked out with it.

About an hour or so later, my friend Lyle came in, got gas, and settled into the office for an afternoon beer with me. He told me that the strangest thing happened to him that afternoon. He had been to Quincy, which is a town just to the south of Boston. He stopped at a drugstore near his home, and as he was entering the store, a guy almost knocked him over, rushing past him and out the door. When Lyle got to the counter, he found the pharmacist on the phone with the police, frantically reporting that he had just been robbed at gunpoint. Lyle smiled at me and said, "The guy that banged into me was the robber, and he looked a lot like your friend 'Robbie'!" I said, "Oh my god! I can't believe that you were there just at the exact time! It probably was Robbie." I told Lyle what had transpired between Rob and me, about him asking me for bullets earlier in the day, and I told him the story about the bag of drugs. Lyle just made a comment something like, "That crazy bastard."

Later, when I ran into Robbie, I asked him where he ended up getting bullets for his gun. He said he didn't get any. I never actually asked him if he had robbed the drugstore. That was a confirmation I didn't need or want. Neither did I tell him what Lyle said to me that day. Apparently, if he robbed that store, he did it with an empty gun. I was glad he didn't get himself killed, and I hoped he wouldn't make a habit out of such behavior. I never heard of him doing anything like that again.

Seeing guns was becoming a daily occurrence. I had started dating a girl named "Tina" whom I had met at Kostic's Deli. That store was at the corner of Broadway and I Street. I also was a very good friend with her brother who was a bookmaker at a local tavern. I loved stopping in where her brother worked because I could have a beer, study the Wonderland Greyhound Park racing program, and place bets with my friend right there at the bar.

Seconds after the race was over, the pay-phone would ring. We would have the real-time results and payoff amounts. It was great! The payoffs were exactly the same as if we were at the track, but I didn't have to leave my barstool. Tina's father was a real trip to meet for the first time. He was probably five feet tall and had a badly scarred face. I met him at their house on the night I picked her up for our first real date. He approached me in the living room as I waited for her to finish getting ready. Instead of the usual grilling I expected from a father whose daughter was being picked up for the first time, he asked me a rather unusual question. He asked, "Do you want to buy a pen gun?" I told him I had no idea what that was, so he pulled one out of his pocket. It looked like a regular pen, but he explained that it held one .22 caliber bullet inside instead of an ink cartridge. To demonstrate how it worked he pretended to jam it into my ribs. He explained that the force of ramming it into somebody would release a spring-loaded firing pin, which fired the cartridge within a small barrel. He said, "They can only be used once, so you might want to buy a few." I declined the offer. It was very disturbing to think that a bunch of people were probably running around town with these things. It gave a whole new meaning to the phrase "the pen is mightier than the sword." That would not be my last encounter with a gun while at her house.

Tina's family lived in a third-floor apartment on East Broadway near M Street Park. While on my lunch hour one beautiful summer day, the two of us were sitting on the front steps of her apartment house. We were eating sandwiches I had brought over. The front of the building bowed out near the steps, and there was a window from the first floor apartment overlooking the spot where we were sitting. Out of the blue, we heard a man's deep voice say, "Hey! Get the hell off my stairs!" Tina and I looked at each other with surprise.

I turned and saw a really large guy in the window only about three feet from us. I responded to the guy, "Hey! She lives here!" Tina and I went back to enjoying our lunch. Maybe ten seconds later, we heard the man yell, "Get the f—off my stairs or I'll blow your fu—in' heads off!" I turned to respond to this idiot and was shocked to see a twelve-gauge shotgun pointed out the open window to within a few inches of my head. A split second later, and without thinking about it, I grabbed Tina by the arm and rushed the two of us off the stairs and away from this maniac. We hugged the front of the house as we fled so he couldn't get a clear shot at us. After escaping the danger, we jumped into my Challenger, which was parked a few houses away, and went to a pay-phone down on L Street. I called Station Six at D Street where I knew several cops and explained what had happened. I told them that I was in fear of sending my girlfriend Tina back to her own house. Within just a couple of minutes, there were several police cars at the scene. They entered the first-floor apartment as we watched from outside. Shortly after going in, they were exiting the house carrying several firearms. They asked if I wanted to press charges, and I said yes. They led this monstrous-looking guy from the house. He was probably pushing three hundred pounds and looked like he hadn't bathed in weeks. We quickly had our day in the South Boston Court before a judge for a hearing. While on the stand, the man explained that he was under the care of a psychiatrist and admitted that he was not supposed to possess or have access to any firearms. He explained that it was his brother's apartment and claimed that the guns belonged to his brother. I don't remember there being any family members in court with this guy at all that day. No brother was in sight that I could see. While testifying on the stand he started reaching into his pockets pulling out one bottle after another of prescription drugs.

When he first reached into his pocket I remember getting a little startled, not knowing what the hell he was going to pull out. Even from thirty feet away I couldn't help noticing that all the fingers on his badly shaking hands were bright yellowish brown in color, from chain smoking. The rest of his hands looked filthy and had severely gnawed fingers, where fingernails should be. He placed the prescriptions in front of him one by one until there were 8 or 9 bottles sitting there in total.

He explained again that he was under a doctor's care, and he was very sorry about what he did. He said he would never really hurt anyone. He looked over toward where Tina and I were sitting and begged that if I would drop the charges, he would give up all those weapons and promise to never bother anyone again. Not even thinking about where I was or who was listening at the time, I stood up and spoke directly to the man, addressing the plea for forgiveness he had just made on the stand. I blurted out in a rather threatening tone, "I'll drop the charges if you give up all those guns. But I'm telling you, this girl has to walk right by your door every day, and I am also going to be walking by your door. I will be carrying my gun, which I am legally licensed to carry, and if your door opens just a crack and we feel threatened, I'll shoot first and ask questions later." I noticed several people in the courtroom, including the judge, shaking their heads in disbelief of what they had just heard. In essence, I had threatened to shoot this guy, and I'd done it right in front of around twenty witnesses and a judge. A recess was instantly called, and after a few minutes, I was informed that the defendant had relinquished the guns to the court and the best thing for me to do was to agree to a dismissal right away and put an end to the proceedings. That's exactly what I did. I only ended up going to Tina's house one or two more times, but that guy never opened his door when I was there.

Tina and I had a way of being in the wrong place at the right time. During one of our dates, I decided to stop in at the Coachman Lounge for drinks. That was a bar located on East Broadway. It was not one of my regular hangouts, but I thought it might be nice to go someplace different. I think it was still called the Coachman at the time, but it did change names once or twice over the years. It may have been called Hap's Lounge by the time this incident took place. Tina and I approached the covered, dark entranceway. I had just placed my hand on the doorknob, about to open the door and let Tina walk in ahead of me when we heard *Pop! Pop! Pop! Pop!* The sound of gunfire was coming from inside. I can't remember exactly how many shots there were, but it was multiple. With my hand frozen to the doorknob, I turned to Tina, smiled, and said, "Maybe we should go somewhere else." She returned my smile and nodded her head in agreement. We got back in my car and left. I found out the next day that I knew one of the guys involved in that shooting. I was glad we hadn't arrived a few seconds earlier.

Besides Tina, I had developed several really good friendships at Kostic's Deli over the years. Sue, who pretty much ran the place, was a longtime friend. Every morning, I would stop in around 6:00 AM for coffee with Sue before going to my shop. She and I would exchange stories about our escapades of the night before and sometimes sympathize with each other's hangovers. Several people who worked in downtown Boston would regularly enjoy coffee and a danish pastry as they waited for the bus that stopped in front of Kostic's. That deli also had the best hot-pastrami around. Over time, I got to know some of the morning commuters well. A very attractive nurse was there every morning waiting for the bus. "Carol" turned out to be a really nice person. Seeing her in that white uniform every morning was something I looked forward to.

We would talk every morning, and eventually, I asked her out. We dated quite a while, and I soon got to know her brother and her sister. Her brother "Jason" started coming in for gas quite often. He would always spend a few minutes shooting the breeze with me and then go about his business. He was a very nice guy, and I always enjoyed his company and conversation. While I was pumping gas for him one day, he called me over to his window, saying he wanted to show me something. He was holding a pistol that he said he had "just picked up." He seemed very nervous and agitated as he held the gun down low in the car for me to see. I asked him why he had bought a gun, but I got an unclear answer. He mumbled something like, "I have something I gotta do." I asked him if everything was all right. He said, "Yeah, I'm fine." He paid for his gas and drove away.

The next morning, a guy who knew I was dating Jason's sister came in and asked if I had heard what Jason had done the night before. I told him "No! What?" He said that Jason had gone into the Combat Zone, walked up to a group on the street, and shot five guys. Some of them had died. He told me Jason had been dating a fifteen-year-old girl from "the zone," and he was pissed off because these guys were feeding his girlfriend drugs and had gotten her hooked. He had gone in there to blow them all away. Jason apparently made no effort to hide what he had done and was arrested for the murders. He ended up in prison, but I don't know for how long. He may still be there. Here is a case of a guy that you would never expect could be capable of murder, yet given the right circumstances, he showed no hesitation.

As for myself, I only fired my Beretta a couple of times in Southie, but never at a person. One day I had six or seven construction workers in my office along with the guys that worked for me.

The construction crew worked for the company that was building the infrastructure for Boston's first cable TV system. They were a rough but likable group of guys. I got to know them well because I serviced and gassed up all their trucks. At the end of the day, we would sometimes grab some beers and have them in the office before going home. This particular day must have been a Friday and probably hotter than usual because the beers were going down real easy. The hours went by, and eventually it was time to call it a day and send everyone home. The problem was, these guys had no homes. They lived in grungy motels as they traveled around the country, building cable systems in various cities. They were perfectly happy staying right where they were and drinking until they could drink no more. No matter what I said, they ignored me and kept drinking. I couldn't get them to leave! I closed up the gas pumps and was putting the cash away when I spotted my gun in the safe. I took the Beretta out and while standing in the center of the 8' x 10' office among all these guys, I aimed through the doorway into the shop. There was a pile of discarded tires about ten feet away that I trained my sights on and fired off a couple of rounds. *Bang! Bang!* That got everybody's attention. I repeated that it was time to leave, and this time they listened.

I then left the garage, but decided to stop at my friend's roofing shop to see if he wanted to go to the I & A Restaurant for a quick beer before going home for the weekend. Marshall operated a very specialized roofing company. He could always be found in his shop late in the day creating ornate copper fascia for the tall buildings in downtown Boston. He was one of the few craftsmen in the country with his level of skill. I expected it would take some convincing to get him to stop working and take a break. I drove the two blocks to his shop and rang the doorbell with my signature three short rings.

He let me in, and as usual, his nasty but good-natured greeting was "What the hell do you want? I have work to do!" He walked back toward the metal fabrication area and proceeded with his work, ignoring my suggestion to quit and come have a beer with me. To get his attention, and to shake things up a bit, I took my gun out of my pocket and fired a round into the bags of concrete that he had piled against the wall. It was very loud because of the enclosed concrete block area we were in, but he was unfazed by the unexpected explosion. I said, "Come on! Quit for a while!" He called me a crazy bastard, but stood his ground to finish what he was doing before joining me at the I & A Restaurant.

There was another day that I couldn't get Marshall to quit working and join me at the I & A. I tried to figure out a reason to make him come out and play that he couldn't refuse. I made the mistake of calling him from the pay-phone at the restaurant and whispered, "Marshall! I'm at the I & A. There are three or four guys at the bar giving me a hard time." I was going to continue to say that I thought there was going to be trouble, but Marshall hung up on me before I could say those words. I thought he had seen through my little charade, but within no more than sixty seconds, he had gotten into his truck and driven the short distance to the restaurant. The front door of the restaurant burst open, almost ripping the hinges off the door jamb! He had taken me seriously and was standing in the open doorway like Spider-Man, scanning the bar back and fourth for the troublemakers with his fists clenched for action. Needless to say I felt like a heel, and he was understandably upset with me for crying wolf. He had run off and left his shop wide open. It did feel good to know that if I had been in trouble, he was there in a flash.

When I think of it, "Spider-Man" is a very appropriate reference when thinking of Marshall. He routinely climbed to the most difficult spots on many of Boston's tallest buildings in order to reach the ornate cornice-work. One cold November, he talked me into climbing Mount Washington with him. That New Hampshire mountain boasts a claim to having "the worst weather in the world." In April of 1934, the summit of Mt. Washington experienced winds of 231 miles per hour, the highest surface wind speed ever recorded on earth. The day Marshall and I attempted our climb we were dealing with high winds and ice pellets hitting our faces at what felt like BB-gun speeds. My friend climbed with ease as we made our way up one of the most difficult routes to the summit. Not being used to the constant exertion of climbing, I was out of breath, and kept getting a very painful stitch in my side that would temporarily prevent me from continuing. Marshall waited very patiently for me to catch up numerous times. With ice forming on our beards and eye lashes, we passed signs warning that many people had died along this route. The signs advised only the most prepared climbers to continue, and only in good weather. Marshall explained that there would be no challenge in doing this in nice weather, so we continued. Near the very top of Mount Washington there is what's called the headwall. It was our very last difficult obstacle to the summit, being practically a vertical climb. With no ropes or safety gear of any kind, we took slightly separate routes on this last leg of the journey. Clinging to the ice and snow cover, I was approximately thirty feet from the top of the headwall. Marshall was fifty feet to my right and twenty feet below me, on what turned out to be a much wiser route. As I kicked at the ice sheet several times attempting to make a foothold, the final kick caused a huge section directly below me to break away. At least a ton of snow and ice went crashing down the face of the mountain. I was scared to death as I clung to whatever I could. Because of the ice storm and poor visibility, Marshall couldn't see me as he faced into the wind, but I could see him.

Hearing the loud crashing of the debris and small avalanche below us, Marshall thought it was me that had fallen, and he thought I was a goner. I was frozen solid, afraid to move, as I watched him look down the mountain yelling, *"Tommy! Tom!"* I milked the moment for a few seconds before letting him know I was still alive. After all, it was his fault we were up here in the first place! Then, I yelled over to him, "Marshall! I'm turning back! I don't want to die here on the side of this mountain!" Slowly navigating sideways, away from the gaping hole left below me, I somehow made it off the headwall. Marshall was very understanding when I refused to continue the final thirty feet to the top. Spider-Man and I started our descent. We hadn't made it to the summit, but at least my friend knew I had given it my best shot.

This narrative of the Mount Washington climb was a detour from my explanation of the role the Beretta played during my years at the garage. But I wanted to include it because it was another example of how I would compromise better judgment, placing myself in danger in order to fit in and be accepted among friends.

The Beretta came in handy as a persuasive tool at times. There were two occasions when I got extremely fed up with the excuses company owners would give me when their monthly account statements went unpaid. They would keep saying, "I'll send a check up to you in the morning, or next week." In the meantime, they would continue sending their trucks and cars up for gas and repairs. The bills would get up in the thousands, which was a big loss for a small-business owner like me to absorb if they didn't pay. In two instances that I can recall, I resorted to subtle persuasion. I would stick that gun in my belt and make sure it was in plain sight when I personally paid a visit to the tardy company's office. I would lean over the guy's desk, stare him in the eye, and tell him, "I came up to save you the trouble of having to deliver my check to the station." I wasn't leaving until I had a check in my hand. That tactic worked on both occasions, although the check from one of those companies bounced. I was unaware that the company had quietly filed for bankruptcy. When I returned to make them honor their rubber check, their trucks and equipment were gone, and their offices were vacant.

The most lucrative commercial account that Emerson Auto ever had was landed purely by chance and was the result of being in the right place at the right time. Please don't think that every day was a heavy-drinking day. That was not the case. These events took place over the course of several years, and it just so happens that drinking was part of many notable situations. For me, most days consisted of working very long hours in all types of weather and often dealing with difficult people. After a tough day, I might stop and have one or two drinks and then head home. On the weekend, it wasn't unusual to really tie one on. That said, I was having a beer at Gavin's one Saturday afternoon when a stranger came up to the bar and sat directly to my right. He was about six foot three and had curly red hair. He was dressed in construction clothes, so nobody paid much attention to him when he came in.

The guys on my left were talking cars with me. After a while, the redheaded stranger joined in the conversation. He seemed to be a very pleasant guy. After talking with him for a while, he asked me where I worked. I told him I owned the gas station and repair shop up the street. He explained that he was new in town, and his company had sent him to Boston because they were under contract to install the underground and overhead infrastructure for cable TV. At the time, Boston had no cable TV at all. I guess you could say this took place "BC," (before cable). He went on to say that he was in charge of the company's operations in Boston and that he anticipated being in town for at least a couple of years.

He told me that he had opened up a charge account at the Texaco down by the beach, near City Point, but he wasn't thrilled with the way he was being treated there. He said they made him feel like they really didn't want his business. I knew the owners of that Texaco station pretty well. I told him they were good people, and I always found them to be very nice and easy to get along with. I suggested that maybe they were just having a bad day when he was made to feel that way. He said that it wasn't just a one-time occurrence, and he asked if I would consider opening an account with his company to service their vehicles. I was hesitant to take business away from a fellow station owner that I knew, but this guy was insistent, and I wasn't about to turn away good business. I suggested that he open an account with me and also keep his other account open for a while longer to see if he would be happy dealing with me. He agreed. I asked him how many vehicles they had here. He said, "Right now we have my van and three trucks, but I expect that more trucks will be sent here as the job picks up steam." He said he would cut me a check each week. I agreed, saying, "That would be great." All my other accounts were on a monthly basis. By being paid weekly, I figured I couldn't get hurt too badly if they left town.

The weeks went by, and they proved to be a wonderful company to deal with. I never had to ask where my check was, and I never had to carry my trusty Beretta to their office to intimidate them into paying. Every Friday afternoon, they would hand deliver a check up to the shop, like clockwork. The name of the company was A M Cable TV. The redheaded boss was named Randy, and we became friends. He would gladly share a beer with me at the garage or at the tavern at the end of a long day. One afternoon, as he gassed up his van, I asked him when they might be sending more vehicles to Boston. He replied "Any time now." He said it with a mysterious smile on his face that I did not understand.

I soon found out the reason for his smile. Have you ever been watching the lottery numbers being drawn on TV and the first ball drops and it's your number? Then another and another! After the fourth of your numbers appeared on the screen, you sat up and stopped breathing. Your eyes popped out of your head as your fifth number came out! Then you woke up and realized it was all a dream. Well, I had a similar thing happen, but it wasn't a dream. It was a hot summer afternoon and I had dragged a chair outside of the front office. I was sitting with my feet up on the little concrete wall, enjoying the sunshine, when I heard the roar of a heavy diesel engine making its way around the corner at Dorchester and Emerson Streets. As the monster-sized tractor-trailer passed by me, I saw that it was a car carrier. Loaded on the trailer were six utility trucks. Immediately following that car carrier was a second identical one. The second one was hauling six full-size vans. As I lounged in my chair, I couldn't help but notice that each and every one of those vehicles was as shiny as could be, and the two tractors that were pulling the loads matched the yellowish/tan color of the trucks they were hauling. Then I saw the balls of the lottery fall into place! The cabs of each vehicle on the trailers, and the cabs of the tractors pulling them, were all lettered "A M Cable TV!" These were not like the rusty old trucks I had been servicing for the past few weeks. They all appeared to be band new! That's why I didn't recognize the lettering right off the bat.

I remember saying out loud, "Holy Shit!" This company had so many vehicles that they owned their own matching car carriers! All those trucks would be gassing up and getting serviced right here with me, all because I had a friendly beer with a redheaded stranger at Gavin's Tavern. My father had retired from the garage by this time, but he had stopped in for one of his short visits. When I told him what was happening, he just calmly said, "Yeah? Good."

That was it. He wasn't one to go nuts with excitement or tell me "You did good securing that account!" I do remember him telling me on numerous occasions, "You'll never be a businessman." He would say that because sometimes, if a customer was broke, I would cut them more slack than he thought I should.

Every few days for the next week or so, I would break into a smile as more car carriers loaded with more and more vehicles drove by. They topped out at between thirty-five or forty trucks and vans. There were times during the day when I would have six or seven A M Cable TV trucks lined up at the gas pumps, waiting their turn, and two or three would be in the shop for routine maintenance. I was really glad the gas shortage was over. They remained great customers and paid on time right up until their work was completed in Boston. I hated to see them go.

The business relationship with A M Cable TV had resulted because of the pure luck of meeting that gentleman at the bar and striking up a conversation with a stranger. I had expressed my optimism and wishful thinking to my father that I hoped it would mushroom into a major account, and it did just that. I'm a big believer that luck and positive thinking each play a major role in the outcomes of our lives. I've always vocalized my dreams. It's just the way I am. An amazing instance of what skeptics will call just a fantastic coincidence happened at the garage one day. We were in the middle of a heat wave with high humidity and temperatures pushing a hundred degrees. After finishing our work in the shop, the two mechanics, Bucky and Ken, and I were sitting outside in front of the office. The guys were complaining about how miserable they were. I blurted out loud, "Boy, wouldn't an ice-cold Miller Lite taste really great right about now?" They both agreed. *Seconds* after I made that statement, a beer truck came around the corner and was speeding down the road. Just before it passed the gas pumps, it hit a pothole, and we heard a crash accompanied by the sound of breaking glass. It was a Miller truck. A full case of Miller Lite had fallen out of the back of the truck when it bounced over the pothole! Half of the bottles had smashed all over the road, but the other twelve were still in the case and just fine. The box slid along the pavement, coming to rest about twenty feet from where we were sitting. It was like a miracle! The guys just stared at me in awe of what they had just witnessed. I went over and picked up those beers and they were ice cold! As we took our first few sips and talked about how unbelievable that was, I said, "Is there anything else you want me to wish for?" What are the chances of that ever happening at all? Never mind right after somebody expressed a wish for it. We didn't just get cold beers. We got the exact brand and type I had asked for. I've heard the saying that "we create what we fear." I prefer the saying "we get what we ask for."

While climbing Mount Washington, the ice build-up on my beard was testimony to the mountains claim to fame, which is, having the worst weather in the world.

Sign reads: "Try this trail *only* if you are in top physical condition. Many have died above the timberline from exposure. Turn back at the first sign of bad weather." Good advice!

I thanked my friend later for inviting me on this fun climb.
Frozen in pain, I try to shield myself from the wind driven ice
pellets which were stinging my face. There was nowhere to hide.

Chapter XX

Scary Neighbors and Friends With Nine Lives

Many of the people that lived within close proximity of the shop were loyal customers, and I got to know just about all of them extremely well. I always suspected that one such neighbor was a prominent member of the Boston underworld. While filling up his car at the pumps, my father and this particular neighbor would often have conversations about the horses that were racing that day at Suffolk Downs, and they would compare opinions. Soon after, Dad would be on the phone, calling to place his bets, or he would send me down to the bookie joint next door. That neighbor spoke very little with me when he came in for gas, and I don't think I ever saw him crack a smile. On occasion, there would be a stream of guys going up his front stairs and into the house. Some of them I recognized as local bookies and loan sharks. The cast of characters sometimes included the guy who had offered to kill somebody for me for 67¢. From the mixture of ethnicities that sometimes gathered, I always assumed that there was a definite connection and cooperation between the Italian Mob and the Irish gang from the west side of Southie. I doubt they were gathering for afternoon tea. It was one of those obvious goings-on that I would observe, think about, but never mention to anyone. I'm sure I couldn't have been the only person to notice things like this taking place. This was Southie, and you just minded your own business if you wanted to survive here. If things got out of hand, the area had a way of policing itself and protecting its own.

Dad and I had endured a decades-long struggle with several of the neighbors over parking. This resulted in too many arguments to count. A certain few would come home late at night and park right in front of our garage doors or at the pumps. In the morning when we opened up, we couldn't get cars in for gas or in and out of the shop. I would be the one elected to go over and bang at their respective doors at 6:30 AM and tell them to move their cars. Sometimes they would just throw me the keys and tell me to move their cars myself. We would threaten them with parking tickets if this went on for, say, three days in a row. It was a real nuisance having to deal with this ongoing problem almost on a daily basis. Finally, we would have to follow through with our threats and call the police who would come and ticket the cars.

Nothing we did stopped some of these people, especially one neighbor named "Sammy." He was the worst parking offender, and we had several bad arguments with him over the years. He would eventually come out, take the ticket off his windshield, and toss it to the ground without even looking at it. Then he would just drive away. He might even come in for gas later that same day as if nothing had happened. This went on for years and years.

At times, even though he was a large and intimidating person with a chip on his shoulder, Sammy could come across as being a very nice guy. However, mostly I found him to be very moody and hard to get along with. Eventually, Sammy partnered up with another neighbor who happened to be a good friend of mine called "Chad."

Together, they opened up a bar down toward the west side of Southie. At the bar, they had an open brick barbecue pit, which was fired by real wood and charcoal. Chad had concocted his own sandwich, which gained a reputation all over Southie. He would split these large and spicy Italian sausages down the middle and flame broil them right in front of you. When they were just right, with fire shooting everywhere, he would top the sausage with a big slice of his secret cheese. It would all melt together as he placed the ingredients into the freshest bulkie roll ever! It was immediately wrapped in heavy aluminum foil. I would drive to the bar, watch him prepare my order, and bring these scrumptious sandwiches back to the shop for lunch. They would still be piping hot when I got back to work. Life was good, and I became very good friends with Chad.

Chad had an antique car collection. One of his cars was a 1930s Cadillac La Salle. He also had an old Riviera and several other rare collectable cars. He would bring many of those cars into the garage and I would work on them. I felt a real sense of accomplishment when I was able to locate a starter or some other hard-to-find part for one of his cars and get the vehicle up and running again. Chad was very likable, easy going, and even tempered. Sammy, on the other hand, was high strung and unpredictable. To me, theirs was an "odd couple" partnership. Chad had moved into a three-decker across the street from my shop, right next to where Sammy had previously lived. Sammy had moved to another neighborhood by this time.

One day, Sammy drove up when I was outside of the shop and said he had a gas tank leak. He asked if I could fix it. I was always a little uneasy at the sight of him pulling up, not knowing what to expect. I had him pull the car inside the shop so I could take a look at it. I got down on a creeper and slid myself under the back end of his car. When I inspected for leaks, I was surprised to see a bullet hole in the gas tank, about an inch or two up from the bottom. I looked around and saw a couple of other bullet holes that were evident in the back of the car. I slid myself out from under the chassis and looked up at Sammy. As I lay on the creeper at his feet, I informed him of the bullet hole in his tank. By this time, I was very nervous being around Sammy because I had heard he was heavily into cocaine. Plus, on this particular day, he gave me the impression of being unpredictable and paranoid. He was mean enough before he ever got into coke, and now, he was most assuredly armed with a gun and probably high for all I knew. This was not a good combination at all. I have to admit that even though there was no hostility between Sammy and me on this day, I felt very vulnerable, lying there at his feet, looking up at him from my creeper. I really felt that all I would have to do was say one wrong thing to him and he would pull out his gun, shoot me, and then just go about his daily business. After I told him about the bullet hole in his tank, he just responded, "Can you patch it?" I said I would try. As he waited there, I drove down to Ross Motor Parts and half jokingly asked if they had anything that was good for patching bullet holes in gas tanks. After a good laugh with the owner's son, Gary, I bought an epoxy he recommended that was specially made to repair fuel tank leaks. When I got back to the shop, I mixed up the ingredients and patched up the tank. It worked like a charm, hardening like iron within minutes. Sammy left happy, with a full tank of gas.

Because he no longer lived across the street, I thought that my arguments with Sammy over parking were finally a thing of the past. I was very wrong. It was around 9:00 AM one day when Sammy pulled up, directly at the gas pumps. He just parked there, got out of his car, and walked away! He was headed across the street toward his partner Chad's house. I came out of the office and called to him as he walked away, asking if he wanted gas. He said no and continued walking.

I said, "Sammy! You can't leave your car here! We're open for business! You're blocking my pumps!" He stopped as he was almost to the other side of the street, near the steps to Chad's building. He yelled, "I'll only be a minute!" He had a wild look in his eyes that I had never seen before. I knew that "a minute" to him might be an hour, so I yelled back loudly, "Move the car! I can't get customers in for gas!" It was as if he had no idea that it was daytime and that I was open for business. He must have been high because he had never parked at the pumps in broad daylight like this before. He was furious as he came stomping back across the street, cursing me as he walked toward me. He got into his car and slammed the door. Instead of just moving the car across the street where there were plenty of parking spots, he revved the engine loudly in obvious anger and sped away like a madman. He didn't return that day at all.

The very next morning, my dad happened to be visiting me at the shop. I asked him to watch the front for a few minutes while I went to Ross Motors for parts. It was once again around 9:00 AM. While I was standing at the parts counter, their phone rang and they said it was for me. That was strange. They handed the phone to me, saying it was Vito, my dad. He sounded very excited as he said, "Come back to the shop! Your friend Chad just got shot!" He said Sammy parked across the street, went into Chad's apartment, and shot him. Then he got in his car and drove away. Dad knew Chad was a friend of mine and that I would want to see if he was going to be okay. I jumped into the tow truck and headed back to the shop with the emergency lights flashing. When I arrived, there were several police cars there and an ambulance was just pulling up. I went to the front door of the house, but the police stopped me before I could go in. As I stood outside waiting for information, TV news crews began showing up and filming. Within a few minutes, they carried Chad out on a stretcher.

He was conscious, and his eyes were wide open. As an EMT wheeled him past, within a few feet of where I stood, he looked right up at me, gave me a smile and a thumbs up sign. I stood there thinking to myself, "What a guy! He just got shot, but he still mustered up a smile and a reassuring signal for my benefit." I went home that night and was surprised to find myself on the six o'clock news. I was filmed while standing outside Chad's house, looking up at his window. They reported that a South Boston man had been shot *eleven times* at point-blank range with a nine-millimeter automatic. Amazingly he lived! Sammy had emptied an entire clip into Chad, but hadn't killed him.

Shortly after seeing the news, a scary thought occurred to me. Sammy had most likely come to shoot Chad the morning before, when he parked at my gas pumps! I believe I had interrupted a killer's plan by making him move his car and pissing him off to the point that he just left without carrying out his plan. That morning, I had no idea I was arguing with a guy whose mission at that moment was to kill another human being. I'm surprised he didn't just shoot me too! I bet he thought about it.

Who knows, maybe Sammy's aim would have been better that previous morning. If I hadn't interrupted the would-be shooter's schedule, maybe Chad would have been sound asleep; therefore making him an easier target, and he would have died. By arguing with Sammy, it's possible I may have inadvertently saved Chad's life and maybe saved Sammy from a full-blown murder charge. Both Chad and the girl who happened to be in his apartment that morning must have identified Sammy as the shooter. He was arrested and charged with attempted murder. He was back out on the street in no time, awaiting trial. A short time later while he was out on bail, I heard that Sammy took a .45 caliber bullet to the back while standing on the street.

He survived that attack. Eventually he was found guilty of the attempted murder charge and went to prison. Possibly, he has served his time by now and hopefully has turned his life around.

A couple of days after Chad got shot, I went to Boston City Hospital to see if I could get in to visit him. He was in a secured section of the hospital, and there was a police guard posted at the door to his room. I seriously doubted that I would be allowed in to see Chad because I was not a relative or his attorney. After having worked several hours in the shop, and still dressed in my garage uniform, I looked pretty grubby. To my surprise, I had no problem getting into his room. They just believed me when I told them I was Chad's friend, and they let me right in! I had a long sharp screwdriver in my pocket and some other tools that could have easily been used as a deadly weapon. After being allowed into his room and we were alone, I pulled out the long sharp screwdriver and showed Chad, saying, "Look! They let me right in here with this! They didn't even search me for guns or knives! I could finish you off right now with no problem, if that's what I had come for!" I was worried that the security being provided to my nearly murdered friend was very poor to say the least. Surprisingly, Chad didn't seem concerned at all.

I was glad to see my friend looking so good. He was glad to see me, and I asked him how the hell he survived this attack! He said he was in bed when he saw Sammy enter his bedroom with a gun in his hand. When Sammy started shooting, Chad told me he rolled up into a ball and slid off of the bed. All the shots were hitting him in the legs and buttocks as he rolled around on the floor, trying to make himself into a moving target. He said he kept his ass facing Sammy. I asked him if any of the bullets had hit his privates. He immediately lifted his hospital gown and showed me several bullet wounds within an inch or two of his family jewels. He was very lucky.

Many of the bullets could not be safely removed, so he was still carrying them around inside of him. I haven't been able to find Chad in years. If you're still out there my friend, give me a call!

Chad attended my wedding, and his gift was one of the most unique that Diane and I received that day. While we were given many of the usual gifts, such as checks and savings bonds, which we really appreciated, his gift was a music box with a bride and groom dancing in a glass dome. I thought it was a very thoughtful gift. Every once in a while, I wind it up and enjoy remembering the day we received it.

On the opposite side of the gas station lived another man whom I didn't really know very well because he was relatively new to the neighborhood. He seemed friendly and nice enough when he would come in for gas and we had plenty of amiable conversations, mostly just small talk. He was a tall Irishman, probably in his mid-thirties. I can't even remember his name or if we ever discussed what he did for a living. He only lived there for a year or so. All I do know about him is that he had nine lives, just like my friend Chad. The following took place on a Saturday, just minutes after I had left the shop for the weekend and gone home. My ever observant neighbor, John Foley, told me that right after I closed up at 1:00 PM, that neighbor parked at my gas pumps and was getting out of his car to walk across the street to his apartment. A black Oldsmobile immediately pulled up on the opposite side of the pumps. Two guys jumped out of that car, wearing ski masks. One had a shotgun and the other had a .44 magnum handgun. They both opened fire on the guy that had just parked, hitting him numerous times. John, who had previously observed my gas pumps getting smashed, saw this shooting happening while he sat at the same window. He told me that the shooters' car looked very similar to the black Oldsmobile that had previously destroyed my pumps. I hoped they hadn't come there looking for me!

Unbelievably, after those guys unloaded their weapons into their target, the guy was still able to run away! The two assailants jumped back in their car and burnt rubber as they headed up toward Broadway. John said the wounded neighbor made it all the way to the front of his house, about a hundred feet away, before collapsing to the sidewalk. He was wearing a white T-shirt when he got out of his car, but John said it now was a bright red T-shirt.

Regardless of whom the intended target was, this was not a random shooting. It was a well-planned hit. The black Oldsmobile that was used in the shooting was found abandoned at the corner of Broadway and I Street, near Kostic's Deli. It had burst into flames shortly after the two guys got out and it totally burned up. The shooters had a second car parked on Broadway waiting for them. They had gotten into the second car and driven away just before the Olds went up in flames.

Miraculously, the neighbor survived! When he came in for gas several weeks later, I told him I was glad he was all right and how lucky he was to be alive. He was more than happy to lift his shirt to show me the damage that had been done to him. I was shocked to see how horribly disfigured he was. His back was one massive web of scar tissue. I never asked him what his problem with those guys was all about. He came in a few more times, and then I never saw him again.

(Left to right) Vito, Tony Banna, and Ken

Over time, within the area of view from the office door, a man was shot several times. A boy was beaten unconscious and kicked in the face. A black man was brutally attacked. Whitey Bulger threatened me with a gun. Farther down E. Third Street, Whitey was killing people and burying them in the cellar of a house. Another would-be killer parked at my pumps. A dealer tossed drugs from his car. It was never dull in Southie during the 1970s and 1980s.

This view from the office into the shop shows the small doorway leading into the largest and most secluded rear bay. That is where the Mob wanted to hold its high-stakes poker games. Directly on the other side of the farthest concrete wall was "Wally's" bookie joint.

Neighbor and friend, John Foley, took this shot from his third-floor window. From this very same window, he watched as a car intentionally smash into the gas pumps late one night. He also watched two masked gunmen pull up and shoot another neighbor several times as he parked his car at the gas pumps.

Chapter XXI

Friends In High Places

From a very young age I was aware that John E. Powers, and his wife Dorothy, were my godparents. John is remembered as one of Southie's most revered and powerful political figures. He was President of the Massachusetts Senate for several years as well as clerk of Massachusetts Superior Courts. When I was just a young boy, I remember my mom and I would take the train into downtown Boston from Dorchester and go to the State House. I remember gazing up at its beautiful golden dome. We would approach the reception desk in the office of the President of the Senate. There were always several important-looking men in suits seated there, waiting for an audience with John. My mom would tell the receptionist that John's "godson" was there to see him. We had no appointment, but we would immediately be led into his beautiful office while all others had to wait. I remember being instantly impressed with Mr. Powers. He was not a large man, but he had a big personality that commanded respect while at the same time making you feel very comfortable in his presence. I must have been only seven or eight years old when I asked him straight out one day, "*How did you get to be such a big shot?*" Those were my exact words.

Without hesitation, he led me by the hand over to the wall bookcase next to his desk. It was packed full of very large books. He said to me, "Do you see all these books? I've read every one of them. That's how you get to be a *big shot.*" I remember those fifteen seconds of my life as though they took place yesterday.

When I asked my dad how John E. Powers ended up being my godfather, he told me they became friends many years ago. He said they had sat next to each other at quite a few functions at the South Boston Social Club. Dad also told me that he had sat directly next to John F. Kennedy at one of those club functions. That took place before the then young Kennedy ran for the office of President of the United States. I would have been thrilled to be able to say I had sat next to JFK, but Dad wasn't. He expressed a very strong dislike for the Kennedy family for some reason. I never understood why. He would refer to the Kennedys as "a bunch of crooks." Personally, I see them as having sacrificed much more in service to this country than most families could ever bear. Even though I may not agree with some of his views, I still respect and admire Ted Kennedy for his continued dedication. Regarding John E. Powers, during his early runs for office, my father had donated gasoline to his campaign workers as his contribution. That surprised me because Dad was not a politically active guy. I know for a fact that my father, Vito, had been treated as an outsider for most of his life. Even within his own family, he was treated that way. He had fought hard for all that he had accomplished. His financial support of John E. Powers' campaigns may have been a gamble on his part to become more of an insider. I'm sure Dad had figured out that there might be future benefits to being friends with a powerful political figure. I know Dad was not opposed to calling in a favor from a police officer friend once in a while in order to get a speeding ticket "squashed," as he would put it. We had both Massachusetts State Troopers and Boston Police Officers as regular customers. It's possible that having John E. Powers as a friend might explain why Dad was successful in several permit applications. The majority of our gasoline storage tanks were located under land owned by the City of Boston. He didn't own enough land under which he could install larger fuel tanks without encroaching farther into city property. Special permitting allowed him to expand the underground storage capacity of the gas station. I never heard Dad indicate that he had ever asked for John's help, although I imagine that if needed, his friendship with Mr. Powers couldn't have hurt. Dad had also been able to secure permits to knock down three residential homes in order to expand the shop area. It was most likely easier back in the 1950s to get those types of things accomplished anyway.

As for me, I never personally benefited from my godfather's status, other than the VIP treatment I received during those State House visits as a child. There was just one occasion when I discussed my future plans with John. That took place at his Clerk of Superior Courts office. I was having my usual back problems at the garage, and I was considering a career change. I spoke to him about the possibility of a court officer position. It would have been a very secure job, and it would have provided great benefits. Although I'm sure that job would have been mine if I had really wanted it, John actually advised me against it. He felt that, knowing me the way he did, I would hate the boredom of being stuck in a courtroom day in and day out, year after year. I took his advice and stuck it out at the garage. I knew he was right, and he had my best interests at heart.

The only friendship in high places that I had personally developed was with a wonderful Irish cop I'll call "Paul." I became a good friend with Paul after working on his personal vehicles for several years.

He was single and usually had one of his fantastic-looking girlfriends at his side when he came into the shop. He was a large, well-built man who had Irish written all over him. He took great pride in his vehicles, which I admired. Looking back, I was sort of like the mechanic on the TV series *Seinfeld*. Jerry Seinfeld's mechanic stole his car because he believed Jerry wasn't taking good enough care of it. Similarly, I would scold those who would neglect their cars.

Paul would always greet me with a great big "*Hello there, laddie!*" Like most of my customers, he had faith in me as a mechanic and as an honest businessman. I always prided myself in being more than fair, and I never sold anybody a service or a part they didn't really need. In thinking back, I guess honesty was a luxury I could afford because we owed no mortgage on the business, thanks to my dad's years of hard work. I was thrilled when Paul introduced me to a private police club that was located on K Street. I think I was the only private citizen that was allowed in there to drink. Even when Paul wasn't there, I was allowed in. There were no signs or markings on the reinforced door of the entry. It was located on the first floor of a three-decker residential building, and there was no doorbell, just a peephole. All the members had a key, but I would have to knock on the door. A voice from inside would ask me what I wanted. I would say that "Paul—sent me," and I would immediately be let in. After they got to know my face, they would just open the door and let me in. Cops, in and out of uniform, would be sitting around, having a drink. Sometimes they would be cleaning their guns at the bar or at a table. It reminded me of an old Wild West saloon, with guns visible everywhere. Beers were almost free. I think the price was whatever the beverage cost at the liquor store. It was just a guys' place. I never saw a woman in there during any of my numerous visits. I have to admit, I felt very special being welcomed into this close-knit group. I got to know some great guys in that club.

As friends often do, Paul and I traded handguns one time. I had an antique Colt .38 with a long barrel, and adjustable sights. I hated that gun because it had a hair trigger. If I was in a firing stance, and tried to adjust my grip slightly, the gun would sometimes go off unintentionally if I happened to just *touch* the trigger. He said those features made that gun perfect for him to use on the target range and for competitive shooting. I, in turn, wanted his stainless-steel police model .357 Magnum, which would be perfect protection when I was out in the salt air of the ocean in my boat. The exchange worked out great for us both.

Having a policeman as a friend saved me from big trouble on two occasions. Sometimes, organized criminals had ways of involving unsuspecting people in their illegal activities without the innocent party even realizing it. Sure, there were the open propositions that I had been approached with on several occasions, to which I said "no thanks", but this was different. These were sly thugs who used deceit to get me involved. One morning, a tough-looking tall young man in his mid-twenties brought a fairly new car into my shop. He told me it was his deceased aunt's car, and they were liquidating her estate. "We're trading the car in, but we don't want to trade it with these new tires on it." He pointed to the big pile of junk tires that was sitting in my shop and asked if I would remove the new tires and put a set of the bald ones on. I didn't question his motives and took the job in like I would any other job. The guy left the car with me, jumped on the back of a waiting motorcycle, and drove away. At the time, it was only an eight- or ten-dollar job to change four tires. A couple of hours later, the motorcycle returned.

The guy came walking back in and paid me for the job, plus he handed me an eight-dollar tip! That was very unusual, and I was happy getting paid double the going rate for the job. The very next morning, around 9:00 AM, in came the same guy driving up with another new car. His motorcycle friend was following right behind him. He said he wanted to do the same thing with the tires on this car. Both of the cars he had brought in had New York license plates. I got a little nervous and sensed that something just wasn't right. I believe he could see the uneasiness in my eyes. He explained that this was his uncle's car, and they were trading this one in too. I apprehensively went ahead and did the job. When they returned, I presented the bill for my services. This time, the bill was paid, and I was given a ten-dollar tip! Now I knew for sure that something wasn't right with this situation. Nobody gives this kind of tip for a tire-change job. I knew I didn't want to do any more work for these guys. I tried to hand him the tip back saying, "I don't want this." He refused to take it.

I told him, "I think I know what's going on here, and I'd rather you don't bring any more cars into my shop." He gave me a wise-looking smile and said, "Don't worry about it." He walked away, leaving the tip behind.

On the third morning, I couldn't believe what I was seeing. It was the same pair of guys, with yet another car with NY plates. The requested work was the same as on the previous days. There was no doubt now that I was dealing with the wrong people. For some guys, this would have been a golden opportunity. The money was great, and who knows what this might lead to in the future if I played ball with these guys. All I had to do was play dumb and collect the money. But I just couldn't do it. This was not what my parents brought me up to do. With an instant knot forming in my stomach, I refused the job, saying,

"I told you yesterday that I don't want to do any more tires for you. I don't want to be involved with this." Upon overhearing my refusal to take the job, the guy who was waiting outside on the motorcycle came walking in with an aggressive and determined gait. Stopping just six inches from my face and staring down at me like a crazed drill sergeant, he growled in a deep, raspy voice, "What's the problem?" This second guy was a really intimidating character. I was not as tough on the inside as the facade I had to put forth every day. At this point, I was counting my heartbeats as my chest pounded, hoping it wouldn't stop beating altogether.

These situations always seemed to happen when I was all alone. Trouble was often timed perfectly for when my guys were out to lunch, out on a road job or under a car way out back. It was as if these people were watching, and knew exactly when to come in. I would have felt much safer in refusing that job if my big protective friend Barney or my cop friend Paul happened to be at the shop, but they weren't. This thug had large scars on his bright red face, and when he looked down at me, his eyes resembled cold stones. It's hard to explain, but I could tell that these guys would not hesitate to just slash my throat and drive away. I had seen their type before. They were not the intelligent organized-criminal type. They were the workhorses. These guys had an assignment to accomplish. They were doing the bidding of somebody else without question or regret. I really had no choice but to take that job. As I did their dirty work, I racked my brain trying to figure out how I could get rid of these guys once and for all. I knew I couldn't live like this. I could envision my mom and dad sitting at home, watching an evening news report about how a shop in South Boston had been busted for stripping stolen vehicles from out of state, which was a federal offense. The situation seemed hopeless, until an idea came to me out of nowhere.

The more I thought about it, I felt it was a brilliant idea at that! If my plan worked, it would free me from having any further contact with those guys, and it would not put me in jeopardy of reprisal.

Thankfully, for once, there were other customers in the office when those two thugs arrived that afternoon to pick up the car. That saved me from having to converse with them. They paid the bill and handed me the expected gratuity. As soon as they left, I decided to head down to the police club, hoping to run into Paul. My employees at the shop knew nothing of this whole situation. I told them I was going out for a while, and I didn't know when I would be back. Paul was not at the club when I arrived, but I was glad to hear that they expected him to stop in. I waited and had a couple of beers while pondering the best way to recruit Paul's help with my plan.

Finally, Paul arrived. I was so relieved to see him walk through that door. We were at the bar, and there were a couple of officers sitting there with us, so I asked Paul if I could talk to him for a minute at a table. He saw a serious look on my face and moved to a table without saying a word. Usually when I was with Paul at the club, I was a fun-loving young man out to enjoy a beer. He knew this was a different Tom sitting with him and he said, "What's the trouble, laddie?" I said, "Paul, if I ask you to do me a favor and not ask any questions, will you do it for me?" He replied, "Sure, me lad. What can I do for you?" I began, "Can you get your hands on a detective's car tomorrow morning, a little before 9:00 AM, and just park a little ways up the street from my shop doors, maybe near the post office? That's all I want you to do; just park there for a while. I'll signal you when it's okay to leave." He said, "I can do that." He didn't ask any questions, and as requested, around 8:30 the next morning, he was parked seventy-five yards up the street from the gas station. He was a true friend. Now I was praying that those guys would show up at the usual time of 9:00 AM with another car.

Sure enough, here they came. They drove right past Paul as he sat in the unmarked police car. As the car and the motorcycle pulled up to the garage bay door, I approached the passenger side, and leaned into the open window. With a concerned look on my face, I said to my slimy friend, "I have a funny feeling we're being watched. There has been that same Chevy parked down the road with that guy sitting in it for two days now." The driver glanced in his side view mirror, and Paul was perfectly situated where he could be seen. Before I could even say another word, the scumbag restarted the vehicle and drove off, barely giving me enough time to back my head out of the car. The scary guy on the motorcycle followed him. It had worked like a charm! I was so happy, but more importantly, I was relieved. I looked up the road toward Paul and gave him a "thumbs up" signal and a big smile. He drove away and lightly tooted his horn as he passed by me. We never talked about the situation except for the "thank you" I expressed to him the next time I saw him. Those guys never showed up at the shop again. I did see them come into the I & A Restaurant one night, looking as evil and menacing as ever, but they didn't talk to me. The whole atmosphere in the place changed just knowing they were there and wondering why. They walked right by, just giving me a quick glance as if they didn't know me at all. They looked like they were on a mission, but thankfully it didn't involve me.

The second time that my friendship with Paul helped me out was late one night after I had just left Gavin's Tavern. I certainly would have qualified as being over the legal limit and could have gotten a DUI that night. As I was getting into the Challenger to head home to G Street, a guy that was at the tavern asked me for a ride up the street.

I didn't really know him, but I said "Sure, get in." Along the way, I figured I'd show this stranger what my car could do. I nailed the gas pedal as we left Gavin's. By the time we were passing through the elongated X-shaped intersection at Emerson and Third Streets I must have been hitting close to sixty. As I passed the gas pumps I caught just a glimpse of a white car out of the corner of my eye. It was going in the same direction, but on the other street as I zoomed by in the darkness. Blue lights were immediately flashing in my rear view mirror, and a siren was screaming. I yelled, "Shit!" as I started to shut it down, trying to stop by the end of the next block. The police were right behind me. As I was bringing the car to a halt, my passenger yelled, "What are you doing?" I said, "I'm stopping!" He said, "I've got a pocket full of cocaine!" I had no idea who this guy was or that he was carrying drugs. Before I could completely stop the car, he whipped open the passenger door and jumped out of the moving vehicle, leaving the door wide open! He ran off as fast as he could. I stopped the car just as I reached the front door of Tom English's Tavern. The police car couldn't get past my Challenger on this narrow street with vehicles parked along the curb. I was stopped in the middle of the street, and my fleeing passenger disappeared into the darkness. It was a warm summer night, so there were several guys congregating in front of English's Tavern, drinking. It must have made quite an interesting scene for those bar patrons, seeing my shiny black car roar up the road with the cops in hot pursuit and then to see a guy leap from the moving car and take off running. I got out with my hands in the air in order to show that I wasn't a threat, as the cops approached me with their guns drawn. These encounters with the police were getting to be a far too regular occurrence. They pushed me face forward onto the hood. I yelled at them, "Easy on the car!" After they frisked me and stood me back up, they asked why my friend had run away and who he was. I told them I didn't know him, and I was just giving him a lift up the road from Gavin's. Then they asked me for my license and registration. By this time, Tom English's Tavern had emptied out onto the sidewalk to watch the goings-on. It probably looked like they had bagged Whitey Bulger or some other dangerous criminal by the way it all went down. I handed them my license, and as I walked back to get the registration out of the glove compartment, I turned to one of the cops and nonchalantly asked, "Is Paul—working tonight? He'll vouch for me and tell you that I'm *okay*." When they heard those words, everything changed. It was as if I had told them I was a cop too. Had I stumbled upon a secret code used by undercover? I don't know, but they immediately tossed my license onto the hood of the car, turned around, and walked back to their cruiser. They didn't wait to see my registration, and they appeared to be very irritated as they were leaving me. They never said one word. It was as if I had hit a switch that made them instantly retreat to their vehicle. They waited patiently for me to move my car, which I pulled into a nearby parking spot across from the tavern.

As the police car drove away, I figured this was a great opportunity to go into Tom English's Tavern for a drink. I had never been in there before. I felt it was very unlikely that anyone in the bar would bother me as a stranger after having seen what just took place outside. They must have wondered who the hell I was and what the hell I had done in order to get rid of those cops like that. I was wondering the same thing myself. I will admit that it felt pretty cool! Thanks again, Paul.

John E. Powers and his wife Dorothy, my godparents, enjoy a meal at our Dorchester home on the day of my Christening in 1952.

To their right are Mom, Grandma Cirignano, and my brother John.

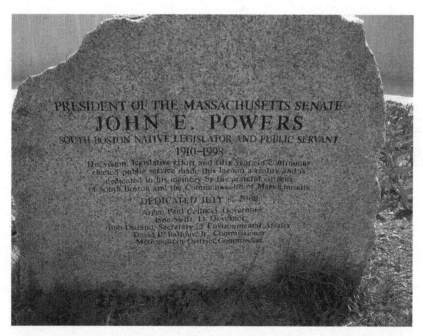

This memorial to John E. Powers is located on Day Boulevard, at Castle Island's "Sugar Bowl" pathway entrance, in South Boston.

John and Dorothy hold their new godson

Southie was home to a nightclub named Patcheesi's.
Barney and I would see many of the Stanley Cup Champion
Boston Bruins at the club. Above, we are visiting with goaltender
Jerry Cheevers, and below, I was thrilled to be hanging out with
Johnny "Pie" McKenzie. To me, he was the toughest guy on skates.

Ali Fiumedoro: candidate, inventor,
musician. At St. Patrick's Day
Parade. March, 1987

Photo courtesy of Chris Lovett. www.NNNonline.org
My Mom's brother, our Uncle Ali, was a well known resident of
South Boston and a regular at the annual parade. Here he is
shown playing an instrument that he invented. Ali held numerous
US patents and was a master magician, having developed many
amazing illusions. Unfortunately, he was unsuccessful in his
political campaign to become mayor of Boston.

Chapter XXII

Danger On The High Seas

By the spring of 1980, I had recovered nicely from my surgery and it was time to reclaim my independence. Interest rates on home mortgages were averaging an unbelievable 13-14% at the time. Thankfully, I had always made a habit of saving, so I had a nice chunk of change to use as a down payment. I found a broken-down cottage-type house on the water in Weymouth Landing. After two attempts spanning several months, the seller finally accepted my $30,000 offer. With its assumable VA mortgage at a bargain rate of 7.5%, the payments were about the same amount as my rent would be if I moved back to Southie. So, I figured it would be better to own than rent. The house was located on a small saltwater inlet called Mill Cove. Looking to the left over the water from the backyard was the Quincy Ship Yard. It was interesting watching the huge ships from all around the world come in for repairs. The sun would set directly next to the huge crane at the yard. That crane, which was nicknamed "Goliath," also served as a landmark whenever I would fly into Boston's Logan Airport after being away on vacation. I could spot the crane as we circled around Boston, and using the shipyard as a marker, I could find and point directly to that little house on the shoreline.

It was a tiny lot with a tiny house, but I had always wanted to live on the water. My dad did not hesitate to give me his opinion when I showed him the house. He said, "You've got rocks in your head buying this house!" I did not let that deter me. I told him I didn't care if there was only a tent on this piece of land. I would still buy it. Going ahead with that purchase ended up being one of the best moves I have ever made. All of my friends and relatives loved to visit there because they could go swimming, fishing, boating, or clam digging all the time. There were swans, ducks and an occasional seal that would visit our dock. Around that same time in my life, I started dating the girl I would eventually marry. Diane had worked at King's Department Store when I was introduced to her, and then she worked at the VA Hospital in Brockton. Both of our lives were taking turns for the better. In May of 1984, Diane and I were married. We were living at the Weymouth house and hard at work remodeling it with every available dollar. Once we had the house fixed up, my dad, ironically, was the one who enjoyed being there the most. I was so glad I had listened to nobody but myself with regard to buying that house.

Soon after moving in, I bought a boat. The dream of somehow being able to commute to work by boat was very enticing to me, and it would soon become a reality. I started looking at charts of the coastline in hopes of mapping a route and scoping out a place to park the boat once I got into South Boston. Any commuting trips would also have to be carefully coordinated with the tides. The cove behind my house was reduced to a mudflat at low tide, yet at high tide the water was ten feet deep at the end of the ninety-foot dock that I built. My pal Robbie clued me in on a spot where I could park my boat once I arrived in Southie. It was located near the end of Fort Point Channel, just on the other side of Castle Island. The channel passed directly behind the Boston Edison Electric plant, which uses the saltwater for cooling.

Robbie referred to this mooring spot as the "Gypsy Yacht Club" because anybody could tie up there. It consisted of an abandoned and dilapidated dock, if you could even call it that. Robbie had used this spot after somebody "gave" him a twenty-five-foot boat for free. He had kept his boat there for a while until, one night, it mysteriously caught fire and burned up. My free Boston mooring place was located where the channel met up with Summer Street. Once I tied up to the dock, which was no more than debris lashed together, I would have to climb around eight to ten feet up to the street using a makeshift ladder that somebody had nailed together years ago. I was so excited because this would work out great for me! I could tie up there and walk around a quarter mile to the gas station. It would surely be more enjoyable and more adventurous than fighting the bumper-to-bumper traffic on the Southeast Expressway.

The first boat that I purchased was a sixteen-foot open aluminum hull with a forty horsepower outboard motor. It was large enough for bay travel, and it was within my price range, cheap.

My virgin voyage into Southie by boat was absolutely wonderful. I don't think I ever felt more alive having fulfilled my small dream of commuting by sea. Whenever the weather and the tide schedule allowed, I would go to work by boat. Usually, as I would walk the short distance from the boat to the garage, somebody I knew would recognize me and offer me a ride to work. After several such uneventful commutes, I had once again enjoyed a morning cruise into work on the boat. Upon closing up the shop, I decided to stop for a beer with my friends Marshall and Barney. During the day, unexpected storms had been brewing of which I was unaware. As Barney and Marshall were dropping me off at my boat, we all noticed that the sky off in the distance was as black as it could get. Warning me not to take the boat home, each of my friends offered to drive me to Weymouth and then pick me up the next day to get to work. The water was as calm as could be where we were, and it looked to me as if those storm clouds were pretty far off in the distance. I decided I could make it home before the storm reached me. I really didn't want to leave my boat there overnight, for fear it would get stolen or meet the same fate that Robbie's boat had met. Ignoring my friends' insistent pleadings that I not risk it, I stubbornly headed out. I didn't get far from the opening of Fort Point Channel to the open harbor when I realized that the storm was approaching much more quickly than I ever thought it would. I brought the boat to full speed, heading directly into the approaching storm. Within minutes, the wind picked up and pretty large swells started to form. The sky had quickly turned black and ominous directly above me. It wasn't until I was startled by the first flash of lightning and heard the clap of thunder that immediately followed that I got really nervous. By the time I had only reached the halfway point to home, conditions had turned much worse! By then, the sky was midnight black, frighteningly black. The rain was coming down so hard that it hurt my face as I tried to race home. The waves and lightning were the scariest I had ever experienced. As the rain changed to hail, I became downright scared. By now, the waves were six to eight feet high, towering over my small open boat. I couldn't even see land unless for a split second I was on the crest of a wave, but even then, the heavy and painful precipitation made it impossible to distinguish any landmarks.

The constant lightning slamming the water was by far the most frightening thing. Deafening claps of thunder sounded all around the boat, and I never felt so all alone and helpless in my life. I kept anticipating that the very next bolt of lightning was going to hit me directly in the head for certain. I started thinking of things like, "They make electric wire out of aluminum. I'm the tallest object out here! At least I won't feel a thing when the lightning hits me.

There's *no way* I'm going to make it home." I had no choice but to continue trying to make my way through the storm. Then, as quickly as conditions had turned deadly, things started to turn around. I saw a glimmer of actual sunlight break through a crack in the clouds ahead of me. The wind started to calm, and the waves were reducing. I was soaked and scared, but alive!

Marshall and Barney had called my house out of concern after I left South Boston. They saw that the storm had come in quickly after I left them and they were really worried. The fact that I hadn't made it home by the time they called only heightened Diane's anxiety. She was frantic with worry and moments from calling the U.S. Coast Guard when I finally came into sight and pulled up to our dock. We were both relieved that I had made it home, yet she still managed to muster up a good tongue lashing for me.

After that harrowing experience in the open aluminum boat, I bought a faster and what I thought would be a safer fiberglass boat. The new boat offered more stability and protection from the elements. It had an eighty-five horsepower engine, which was safer for being out on the ocean. Shortly after buying the "safer" new boat, the tides were just right for a nighttime cruise, so I called my buddy Barney and invited him to go out with me. I asked him what he felt like drinking that evening and he suggested 7 and 7s. The sun was setting as I waited for Barn and loaded the boat for our trip. I packed nuts and chips to munch on, and I placed the cooler in the boat. When Barney arrived, off we went into the night. It was particularly dark with virtually no moonlight, but it was warm, and the water was as calm as could be. It couldn't have been more perfect for cruising as we made our way out into Boston Harbor. A few minutes into our trip Barney decided it was time to prepare a couple of drinks. He reached into the cooler and pulled two insulated mugs and a bottle of Seagram's 7 from the ice. He asked, "Where's the 7-up?" I said, "Damn! I forgot to pack it!" He said "No problem." We would just make do with whiskey on the rocks. I didn't make a habit out of drinking straight whiskey, and it wasn't long before we were both feeling pretty buzzed. Drinking whiskey in this manner is like drinking "liquid stupidity." With no headlights on the boat, it wasn't long before we were blindly blasting around the inland waters, dodging the islands of Boston Harbor. We were yahooing and horsing around at full speed.

As we took turns "piloting" the boat as Barney called it, we were having the best of times. With the tide on its way out, we had time for one last full-blast ride before heading in. I was at the helm, feeling invincible with the throttle wide open. We were speeding through the darkness, feeling as good as could be. Barney and I were looking toward each other, laughing and joking, when we both happened to turn forward at the same exact moment. Horror struck as we saw a huge rock formation directly in our path! We both spotted this menacing and potentially deadly island less than a hundred feet in front of us. We were only a second or two away from slamming into it! There were no lights on this rock formation. There were no warning devices of any kind. It was just a huge pile of boulders, twenty feet high and fifty feet wide, just sitting there, sticking out of the water in the middle of nowhere. In a fraction of a second I *whipped* the wheel all the way to the right and slammed the throttle to the off position. The boat turned onto its right-side rail, almost flipping over, and along with its scared shitless riders, the boat veered away, missing the jagged rocks by no more than a couple of yards. Barney and I fell silent, each of us unable to speak for several seconds. The first words out of our mouths were "Oh my god!" "What the f—!" Had I turned and faced forward *one instant* later, we would have been found the next morning, splattered on those rocks, if we were ever found at all.

We idled our way back to my house without saying much. It was just one more instance of my making a dumb choice. It was a choice that came close to ending our two lives. That night, I learned a lesson the hard way. From that time on, I left the whiskey at home and respected the ocean at night by never speeding in the dark again. Shortly after that very close call, I happened to be looking over a chart that a friend had of the coastal waters near Boston. I spotted that exact rock formation. It is appropriately named "Dead Man's Island", or "Dead Man's Rock." I can't remember which. I haven't been able to find it on several other charts I've examined, probably due to its small size.

When Barney and I were single, we always seemed to get into mischief when we were out on the water together. One night we decided to go out on a Boston Harbor Booze Cruise. Those cruises took place on large commercial vessels that held a couple of hundred passengers. For a reasonable fee, the boat would take you out in the harbor for an evening of drinks and music. Toward the end of the cruise, Barney and I were on the bottom deck and the only bar still serving cocktails was on the second level. With the boat as crowded as it was, it was impossible to get up the stairway to get a drink without a struggle. I was trying to figure out an easy way to get to the bar when I came up with an alcohol-inspired idea that could have proven to be ill-fated. With my secret plan in mind, I suggested to Barney, "We should have one last drink before the boat pulls into shore. Let's have a race to the bar, and the last one there buys the drinks." He eagerly agreed, and wasting no time, he immediately took off en-route to the bar. My scheme was ready to be put into action. I stood right where I was for a few seconds, as Barney struggled to make his way toward the crowded stairway. He glanced back at me with a puzzled look, wondering why I was just standing there wasting time. As soon as he was out of sight, I climbed up onto the railing next to me and grabbed the chain-link fencing that hung down from up above. They had installed this fencing in order to block off most of the opening between the lower deck and the top of the railing on the second level. It was there as a safety measure to keep people from falling overboard, but it also served me in another unintended way. It made a great ladder! I climbed my way up on the outside of the ship to the second level as we steamed along at a fast clip back to shore. During my climb, I paused and looked down at the passing black water in the darkness far below me. I remember thinking, "With all the noise of the music and the people, I better not fall off because they will never know I went overboard." I made it to the top deck in about twenty seconds. There was no shortage of confused looks from the nearby passengers as I climbed over the railing. They were probably thinking, *where the hell did this guy come from*? I jumped onto the deck and walked over to the bar. About twenty seconds later, Barney appeared and he was all out of breath. He was totally confused as to how I could have possibly gotten to the bar before him. As he bought our final drinks of the evening, I told him, "I climbed up on the outside of the ship." He looked at me, gave me one of his signature laughs, and said, "*Yeah, right!*" He never did believe me about that.

Another very close call I had involving the ocean resulted from yet another instance of poor judgment. This time, it happened from the air. I owned a "ParaPlane" which is a twin-engine, single-seat aircraft. It is a type of aircraft categorized as an ultralight. Because they are under a certain weight limit, weighing only a few hundred pounds, they do not require a pilot's license. Ultralights are a blast to fly. If you can get up high enough, and far enough away from obstacles, they are even more fun! I had flown my ParaPlane a couple of times at the field where I purchased it. The manufacturer mandated that buyers take lessons and do solo flights prior to taking the planes home.

I must admit, going up alone for the very first time was quite scary. I realized that nobody would be there to take over the controls if I screwed up. Surprisingly, I became comfortable piloting the ParaPlane very quickly. On my second flight, I took the plane up to an altitude of a few thousand feet. The sky was so clear that I could see the White Mountains in New Hampshire, and the Atlantic Ocean, all the way from where I was flying, in central Massachusetts. It was truly a hypnotic sensation being up there all alone, just guiding the plane wherever I wanted it to go. During that flight, my instructor actually had to break me out of a trance. He had to yell loudly over the two-way radio in my helmet's headset in order to get me to come back down to earth. I was totally oblivious to the fact that he was talking to me and giving me flight instructions. Only when he raised his voice did I realize someone wanted my attention.

The one aspect of my ultralight hobby that I disliked was that I had to break the aircraft down and transport it to a suitable take-off and landing strip. I couldn't just jump on it and fly from my back yard. The flight manual specified a field with a minimum of three hundred feet of unobstructed area; in other words, a football field. I was determined to find a way to fly it from somewhere near my home where I wouldn't have to load it in a vehicle and transport it. There was a Little League baseball diamond located a few hundred feet from our house in Weymouth. Although it was nowhere near three hundred feet long in itself, the field ended at the waterfront where there was a steep drop off to the water. I figured that if I could get the wheels off the ground by the time I got to the outfield, I would be just fine heading out over the saltwater of the cove. The flight was planned for early in the morning, so there should be no crosswind to contend with which might prevent me from being able to go straight out over the water. My friend Marshall came to see me take off and I had arranged for a couple of neighbors to help me push the plane over to the baseball field. Everyone was excited, and I was confident that I could pull this off. Coming in for a landing in such a small area would be extremely tricky, but I was going to worry about one thing at a time. First, I needed to get up in the air. I would worry about getting back down later. I always felt that if I overanalyzed everything I wanted to do, I would eventually talk myself out of taking *any* chances at all in life.

As planned, not long after sunrise, the winds of the day had not had time to build. I bid farewell to Diane as she slept in. She had decided she didn't want to watch what she considered an ill-advised take-off attempt. I think she actually used stronger words than those when I told her what I was going to try. But nonetheless, she raised her head off the pillow and said, "Have a good flight."

Quite a group of friends and neighbors had gathered to help me launch the plane and give me moral support that morning. We backed the plane up to the far edge of the field. I started the two engines and strapped myself in with the seatbelt, shoulder harness, and put on my helmet. It was time to give it a try. I gave both engines full throttle as my friends guided the wing until I got moving. It was as if everything was happening in slow motion. The engines roared loudly, and I was going faster and faster. The edge of the field and the ocean were approaching, but I was still not in the air. I wouldn't allow myself to wimp out. I was mentally committed. I knew I could make it!

Later, my friends told me they were all yelling, "Shut it down! Shut it down!" as I approached the end of the field. They thought I wasn't going to make it off the ground in time. Of course, I couldn't hear them over the engine noise. It wouldn't have mattered if I had heard them. I had dreamt about trying this for way too long to just give up. I wasn't about to shut anything down.

About ten feet from the end of the grassy field, I finally saw the front wheel lift off the ground! The rear wheels followed. Just in time, I was up in the air, and smiling! I gained altitude as I exited the field and flew over the rocks of the seawall as it sloped down to the water's edge. I truly felt I had safely achieved my goal as I reached twenty and then thirty feet of altitude. Suddenly, a sick feeling set in. You know—the feeling that takes over your gut the moment you realize things are about to go downhill fast. As I got farther out over the cold seawater, I felt a sinking sensation, in more ways than one. I was losing my lift. I had failed to take into consideration one of the basic fundamentals of flight. Air over a warm grassy field will rise, giving lift. Air over cold ocean water will fall, causing down drafts as the air cools. Even with both engines at full throttle, I was losing altitude. My heart sank with disappointment. There was nothing I could do. Lower and lower I went, and I realized it was hopeless. I was going to crash. If I hit the water with those propellers spinning at thousands of revolutions per minute, they would splinter into hundreds of pieces and possibly hurt or kill me. I shut down the two ignition switches and killed both engines just prior to hitting the water. I also took in a really deep breath. The moment I crashed, the aircraft flipped upside down and sank like a rock to the bottom. It flipped over because the heavy engines were mounted up high, right behind my seat.

I came to rest on the rocks of the ocean floor, hanging upside down, still strapped in with a shoulder harness, seatbelt, and wearing my helmet. Thankfully, I was only in ten to twelve feet of water, although it was ice cold. I knew that if I panicked and fumbled while trying to undo all the clasps of my safety gear I was a goner. I could only hold my breath for so long and I thought to myself, "Everything better go smoothly." While I was underwater, restrained and holding my breath, time seemed to stand still. I experienced a very eerie feeling of being *all alone*. It was totally different from the wonderful, euphoric, *all alone* feeling I had experienced while flying the ParaPlane at three thousand feet. In the darkness and silence of being underwater, I blindly felt around for the release clasps and easily found them. It was something I had practiced, just in case the need ever arose. I undid my shoulder restraints first and then my seatbelt. Thankfully, all buckles and straps released without a problem and I swam away from my seat. During my first attempt to surface, I found myself trapped under the fabric wing, so I dove back down and swam to the side until I could safely surface. That was a move I remembered from reading the section of the flight manual titled, "In the event of a water landing." My friends were relieved and clapping when my white helmet broke the surface of the water. I was a little surprised that everyone was still nice and dry on shore, watching. Marshall said he was just about to jump in and assist me when he saw me come to the surface. He asked me how I knew enough to shut down the engines before hitting the water, and I said, "I just knew I should."

The rest of the day was spent undoing the damage that my failed attempt had caused. Wearing a long face, I walked home by myself to get a rope. While at the house, I checked on Diane in the bedroom. She raised her head off her pillow once again and saw that I was soaked from head to toe. She smiled and jokingly said, "How was your flight?" That was her way of saying, "I told you that was a stupid idea." I returned her smile and told her I would fill her in on the details after I dragged the plane out of the water. I headed back to the field.

I was feeling quite downhearted as I got back into the cold water. I dove down and tied the rope to the plane so my friends and I could drag it out of the bay. When I got it back to my yard, I had to flush and wash out everything with fresh water. I dried the engines out, got them running, and ran them until they were hot enough to get rid of any residual moisture.

Just to be safe, I decided to ship both engines back to the factory and have them completely rebuilt and upgraded to "high performance." The extra few horsepower available with the high performance upgrade would have been enough to keep me in the air. The next time I flew, I wanted to make sure I would have that power at my disposal. When my friend Lyle came into the shop in Southie and saw me packing up the engines for shipment, he offered to take care of that for me. He summoned a tractor-trailer truck right to my shop to pick up the engines. He took care of transporting them out of state and back again, at no cost to me. He had friends in all trades. Within a couple of months the motors were back from the factory. Everything was up and running again, actually better than new, and the ParaPlane was ready to fly another day.

After that accident, I happened to see the movie *An Officer and A Gentleman*. There is a segment in that movie that *exactly* reenacted what I had to do in the water the day of my crash. The scene shows the pilot trainees sliding down a ramp while strapped into an ejection seat and wearing flight gear and helmets. Their seats hit the pool water and immediately flip upside down as they sink to the bottom. They have to undo all their safety straps and swim to the surface. I don't think anybody knows how they will react in a situation like that. With all the training in the world, a person may still panic.

The next attempted flight was over the dry streets of a not-yet-developed section of Cape Coral, Florida. This time I got up with no problem, except for one thing. The steering was totally unresponsive. Some lines had inadvertently gotten crossed during reassembly after transporting the plane to Florida. Once I was up in the air I realized that the ParaPlane was flying wherever it wanted to go, which was in large circles to the left. I was determined to get in as much airtime as I possibly could before landing. I just kept flying the plane at a low altitude and let it go wherever it wanted to go. Eventually, I had to put it down because of an approaching bank of tall pine trees. When I got her home, I straightened out the steering lines. Later, while viewing a videotape of that flight, I could actually see that the front edge of the wing was folding under while I was in the air. I was lucky it hadn't completely folded. If it had, I would have dropped like a stone from the sky.

Not every memorable experience on the water was life threatening. One unfortunate episode was extremely memorable just the same. Diane and I had scheduled a big Fourth of July party that was to take place outside by the waterfront in our yard. We had to plan it as an outside gathering because the house could only accommodate a few people inside. The invitations were out, and we hoped for good weather.

I planned to cook out on the grill, and Diane made delicious desserts. She also had prepared an extra large fruit salad for our thirty-or-so expected guests. She used all the freshest ingredients, including cherries, watermelon, blueberries, grapes, bananas, cantaloupe, and pineapple. That fruit salad looked absolutely wonderful as it sat there in a great big bowl in the fridge.

Unfortunately, we were in for a disappointment on the Sunday morning of the party. It started raining early and it was obvious that it wasn't going to let up. The phone started to ring with cancellations.

As it turned out, only a couple of the people we had invited showed up. We had all this food and very few people to eat it. But with the friends that did show up, we had a really good time.

I sampled some of Diane's delicious fruit salad during the morning, and I got hooked on it. As the day progressed, I couldn't pass the refrigerator without filling up my bowl. I would enjoy a large serving, and before long, I was back, filling my bowl again. Diane warned me saying, "You really shouldn't overdo it with that fruit salad!" Defending myself, I replied to her more than once that day saying, "Fruit salad needs to be eaten when it's fresh. I don't want it to go to waste!" For supper that night, I had more fruit salad. Finito! It was all gone.

Well, the following morning, the weather was exceptionally nice, and the tides were perfectly timed in order for me to commute to Southie in the aluminum boat. I was glad I wouldn't have to fight traffic on the expressway with the slight hangover I had earned from the previous day. I kissed Diane goodbye and headed out from my dock for what should have been an uneventful ride to work.

I was cruising along, gently bouncing over the small waves in the harbor and had made it about halfway to Southie. Suddenly, I started to hear and feel a horrible rumbling in my stomach. It came on me so quickly it was as if there was something *alien and alive* in there. I had no idea what could possibly be going on inside me. Within a minute or so, the rumble had turned into excruciating cramps. I realized then that I had to go to the bathroom very badly! This was a bad situation to be in. With no facilities on the boat and miles of water ahead of me, I prayed I would make it to shore and to the gas station in time. When I arrived at my usual berth at the "Gypsy Yacht Club," I thought I just might be able to make it into work to relieve myself. Even trying to walk there would be pressing my luck, but what choice did I have? You can't hang over the side of a lightweight aluminum boat because it would probably tip over. By this time, I was in absolute agony when making even the slightest movement.

I quickly tied up the boat and rushed to get to the ladder so I could climb up to the street. I couldn't believe my eyes when I got to my usual exit spot and found that somebody had *stolen the ladder*! It was gone, and there was no way for me to get up to the street ten feet above me. There could not have been a worse time for this to happen. The situation was quickly turning into a nightmare, and I had no more time to spare. I looked up and saw nicely dressed men and women scurrying along the sidewalk above me on their way to their office jobs. Nobody seemed to be paying much attention to me, thank goodness. Approximately forty feet to my right was a small, but legitimate yacht club where a man, two young girls, and a little boy were walking down the long ramp to their yacht. The kids were all dressed in matching white outfits. They were busy loading their expensive yacht with goodies for a day of cruising. I was in plain sight of all of these people, and the time for procrastination had expired. I could either take some drastic action right at that moment or make a horrible mess of myself.

I desperately surveyed the boat, looking for some kind of vessel in which to do nature's most primitive deed. The only thing I had that might work was a huge funnel. It was the one I used to put gasoline in the motor. The funnel was probably ten inches across at the top, and a foot tall. Being the ingenious guy that I am, I ripped a small piece off of a rag and stuffed it inside the funnel to block the exit hole. Pretending that I was working on my fishing rod, I dropped my drawers and squatted down onto the large improvised funnel. It was a great fit! I held what was left of the rag in front of me in one hand, and a fishing pole with the other, trying to cover up as much as possible as I sat there on the funnel.

I prayed that nobody would notice what I was really up to. I had squatted not a second too soon. What exited my body was like nothing I had ever seen before. Molasses from another planet instantly filled the funnel to the brim. I was *so relieved* and *so proud* that I had pulled this off!

With my pants still down around my ankles, I decided to rise up just a couple of inches off my self-made toilet and clean myself with the rag before pulling my pants up. My relief immediately turned to disaster. I forgot that I was sitting on a funnel, which had a point on the end. It would not stand up on its own. Of course, it could have fallen backward, and that would have been wonderful. But with my trusty rag in one hand, and the fishing pole in the other, I helplessly watched as the overflowing funnel decided to tip forward, right into my pants, which were still down around my ankles. It was a bull's-eye! The disgusting contents of the funnel now filled my pants like a pool of bubbling toxic waste.

I froze in disbelief as I cursed loudly, **"F—! Now what do I do?"** I looked around at the Boston Harbor water surrounding my boat, thinking maybe I should just throw modesty to the wind and wash the pants off in the ocean water. Unfortunately, Boston was still pumping raw sewage into the harbor back in those days and the scummy film on that water looked no more appealing than what was in my pants. There were all sorts of niceties floating along next to the boat, which included, but were not limited to, a couple of dead fish, a dead rat, and some undesirable latex items. Also, some people who were close by had heard my uncontrollable loud cursing and were now staring down, checking out the situation. It was absolutely awful.

I said to myself, "Oh my god! I have no choice but to pull my pants up as they are!" I couldn't just stay there, squatted down, staring at the stuff in my pants with people looking on. Pulling up those pants was the most unpleasant process to endure. It was a truly horrible experience. The molasses-like substance was oozing down my legs and out of my pant legs, but what else could I have done?

Now I was faced with the previous problem of getting up to the street with no ladder. If this were to happen to me now, all I would have done was call one of the guys that worked for me on my cell phone, and told them to open up the shop. I could have just turned around and headed back home in the boat. Unfortunately, this took place, once again, BC (before cell phones). Somebody needed to open the shop, and I had no way to reach anyone.

My only way up to the street was to leap three feet over the water to a massive pylon, and climb up. The ancient pole was thick with smelly green sea slime that had built up from the tides going in and out, year after year. I had no choice. I took the leap! I was now wrapped around and bear-hugging the slimy monster of a post. I began shimmying up, using barnacles and protruding spikes to work my way up the thick log. When I finally made it up to the street, I was an awful sight. I was cut and bleeding, covered from face to feet in green slime, and had *crap* running out of my pants. This was the roughest start to a day that I had ever had. I began the quarter mile stroll to work, walking with my legs spread apart because of the utter discomfort caused by what was in my pants. People who happened to be approaching me on the same side of the road got within a hundred feet of me and crossed over to the other side. They stared in disbelief. Certainly, they had never seen a sight like me before. I looked like the "Creature from the Black Lagoon," and my mood was not much better. I got about halfway to the shop when a pickup truck slowly passed by me. The driver stared, trying to figure out what he was looking at. Then the truck turned around and came back.

I was so glad to see that it was my friend Chad. He had somehow recognized me. As he pulled up across the street, he yelled out, "*Tom! What the hell happened to you?*" I walked over and said, "Please! Just get me to work. I'll tell you later." Laughing, he said, "There's *no way* your gonna sit in here with me!" He told me to get into the back body of his pickup, and he took me to the shop.

By now, I was forty-five minutes late for the opening of the gas station. This happened during a time when I had lots of commercial accounts, and most of their vehicles gassed up bright and early each morning, before my mechanics would come to work. As Chad and I drove up, I saw that there were trucks lined up all the way down the street to the post office. Although I knew all those impatient drivers very well, they just stared at me and said nothing as I climbed out of the back of Chad's pickup. They had never seen me looking like *this* before. It's safe to say I looked like *shit*. I threw them the keys to the gas pumps and said, "Take care of yourselves." Thank God I had spare clothes and a place to wash up at the garage. I placed all the clothes I had worn that morning in three layers of plastic bags, and in the barrel they went. I was really glad that my good friend, Tony, was standing by the door waiting for me when I got to the shop. He made sure everyone signed for their gas as I was cleaning up.

Whenever I took the boat to work, Diane wanted me to call her when I arrived at the shop, so she wouldn't have to worry. After things were under control and everybody at the shop had their fill of laughter, I called my wife at her work. When she got on the line, she already knew I was calling later than usual. All I said to her was, "Guess what happened to me during the boat ride to work this morning? Remember all the fruit salad I ate yesterday?" That's all I had to say. She fell into uncontrollable laughter on the phone. I told her I'd fill her in on all the juicy details when I got home. As I hung up, she was still laughing so hard, she was unable to converse with me.

Even after all these years, people still want me to tell the "Fruit Salad Story" at family gatherings, or while sitting around a campfire. They laugh all over again. My sister Fran, from Colorado, was visiting us one summer at the house in Weymouth. After hearing this account, she actually made me drive her into South Boston because she had to see the spot where I had parked my boat that day. She also wanted to see the road I was on as I walked to work and where Chad had picked me up. I drove her in, and I showed her. We laughed all the way in and all the way back home. The moral of the story is "everything in moderation." Even the healthy stuff!

Drying out the ultralight in my yard after the crash in the ocean

Pictured here is my wife Diane. I was *hooked* on her the moment I met her.
Several changes for the better mysteriously took place after meeting Diane.
The traffic tickets stopped, the car crashes stopped, and with
her insightful input, the excessive drinking faded away. I still
remember how to have a good time, but now I have somebody to
help pull in the reins a bit when necessary. On the other hand, my
adventurous side has been good for her as well.

Chapter XXIII

Mid-1980s: Craziest Time Ever In Southie

Certain customers and friends from my Southie days will always remain in my memory. There was one woman especially that I will never forget. She was a very nice, hardworking middle-aged woman. Regardless of how bad things might be going for her, she always had a ready smile for me. Over time, I felt a strong connection between us as if we were family. She had a daughter and a son, both in their twenties, and they were still living at home with her. For all the years I had known her, "Helen" had old cars that needed a lot of my attention. She had consistently worked at least two jobs to support her family. I always took special care of her car and gave her a few price breaks that she never knew about. I would think about how I would want my mother to be treated if she was ever in such a tough situation. I would sometimes install an entire new set of spark plugs and tell Helen I had replaced only one. When my dad would notice me doing things like that, he would tell me, "You'll never be a businessman." But Dad's deeds spoke louder than his words. I noticed that he had a soft spot in his heart for certain people too, which he tried to hide. Maybe he thought to show compassion around me was to show weakness. I saw through his tough façade and learned well.

Helen never made any mention of a husband, so I assumed that he was long gone. Her daughter, who I'll call "Angel", was very nice. That young lady enlightened me to the fact that my occasional heavy drinking was having a negative effect on me. Like many of my more familiar customers, Angel put up with my nasty moods, until one day she said to me, "You were out drinking a couple of days ago, weren't you?" Puzzled by her comment, I replied, "Yes, I was! How can you tell?" She said, "You're going through alcohol withdrawal and you're being nasty to everyone." When I realized that she was right, I decided to attend an AA meeting. Listening to the stories of those people opened my eyes. I realized that I had better start to curb my excessive drinking, which I did. We were that close that Angel was able to tell me something like that without me taking offense. Later, I thanked her for her observation and candor. I had never associated drinking, and my occasional nasty moods as being related. I would soon find out that this girl was very familiar with the effects of substance abuse and addiction, and she could easily recognize the signs.

Many times, Helen would bring her car in for service and have one of the kids pick it up at the end of the day, while she was still at work. One day when her son "Red" came in to pick up her car, he said to me, "Do me a favor and add forty or fifty dollars to Mom's bill. We can split the extra money. She'll never know." I was flabbergasted. I asked him if he was joking, and he said he wasn't. I got really upset and called him a few choice names. I asked him how he could even think of doing such a thing to his own mother. The thought of a son capable of even requesting such a thing was totally foreign to me. I told him to take the car and leave before I let my anger get the best of me.

That incident bothered me so much that after seeing Helen a couple of more times, I felt compelled to warn her about her son.

I just had to do it. She didn't deserve to be treated this way. I said to her, "Helen, I have to tell you something that's going to be very hard to hear. You can't trust your son. He tried to have me pad your bill so he could have some of the extra money. I don't understand how he could do this. I'm very sorry to have to tell you this, but I just had to." With a solemn look on her face she said, "I already know that, Tom, but thanks for telling me." A short time later, her daughter came in for gas and said her mom told her what happened. She told me her brother was a heroin addict, and he had stolen from them both several times before. He had even taken their TV and stereo from their house one time and sold them on the street in order to get his drug money. Her mom just didn't have the heart to throw him out. This was the first time I had seen, firsthand, just how far an addict would go in order to supply a habit. It was a sad education. When drugs take control, you can't trust anybody.

About a year later, up drove Helen in a brand new Chrysler! It was the very first new car she had ever owned, and she was so proud of it. I congratulated her and told her how happy I was for her. The very next day, her redheaded pride and joy drove her new car in for gas. He charged the gas to her tab, of course. As I was pumping the fuel, I happened to glance down at the tires. I couldn't believe my eyes! All four tires were completely bald. That disgusting excuse for a son had sold his mother's brand-new tires, rims and all, right off of her two-day old car. I'm sure he did this in order to get a fix. She now had bald tires and old beaten-up rims. It saddened me so much. The next time Helen came in for gas I asked her if she knew about her tires. She said, "What about my tires?" She hadn't even noticed. She got out of the car and stared down at the wheels. I saw the look of desperation and sadness appear on her face, and it was tough to watch. How absolutely heartbreaking it must be to realize that your own child is working against you.

It wasn't long after that when Helen drove into the station, lacking her usual warm smile and greeting. She told me she was there to say goodbye to me. I asked her, "What do you mean? Where are you going?" With tears in her eyes, she said, "I can't stay here anymore, Tom. I have to get away from my son. I've done all I can possibly do for him, but I'm done. I'm not telling anyone where I'm going, not even you. I haven't told a soul. I don't want him to ever be able to find me." I was glad that she had decided to move on and start living her life free from this awful scourge. At the same time, I knew I would miss her. She finally did let me know which state she was headed to, but that was all she would say. I gave her a big hug, wished her the best of luck, and gassed her up for one last time. I never saw or heard from Helen again.

I knew that drugs could change a person from a Dr. Jekyll to a Mr. Hyde. I had seen my very best friend from high school ruin his life with drugs. The change in him happened unbelievably fast. One week we were happy seniors, skipping high school together to go fishing at the reservoir behind the Colbert School. The next week, after somebody had given him some kind of hallucinogenic drug to try, he was up in a tree, laughing hysterically and making no sense at all. He refused to come down and was totally out of control. It was quite scary to see. He had no idea where he was or what the hell he was doing. Seeing his frightening exhibition was enough to keep me from ever getting into those types of drugs. We suddenly went our separate ways as he continued to experiment with acid and mescaline, which were readily available during the 1970s. Before long, the person I knew and loved hanging out with, was no more. There was a total, almost-instant transformation. He began physically attacking people with no provocation, I imagine out of paranoia. After beating up his girlfriend pretty badly, he had to be institutionalized.

Sadly, he has been in treatment and living in halfway houses ever since. He was a wonderful, caring friend until that happened. Something snapped that never went back in place. You might say, that scared me straight. Drinking and smoking caused enough trouble, and they were bad enough habits for me. Thinking back, one of the things I regret most about the past is that I didn't do *something* to intervene in my friend's downward spiral. Had I been more mature and forceful, I might have been able to help him in some way. At the time, his actions scared me. Regrettably, I just backed away from him. Maybe if I had just expressed my concern or showed that I cared, it may have made a difference. After reading about my regret, I hope others might try to overcome their fear when they recognize a friend or relative in need of intervention and take action on that person's behalf.

During the final six years that I owned Emerson Auto, I was enjoying the relative calm of living in Weymouth Landing, while things were definitely getting way out of control in Southie. By the mid-1980s, it seemed as though drugs had gotten a hold of South Boston right by the neck, and they were strangling all that was good right out of her. Wherever you went, you couldn't help but notice how flagrant drug use had become. It was commonplace to walk into the restroom of a restaurant or bar and find somebody openly chopping up cocaine, or crystal-meth, right on top of the urinal. It seemed they weren't even afraid that a cop might walk in to use the bathroom and bust them.

I was surprised when some of the most respected South Boston business owners became open about their drug use. I'm not implying that the majority of people in Southie used drugs. That was not the case, but some that did were people that my dad had dealt with and respected for many years before he retired.

He would have been shocked at the revelation. I wouldn't have believed these individuals used recreational drugs if I hadn't seen it with my own eyes. When I had business to conduct at one of their offices, such as picking up or delivering a vehicle, there might be lines of cocaine openly sitting there on their desk. It was offered casually, as if they were offering a cup of coffee. I would decline the offer, not needing to acquire any more bad habits. There was no pressure to force it on you, but it was there if you wanted it. In an effort to preserve the high regard that my father held for these people, I never mentioned any of this to him.

The drug dealers were known to many people in the neighborhoods, and they went about their business with impunity. Deals could be seen taking place from cars, from motorcycles, at the bar of a local tavern, or just about anywhere you can imagine. The fact that everybody, including dealers, need to regularly buy gasoline and have their cars fixed, meant that I couldn't avoid getting to know them pretty well. One particular dealer, whom I'll call "Chuck," occasionally would spot one of his friends or customers standing with me while I pumped their gas. As we watched him drive by, Chuck would toss a big fat joint out the window of his car. The joint would either be caught in midair, or roll to our feet. The customer would pick it up and signal his "thanks!" It was Chuck's way of spreading goodwill. Having spent so many years in this environment, I wasn't fazed at all by this. It was just the way things were at that time.

Another local dealer drove an extremely fast motorcycle. He would come screaming through the streets of Southie on his crotch rocket, as if he was invincible. I guess I shouldn't talk. I had done almost the same thing in my Challenger and on my bike at times, but not nearly as recklessly. At least I stopped or slowed down through intersections.

Having gassed up his car and bike a hundred times or so, I got to know and like him. I certainly wished him no harm. But every day, I expected to hear that he had been killed in an accident. The worst that I remember happening to him was two badly broken legs, the result of broad-siding a truck.

One morning, I was picking up a car at a local body shop. I would send some of our bodywork to "J's" shop, and he in turn sent mechanical work to me. I also worked closely with several well-established body shops, but J was just starting out. Because I liked him, I decided to send him some business. I had noticed other activity going on at his shop, involving drugs, but thinking it was just recreational in nature, I ignored it. In reality, I would come to find out that there was much more going on there than I ever imagined. While I was in J's shop having a cup of coffee and a smoke with him, the motorcycle-riding dealer drove in. I soon realized that this was a very special visit for that dealer. He was there to pick up a substantial amount of pure cocaine. He would later "cut it" (dilute it with something to increase its weight and volume) and then distribute it as grams. This would afford him a very large profit. After he was handed the cocaine, I watched as he held the plastic bag full of white powder in his outstretched hand. His eyes were affixed to it as he paced through my friend's shop, seemingly mesmerized by what he was looking at. As he stared at the bag and walked around in a circle, he was in an almost hypnotic trance. It didn't matter to him that two or three people were standing there watching him. After he left, I asked J why the guy had acted so strangely. That's when J told me it was that dealer's *very first time* buying a substantial quantity of uncut cocaine. We guessed he was thinking he had finally entered a new level in his career and made it to the big time. He was probably wallowing in the moment, holding the prize in front of his eyes. It was amazing to see.

The dealer on the motorcycle was one tough bastard with a reputation for violence. I was glad that he, and some of these other guys, liked and got along with me. I have to admit, I genuinely liked them, but I kept a safe distance and didn't get too involved with them. I imagine that if these guys didn't like someone, it would have meant big trouble at the very least.

I never thought of my friend, the body-shop owner, as a high-level cocaine dealer. Years later, I learned that J was actually the person that introduced Whitey Bulger to the money-making potential of the cocaine trade. Whitey bit at the idea, and that was the beginning of a whole new chapter in South Boston history. It was a chapter with sad endings for many.

I would eventually read all about how it was Whitey Bulger who was controlling the cocaine and other drug trafficking, as well as the racketeering in South Boston. He didn't care that it was ruining families, lives, or the town he claimed to love. There was a ton of money being made, and that's all that mattered to him. While I was living in Weymouth during the early 1980s, there were so many shootings taking place in South Boston that when I would come in on Monday mornings to open up the shop, I wouldn't ask the locals how their weekend was. I would ask, "Who got shot this weekend?" Seriously! There were that many shootings and killings. Many of these killings never even made the newspapers. It wasn't newsworthy anymore, I guess.

In addition to the lucrative drug trade, there was also the gambling. During those years, control of the gambling operations in Southie obviously continued to be a point of contention between the local underworld factions, and there was an ongoing struggle as to who would control what and where. The incident that resulted in Gavin's/O'Leary's Tavern being machine-gunned was a perfect example of that struggle. I'm convinced that there must have been many secret meetings during which the groups involved would discuss which bars would have whose bookies working in them and which gang's gambling machines would be allowed in each section of town. Maybe some of the bullet riddled bodies that were turning up each and every week on the streets of Southie, along with those that will never be found, were the direct result of meetings gone badly. Regardless of the cause, it became quite unnerving to see the value of human life quickly evaporating. It hits even harder when the folks that are disappearing from the face of the earth at alarming rates are personally known to you.

One young man who was always pleasant and courteous to me through the years was named Joe. He lived in one of the three-deckers across the street from the shop. One of my most violent South Boston memories involved him. I witnessed him take the most brutal beating I had ever seen. When this took place, I was probably twelve or thirteen, and Joe was a year or two older. I was pumping gas thirty feet away, when I watched a guy walk up to Joe on the sidewalk and hit him with a horrific sucker punch that instantly rendered him unconscious. He dropped, face first, hitting the pavement very hard. Right after he went down, he was viciously kicked directly in the face, full force with a work boot. His head jerked back like a football leaving for a field goal. I remember the horribly loud noise from the kick. It is very hard to describe, but it actually echoed off the surrounding buildings. It sort of sounded like a melon exploding. I don't think I was ever the same after seeing such brutality. That kick certainly could have proven fatal, but miraculously, he survived it. As far as I could see, Joe had done nothing to provoke this attack. I knew his attacker as well, because they both lived in the same building. After Joe recovered consciousness, he stumbled over and sat on the front stairs of his house. Within minutes, he had transformed into a surreal sight, looking almost nonhuman as he sat there all alone. His head and face were bleeding and swollen way past their normal size. His facial features were virtually indistinguishable with one eye completely closed.

It may have been at my father's suggestion that I grabbed a clean towel, soaked it with cold water from the fridge, and wrapped some ice inside. I brought it over to Joe on the stairs, and handed it to him. He nodded a slight thank you as he placed it against his disfigured face. The kid that had attacked Joe eventually became a professional boxer. Several years after that incident, "Rick" came in for gas, as he often did. Even though he was always pleasant to me over the years, that awful day was the only thing I could ever think about whenever I would see this guy drive up. I felt compelled to finally ask him why he had attacked Joe on that day so long ago. He remembered the incident clearly. He told me Joe had thrown a firecracker in the hallway near the door to his family's apartment, and his father was sleeping. He said it wasn't the first time Joe had done it, and he had been warned not to do it again. Rick could have called the cops that day to report somebody throwing firecrackers, but in Southie, I don't think anybody did that at the time. Street justice was swifter, and didn't involve police, lawyers, or judges. In this case, the penalty for throwing a firecracker was almost a death sentence.

More than a decade had passed since I had witnessed that beating. During that time, Joe and I would see each other on the street every so often, saying hi and making small talk. One day as Joe was walking by the gas station, he stopped to talk to me. He said, "You know, we have known each other for years, but we've never had a beer together." I agreed, saying, "We should do that." He asked if I could meet him after work that same day at the Ocean

Kai Chinese restaurant, on the west side of Southie. I was familiar with the bar at that restaurant because I had gone there a few times with my friends, Barney and Peter. Joe and I decided to meet there at 5:30 PM, right after I closed up shop. He said, *"Great! I'll be outside waiting for you."*

As I was closing up the garage and preparing to go meet Joe, a good customer came in with what appeared to be a very minor stalling problem. He lived in the suburbs and needed his car to get home for the weekend. Thinking it was only a bad fuel filter or something like that, I agreed to stay a few minutes and fix it. As usual, because I was in a hurry, everything that could go wrong did go wrong, and it ended up taking me almost two hours to get that guy back on the road. It was too late to meet Joe down at the Chinese restaurant, and I was exhausted after my twelve-hour workday. I headed right home.

The next morning, as I drove up to the shop at 6:30 AM, I noticed two men in suits standing by the front office door. They were waiting for me. As I approached them they asked, "Are you Tom?" I replied, "Yes." Then they asked, "Were you supposed to meet someone at the Ocean Kai Restaurant last night?" I said, "Yes. Why? What's going on?" They took out their badges to show me they were Boston Police Detectives, which I had already figured out. Even though they hadn't answered my question as to what was going on, I told them I was supposed to meet somebody at the restaurant, but I got tied up and couldn't make it. They asked where I was at the time I was supposed to be meeting my friend at the restaurant, and I said, "Right here, working on a customer's car! What's going on?" One of the cops pulled a Polaroid instamatic photo out of his jacket pocket and showed it to me. It was Joe. His eyes were swollen and closed with black and blue under each eye. His entire face looked swollen as well. It was not nearly as swollen as it had been years ago after that beating, but it was very swollen. I said to the cops, "That's Joe. I was supposed to meet him last night. What happened to him? Did he get beat up?" One of the detectives said, "No. He's dead." I looked up at the cop in shock. I was speechless. The detective told me that around the time I was supposed to meet Joe, he was sitting in his car outside of the restaurant. Somebody walked up to his open driver's window, put a gun behind his ear, and fired. They shot him in the back of the head. They asked me if I could confirm from the photo that it was indeed Joe—, and I said, "Yes, that's definitely him."

Apparently, Joe had mentioned to somebody at the restaurant that he was out there waiting for Tom from Emerson Auto that night. That's why the detectives ended up coming to question me. I told them I could contact the customer whose car I had stayed late to work on the night before, if they wanted to confirm my story. They said they would be back in touch if they needed anything else from me. They also mentioned that they had not been able to find any members of Joe's family so they could notify them of what had happened. I said, "His dad lives right over there," as I pointed to the house across the street. The detectives never came back to question me again. In the weeks that followed the killing, I saw that Joe's father was actually driving his son's station wagon around town. It was the car his son had been executed in, with its disgustingly bloodstained front seat. I found that incomprehensible. I could never have driven that car again if a family member of mine had been murdered in it. It was a sad ending to a life that had seen way too much brutality. Little did I know that afternoon, when Joe said, *"Great! I'll be outside waiting for you,"* those would be the last words he would ever say to me.

The murder of my scheduled drinking partner, someone I had known since childhood, hit way too close to home. A grim reality occurred to me. If I had met Joe at the arranged time, and sat outside with him for a smoke, I could very well have been with him when his assassin walked up to that car. The method of his killer, execution by way of a bullet behind the ear, indicated that Joe's death was not a random act of violence. Guys who carried out those deeds in Southie made sure they did not leave live witnesses. I asked around town about Joe's killing. The word on the street was that he had been dealing cocaine out of that restaurant's bar, without paying tribute to the person who controlled trafficking in that area. This murder took place in the middle of Whitey Bulger's territory, so I guess one could speculate and put two and two together. Maybe Joe had a problem with heeding warnings. I had no idea that Joe was a dealer. If I had been with him as planned, I'm sure there would have been no hesitation on the part of the shooter to take me out as well.

I came to the realization that it was impossible to be this close to so much violence and death without eventually having it affect me directly. Things were getting further out of control all the time. Couple that with the fact my back was getting steadily worse and it seemed the time was right to put the business up for sale and move on. It took quite a while, but the shop finally sold. I was very saddened to be leaving a place where I finally felt like part of the community. But, there had to be more to life than the view I had gazed upon from these shattered iron-grate-covered windows since I was a young child. I wanted to explore more of life's options.

Once the garage and the home in Weymouth sold, Diane and I relocated to Florida. I was in heaven. I had dreamt of making that move ever since the very first time I saw Florida and its beautiful canals some ten years earlier. I knew that southern Florida was where I wanted to live someday. The warm weather would be much more tolerable than the cold New England winters, especially for somebody like me with lots of hardware in their back. Starting all over again was a little scary. To the Florida crackers (people born and raised there), we were the pesky northerners that came down to clog their roads and strain their school systems. We were once again outsiders.

We persevered and made friends through the real estate company where I took a job as a sales agent. It was purely by chance that I ended up being a Realtor. I was new to Florida, sitting at the closing table taking ownership of our new home. I turned to my agent, Valerie, and jokingly said, "Well, I have a house. Now all I need is a job." Valerie wasted no time in saying, "Why don't you come to work for us?" At first I didn't think she was serious. But then she explained that her company had its own real estate school. With no other prospects or plan in mind, I said "okay." I immediately enrolled in the real estate school which was located in the building directly behind the office we were sitting in. Within a few weeks, I passed my license exam with the State of Florida. I liked the instructor that taught my real estate licensure course, and we got to know each other fairly well. He was a charismatic man who spoke articulately with a distinctively deep voice. After working for the company a few years, I came to the office one morning and was shocked to hear that he had been found on a deserted dirt road, sitting in the front seat of his car, holding a pistol in his hand. He had shot himself in the head and killed himself. Outwardly, he showed no signs of a person in mental turmoil. Having spoken to him just a day or so before, it was a vivid lesson that you never know what is going on in a person's mind.

It took me about one day to realize that real estate offices are full of people with strong personalities and large egos. It's like having a tribe full of Chiefs, which always kept things interesting to say the least. One of the very strongest personalities I came in contact with was that of my first manager, Dot. She was very tall, and spoke with a southern twang and style that demanded respect. Couple those traits with her confidence, experience and stern demeanor and she was as intimidating to me as any of those tough guys from Southie had ever been. Her in-house training for new agents was intense. I was made to memorize numerous presentation manuals and make hundreds of cold calls, which went against my grain. I had walked the neighborhoods for weeks, going door to door, doing all the things I was taught. Six months of hard work had not produced one listing, one sale, or even one penny of income. After talking the situation over at home with Diane, we agreed that it was time to throw in the towel.

Distraught with the realization that I had failed, I walked into Dot's office the next morning with every intention of quitting. I explained to her that I had worked my ass off for six months, doing all the things she had taught me to do, and I had gotten nowhere. I told her, "It's obvious that this career is not for me. I quit." Dot's reaction was totally unexpected. She quickly stood up from her chair, leaned forward and planted her hands flat on the desk in front of me. She looked me in the eye and said, "You're not quitting. I know you can do this!" I was stunned, and thought, "How can she possibly think I can do this?" I was never comfortable with the canned presentations or the phone calls disturbing people at their homes in the evenings. I also hated going door to door and having kids yell *"Holy Roller!"* out the windows at me. Upon hearing her insistence that I stick it out a while longer, I presented her with a proposition. I said, "I'll stay, on one condition. I'm throwing all those presentation manuals away and I'm going to try doing things my way." She said, "Okay. Now go out and do what I know you can do."

Everything changed dramatically from that point on. My second six months in the business were a whirlwind. Speaking from the heart and listening to people's needs was all it took.

Clients can immediately tell if you are being yourself, as opposed to just reading from a script, and that makes them comfortable dealing with you. I had another advantage. I loved what I was selling and my enthusiasm was contagious. The Florida lifestyle was something I truly believed in and I wanted others to share in that dream. By the end of that first year I had closed more than two million dollars in sales, and I had a sizable inventory of listings. During my second year in the business I closed 4.6 million dollars in sales, which was great, considering 1989's real estate prices. Many of those buyers weren't even looking for waterfront, but I found that I could easily turn them on to the added benefits. Because of those sales, I was able to purchase a brand new boat which had a nice cabin and a head. I started showing property via the water, which was a great way to mix business with pleasure. During one such house-hunt, with Mark and Roz K., Mark, a lawyer, fell overboard! That was fun! They bought a riverfront home, and we became friends. Another memory was formed after I sold a waterfront vacation home to a couple visiting from Germany. After everything was signed and sealed, I invited them out on my boat to revisit the house. I thought they would enjoy seeing it from the water-side before heading back overseas. They were thrilled with the idea. As we approached the house from the river, they spotted a big sign attached to the outside of their sea wall. It had a painting of a large manatee on it and in bright red letters it read, "WARNING! Manatee Area!" In broken English, the buyer asked me, "What is this manatee?" I turned and looked at him very seriously, and answered, "Oh! You never heard of manatees? They are vicious sea creatures that come out only at night. They climb over sea walls searching for anything they can eat. They are *very* dangerous." The man and woman looked at each other in obvious distress, wondering what they had gotten themselves into. When I finally explained that I was kidding, we all had a great laugh. That sign was actually a warning to boaters to go slow and not injure those harmless and endangered vegetarians.

The highest earning years of my entire working career, along with the lasting friendships formed at that real estate office, were entirely the result of one lady showing faith in me when I had lost faith in myself. The impact that her few forceful words had on my life was immeasurable. Eventually, the realization of what she had done for me set in. One day, I bought a dozen roses and brought them to Dot in her office as a thank you. I'm glad I did that when I did. Not long after that, she left the company and moved on.

After a few years in the field as a sales agent with AAIM Realty Group, I accepted the manager's position at the North Fort Myers office. I found out quickly that I enjoyed being out on the front lines selling homes much more than sitting in an office dealing with the problems of eighteen other agents. I decided to give up management after just two or three years to rejoin the sales force. Once again, my back decided to make my life miserable. With no provocation on my part, the pain began to intensify with each passing month. It got to the point that just getting in and out of a car ten to twenty times per day was enough to cause incredible pain that increased as the day went on. Sometimes, I would sit in my car in front of a client's house, trying to decide which hand to carry my briefcase with, because that would affect the amount of pain I would be in as I walked to the home's entrance. Carrying it in my right hand was sometimes less painful, but then I wouldn't be able to shake hands at the door, so I would switch over. I found that being in constant pain made it increasingly difficult to be an effective salesman. It's hard to be cheerful while feeling like a knife is stuck in your back. I scheduled appointments with each of the three top neurosurgeons in Fort Myers, hoping for a surgical solution to the pain.

Every one of them refused to operate after seeing the x-ray evidence of my previous surgery and the hardware in my back. When I got to the point that I couldn't walk, there was a ten day hospitalization during which keeping me medicated and in bed were the only things they were able to do for me. I later found a specialist who made an attempt at steroid injections. But, the rod in my back prevented him from being able to inject the drug into the exact spot where it was needed. I had fought a good battle with my back for almost my entire life and finally I had to admit to myself that my back had won the war. I had no choice but to give up the work I loved.

I cherish the eleven years I spent in Florida as a Realtor. Some of the best friends I will ever have were made during that time. Thankfully, I had found that the majority of people living in that state were from somewhere else, and therefore they were all *outsiders* as well. That fact made it easier to bond with people. But, now that I was unable to work, it seemed that moving back to Massachusetts might be the right thing to do. Diane had never really wanted to live in Florida, so far away from family, and I got to the point where I agreed with her.

Making that move back up north would not be easy for me. It amounted to yet another *start-over* proposition. As we began to pack our belongings, I received a blatant reminder of how some people feel the uncontrollable need to go out of their way to be cruel and rude to anyone they perceive as an outsider. I was standing in line at the customer service counter of the Publix supermarket where we had shopped for over ten years. I knew the woman behind the counter, and I asked her if they had any large boxes I could have. She said, "You're not moving back up north, are you?" I replied that we were, for family reasons. After overhearing our conversation, the man standing behind me tapped me on the shoulder and said, "Moving back up north?"

I smiled at him and said, "Yes." I thought he just wanted to make conversation, but his reply was anything but friendly. He said, "Great! This time, stay there!" He said it loudly enough for all to hear. He was just another cracker jumping at the chance to be rude. I was so mad when I heard this total stranger say those words that my blood boiled. His comment was totally uncalled for, and I felt like knocking him out cold. But not wanting to end up in jail, I gave him a look that showed just how I felt about him. I took my boxes and left the store.

We relocated to a small southeastern Massachusetts town, miles from any of the neighborhoods where either Diane or I had previously lived. Except for a few relatives in the area, we didn't know anybody in town. Even I, "the constant outsider," was surprised at the not-so-subtle comments I received shortly after moving to our new little town. I tried to engage a man in friendly conversation as we waited in line at the local country store. As soon as he figured out that I was new to town, his attitude changed. His comments weren't openly hostile, but they were direct enough that I knew he resented any new faces he saw. In a town where we found the vast majority of people to be welcoming and friendly, I had the uncanny talent for finding the one resident asshole. To him, I was the cause of all the new construction, population growth, and increased traffic in his little private world, and being thus, he went out of his way to make me feel unwelcome. By this time in my life, I had realized that the best response to someone like him was no response at all. I can somewhat understand his feelings, but I didn't appreciate his rudeness. Whether it's out of pride or the pleasure of the act, there will always be somebody dying to remind you that you are an outsider. It starts in early childhood and could possibly be there waiting for you at the nursing home you end up checking into. How we all decide to deal with those situations is what's important. I'm by no means an expert. I'm still learning.

I've found that a great way to meet people in a new area is through volunteering and community service. Shortly after moving to our new town, I was elected to the Freetown-Lakeville Regional School Committee. I ran for that office mostly out of necessity. For weeks, I had read in the local papers that nobody had filed papers to run for that position, and the elections were close at hand. My incentive to run was the fact that I knew there were some important issues that needed to be addressed at the schools my son would be attending. As fulfilling as public office can be, as a newcomer to an area, you can expect a certain amount of resistance to new ideas you present. When suggesting change, you may find that some longtime residents of your new home town will be eager to remind you that, "You are not from around here, and you don't know the history." But with perseverance and a strong belief in your ideas, it is possible to get your points across. Being a school committee member was very demanding and time consuming. After serving in that capacity, I have to admire those who continue doing it term after term. I believe I was part of making some small but important contributions to the betterment of the school system. The one change that I am most happy to have been able to initiate and get approved was an anti-bullying policy. Until that time, there were few guidelines for teachers and administrators to refer to when they observed situations involving ongoing or persistent bullying. There were no uniform procedures to follow when a student would approach a staff member to report an instance of bullying. Unlike some, this new policy was not one that was focused on punishment. It was a policy that required that all reports of bullying be taken seriously and that counseling would be encouraged and made available to all of the parties involved. It assured that kids wouldn't just be told to deal with the problem on their own.

When kids feel they have no place to turn for help, and that they must deal with the situation on their own, that's when things get very dangerous in our schools. With proper guidance and help, kids can learn effective methods of self help, but most are not born with those skills.

Some wonderful and lasting friendships were the result of my four years on the school committee. I was also happy that I was able to serve on two building committees that were related to the school system. I found that being a member of the region's new middle school and high school building committees was a rewarding experience in that I was part of something that will serve the local communities for years to come.

While serving on the Freetown-Lakeville Regional School Committee, I attended a Republican fund raiser for Massachusetts Governor Mitt Romney.
On the right is Bristol County Sheriff Tom Hodgson. I was probably the only Democrat in the room and I was there with a purpose. I approached Mitt twice that evening to lobby him for more state funding for our schools. He looked at me, smiled, and in a humorous way said, "You again!"
Although this occurred prior to him ever announcing aspirations for higher office, I addressed him as "Mr. President." He seemed to really like that.

Chapter XXIV

Something To Think About

There have been far too many instances in my life when whether I lived or died depended on just plain luck. A few inches of variation as to where a telephone pole would make contact with my car has spared me on two occasions. When guns have been pointed at my head, I lived only because the people holding those guns took that extra second to *think* before pulling the trigger. My life has hinged on whether or not safety latches would function properly with a person hanging from them, upside down, underwater. The fact is, I was placed in each of these situations solely because of my own reckless decisions. There was no other reason.

As I hopefully have several more chapters of my life to fill in, I certainly want them to include more adventure and excitement. Will those chapters reflect my having learned from past mistakes, or will I tend to repeat them? Time will tell. When all is said and done, it's all about the choices.

After reading about the events and situations I have encountered throughout my life, it may appear that mine has been an unhappy existence. That is not the case at all. Nobody would want to read a book about all the fun and good times I have had.

Many of my dreams have been fulfilled, although some have been allowed to slip away and will have to be pursued again. I want to someday have a two passenger ultralight that I can fly from my own back yard, and a home back on the water would round things out nicely.

I've endured, and continue to endure the pain that goes hand-in-hand with having major back problems and surgery, as well as a few broken bones. But, most people have, or will have to deal with major pain at some point during their lives. I have also had a life full of excitement and adventure with love and wonderful friendships. I consider the latter two as being the true treasures that we gather throughout life. I believe we all have to create our own happiness and do our best to not dwell on the negative aspects, which are realities in everyone's life. Regardless of whether you believe in God or any higher power at all, the prayer, which starts, *"God, grant me the serenity to accept the things I cannot change; the courage to change the things I can; and the wisdom to know the difference,"* is something to try and remember throughout each and every day. These simple words make so much sense. Putting that philosophy into practice takes a whole lot of pressure off making everyday decisions. Just think about it. It allows *us* to decide what we will let bother us and what we will not. That family member or coworker whose characteristics and personality make you crazy is a perfect example. Can you change that person? No. We have absolutely no control or power to change people. It's so much easier to learn to accept them. Remembering that we possess this *power* of choice is the hard part.

By not being afraid to dream, and striving to make those dreams a reality, our lives can be enriched. If flying an ultralight aircraft looks like something you would love to try, do it! If your dream is to be able to wake up in the morning and jump in the ocean right outside your back door, do it! So what if that back door is from a tent, because maybe that's the only waterfront home you can afford. The water feels just as good. If you envy the guy or girl that cruises by you on a motorcycle on a warm summer night, but think, *I could never do that*, go ahead and experience that feeling at least once in your life, even if it's from the back of a motorcycle driven by somebody you trust. Yeah, you *can* live your life with a capital *L*. I love the saying, "A coward dies a thousand deaths, the brave man dies but once." When you really think about it, it is so true. That doesn't mean we should throw all caution to the wind. I have been extremely scared of many of the things I've tried. It's only natural to be apprehensive. But sometimes, things appear to be more risky or difficult than they really are. Driving a motorcycle at a hundred miles per hour, weaving in and out of traffic, is extremely risky. Driving at the posted speed limit on a beautiful country road with an experienced driver at the controls is a tolerable amount of risk to most people.

It has been tough writing about many of the things in this book. It forced me to relive several unpleasant situations all over again. At times, it brought very strong emotions right back to the surface. In some cases, it got the adrenaline pumping all over again. When you are writing down your experiences in the blank pages of this book, remember;

That which you don't write down is lost forever.

I can't help but wonder what interesting stories some of the people I have known could have shared with me if they had chosen to do so. My dear old friend, Tony, never talked to me about what it was like to have been born in the year 1888 and grow up in that era.

Imagine having lived through the time when the automobile, the airplane, and so many other modern miracles first appeared! What was that like? Why and how had he ended up in this country? I never thought to ask those questions and he never brought those subjects up. I will never know the answers.

Some of the stronger personalities I have known during my lifetime would have supplied extremely interesting reading, I am sure. What seems ordinary to one person can be extraordinary to another. The absolute strongest personality I have ever known was my father. I think many people who knew him would say the same. What an opportunity was lost to me by him never sharing his most personal experiences and feelings with me, or with anyone else for that matter. He came to this country from Italy as a young boy, not knowing English, and he was thrust into a hardworking Irish neighborhood. It must have been anything but fun for him as he grew up. One thing I'm pretty sure of is that he too must have felt like a constant outsider throughout much of his life. What hardships had my father and grandfather encountered? What dangers had they faced? What choices did they regret? I'm sure I would have understood my dad's personality and his stern ways much better if he had shared those deeply personal experiences of his life with me. I will never know the answers to those questions. He took those facts with him to the grave. You can't say that about me. I spilled my guts on these pages. (Most notably in Chapter XXII, boat commute after July 4th party) By digging deeply into my memories, I have gained a greater understanding of why and how I became the person that I am. Now it's your turn. I truly believe that each of us is a book waiting to be written, and that book, if written, results in a person explained.

Although the world of the 1950's through the 1980's was quite different than the world of today, the problems and challenges remain the same. Crime, alcohol and drug abuse, discrimination and injustice all still exist, albeit in their evolved forms. The times have changed, but the choices remain the same. How far should a person go in order to just fit in?

Sometimes, maybe it's better to remain *the constant outsider*.

THE END

Reader comments are welcome at the author's BLOG located on the book's Amazon.Com page.

Signed copies may be available by emailing ConstantOutsider@aol.com, with "Copy Request" in the subject line.

Reader's Final Thoughts
(Need to post some photos? Why not do so here?)

Reader's Final Thoughts

_____

_____

_____

_____

_____

_____

_____

_____

_____

_____

_____

_____

_____

_____

_____

_____

_____

_____

_____

_____

_____

Reader's Final Thoughts

_____

_____

_____

_____

_____

_____

_____

_____

_____

_____

_____

_____

_____

_____

_____

_____

_____

_____

_____

_____

Reader's Final Thoughts

Reader's Final Thoughts

50583378R00220

Made in the USA
Lexington, KY
21 March 2016